WRECKONOMICS

WRECKONOMICS

WHY IT'S TIME TO END THE WAR ON EVERYTHING

RUBEN ANDERSSON
AND
DAVID KEEN

OXFORD
UNIVERSITY PRESS

OXFORD
UNIVERSITY PRESS

Oxford University Press is a department of the University of Oxford. It furthers
the University's objective of excellence in research, scholarship, and education
by publishing worldwide. Oxford is a registered trade mark of Oxford University
Press in the UK and certain other countries.

Published in the United States of America by Oxford University Press
198 Madison Avenue, New York, NY 10016, United States of America.

Library of Congress Cataloging-in-Publication Data
Names: Andersson, Ruben, 1977- author. | Keen, David, 1958- author.
Title: Wreckonomics : why it's time to end the war on everything /
Ruben Andersson, David Keen.
Description: New York, NY : Oxford University Press, [2024] |
Includes bibliographical references and index.
Identifiers: LCCN 2023022523 (print) | LCCN 2023022524 (ebook) |
ISBN 9780197645925 (hardback) | ISBN 9780197645949 (epub)
Subjects: LCSH: Policy sciences—Case studies. | Political ethics—Case
studies. | Political science—Decision making—Case studies.
Classification: LCC H97 .A535 2024 (print) | LCC H97 (ebook) |
DDC 320.6—dc23/eng/20230807
LC record available at https://lccn.loc.gov/2023022523
LC ebook record available at https://lccn.loc.gov/2023022524

DOI: 10.1093/oso/9780197645925.001.0001
Printed and bound in Great Britain by Clays Ltd, Elcograf S.p.A.

Contents

Acknowledgments

This project has been in many ways an example of what it analyzes: an escalating and self-perpetuating endeavor. While this has generated benefits, it has also generated costs. Vivian and Cristina have been truly amazing, bearing the brunt of the costs during our long days and nights of writing and editing; without your love and support this book would not have been possible. Sophia, Aaron, Eirik, and Milo have brought the fun and kept it real. Sara, Vincent, Ann, Roy, and Helen have cheered us on. Our love and thanks to everyone in our respective families. The project would of course also not have been possible without all the people who have generously given their time in our fieldwork in often very difficult circumstances—thank you. Inside and outside academia, Mark Duffield, Mary Kaldor, Alex de Waal, Mats Berdal, Florian Weigand, Ali Ali, Dace Dzenovska, Nayanika Mathur, Loren Landau, Martin Ruhs, Yang Li, James Vincent, Amrita Rangasami, Edward Balke, Adekeye Adebajo, Freda Bear, Henry Bagenal, Gopal Sreenivasan, and Biao Xiang are among the many people who have inspired us through the years. A special thanks to staff at the NGO Saferworld and their important work on conflict and security over many years—especially to Larry Attree, whose insights from a vast range of crises have been an inspiration. Our students at Oxford and the LSE have inspired us too. Thanks to Dave McBride, who believed in the project from the start, as well as to Sarah Ebel, Emily Benitez, Preetham Raj, Judith Hoover, Rachel Perkins, Thomas Kiefer, Kevin Eagan, and all the team at Oxford University Press. Thanks to the anonymous reviewers, whose insightful comments came at just the right time. In the spirit of *Wreckonomics*, we must insist that all failures and errors are, of course, theirs.

I

Crime Scene Investigation

In September 2021, twenty years after the start of the "war on terror," Americans seemed to be reliving Saigon all over again as Kabul Airport thronged with desperate people scrambling to get out amid the Taliban's rapid takeover of Afghanistan. Bombs and a drone attack left scores of civilians dead. Taliban fighters showed off their new US helicopters and took journalists on visits to the dire Tora Bora prison complex, scoring win after propaganda win. At home, President Joe Biden was under siege: his failure, it seemed, was complete.

Yet for all the noise about "collapse" and "Biden's Saigon," failure (as in Vietnam) had been years in the making.[1] Since the occupiers had entered the country in 2001, tens of thousands of Afghans had died, and many more had been driven from their homes, while casualties were adding up for NATO with each passing year. The occupiers had plowed billions into unchecked coffers, fueling corruption and distrust of the state as the promised benefits from military intervention failed to materialize. Among the winners were investors in the machinery of the war on terror, which up until 2021 had cost some 2.3 *trillion* US dollars in the Afghan-Pakistan theater alone.[2] Winners from the debacle also included assorted warlords who played a double game with the occupiers, extracting cash and impunity by issuing threats with one hand and offering to remedy them with the other. US officials were gaming the war, too, as the confidential trove of interviews known as the Afghanistan Papers showed in late 2019. Even the wildest failures to quell the insurgency could, time and again, be presented as a phony "success." More funding could always be found—ranging from the oddest projects (such as spending $486 million on cargo planes that were barely used) to the deadliest ones (such as the deployment of inaccurate B-1 bombers at a cost of $300 million apiece).[3]

"We didn't have the foggiest notion of what we were undertaking," admitted Douglas Lute, the three-star army general and Afghan war czar under the Bush and Obama administrations. "If the American people knew the magnitude of this dysfunction . . ."[4]

And yet: as we sift through the rubble of Afghanistan, we find evidence not of some one-off failure to plan ahead, a policy initiative gone wrong through unexpected circumstances. Rather, we face something akin to a complex crime scene where the damage, the ostensible "mistakes," and the cover-ups have all been *systematic*—with many powerful players succeeding in their most important goals amid the wreckage.

In *Wreckonomics*, we show how the perverse outcomes manifest in Kabul in the autumn of 2021 are far more than a blip or an anomaly. When policies fail (and fail persistently) we need to look not only at "what went wrong" but also at "what went right"—and at who is benefiting from these apparent failures.

We start with the manufactured disaster of Afghanistan since we find that questions of success-amid-failure are especially urgent when it comes to the remarkably persistent habit of going to war against some threat or other. This habit of waging "war on everything" has spread from the early days of the war on Communism and the war on drugs to "fights" against crime, terrorism, migration, and many more complex political problems. By examining the factors that propel such wars and fights forward and outward, we may be able to explain the central puzzles with which the book is concerned: What keeps disastrous interventions and policies ticking over? What renders them acceptable? Why do they get reinvented from one era to another? And why do we never seem to learn?

Wreckonomics offers important tools for piecing together an answer and asks you to join us as a particular kind of detective in sifting through the wreckage of a range of "crime scenes," from old and cold wars to counterterror and border security, from fighting narcotics to combating a virus. We will see how very many problems are persisting and even worsening not so much despite the "wars" and "fights" that are waged against them as *thanks to* these fights. Within dysfunctional systems of intervention, moreover, we discover that failure has repeatedly been presented as glorious success. In order to start dismantling this counterproductive approach, we must first understand who benefits from it—and if we learn this lesson well, we may collectively start to find a way out of the endless crises and destructive wars in which our societies seem to be stuck.

The Puzzle

We are used to hearing today about financial, epidemiological, environmental, democratic, and geopolitical crises coming thick and fast—the list goes on. As citizens and voters, it is easy to despair at the lack of a clear way out of the "permacrisis" or "polycrisis."[5] Yet many of us cannot quite disconnect, however hard we try. "Doom-scrolling" on our phones, nursing a light or heavy addiction to the latest bad news, we seem to inhabit a world where our capacity to be both outraged and depressed by contemporary events greatly exceeds our capacity to understand them—or to begin to put them right. This despair and lack of positive vision may also encourage us to accept (or at least resign ourselves to) whatever heavy-handed solution our governments roll out to remedy the malaise du jour. At the extreme, this "solution" is a war or fight against some vague or specific enemy, and we will focus on a number of such "war fixes" in this book. Yet the habit of reaching for a simple fix to an oversimplified problem extends well beyond such contexts. So too does the wider pattern of self-serving malaise—or functional dysfunction—that we label "wreckonomics."

We will return to that wider pattern as the book unfolds. For now, let us remind ourselves of the multiple and overlapping disasters and wars affecting both richer and poorer countries. The global "war on terror" has greatly boosted levels of terrorism and violence worldwide, at great human and financial cost: some US$8 trillion and 900,000 deaths between 2001 and 2021, according to Brown University's Costs of War Project. It has also helped non-Western actors to wage their own wars on terror to devastating effect in countries such as Syria and Yemen, as we will see in chapter 4.[6] At the borders of the West and elsewhere, a variety of walls and other barriers have been put up to halt migration (and sometimes ostensibly to preempt extreme right-wing movements), but these walls have fueled political tensions while prompting migrants and refugees to adopt ever more dangerous routes.[7] Inside the walls, our politics is increasingly fractious and polarized, in hock to "culture wars" and deep ideological and identitarian divides, as seen from India to the United States and beyond.[8] Meanwhile, a seemingly endless "war on drugs" has strongly contributed to ill health, incarceration, corruption, and criminal violence wherever drugs are produced, transported, or consumed, including 150,000 deaths in Mexico alone since 2007.[9]

Amid all these wars and crises, humanity's largest challenges remain relatively neglected—as with rising inequality—while presenting further opportunities for militarization, as when global warming becomes yet another plug for more funding for defense and border security.[10] Add to this the austerity policies in the wake of the 2007–8 financial crisis as well as the error-ridden responses to the COVID-19 pandemic, and the list of calamities is long indeed. To top off this litany of doom, interstate war has roared back in the picture with Russia's invasion of Ukraine, which is generating huge knock-on effects, from the risk of nuclear conflagration to an acute global inflationary crisis as well as a looming debt crisis for poorer nations.[11] With such a bleak picture, there's every incentive for citizens to avert their gaze and hope it will all go away.

Yet look we must. In fact, there's a major puzzle here, and a major, even intriguing, challenge to somehow join the dots. Within all of these diverse spheres and across very varied interventions, politicians seem to be strangely wedded—perhaps even addicted—to policies that are manifestly not working even on their own terms. Bad habits and bad policies have exhibited a remarkable capacity to persist even in the face of a growing body of evidence indicating that they are simply not achieving the stated aims—and that they are in many cases making things much worse. Like gamblers, our leaders cannot seem to stop even when they know they are losing big. In fact, losing all too often prompts an increasingly desperate defense of the indefensible, plunging us deeper into the mire. The more crisis responses feed further crises, the more politicians persist in pursuing them. How did it come to this? And how can we escape into something better?

The Burned Thumb

In 2017, a court in Australia pondered a curious criminal case: a Melbourne restaurateur in financial trouble had apparently burned down his own pizza parlor to cash in on the insurance. However absurd this sounds, it was no laughing matter: upstairs in the building, eight people lay sleeping as he set it alight (though thankfully they survived). It turned out the restaurateur had a hand in his own demise. His plan went a little awry since he accidentally spread some of the petrol over himself and set his thumb alight. The digit promptly burned off and its remnants were later matched to the owner, who was duly sentenced to nine years in jail.[12]

Now if we think of a disastrous war or intervention as a crime scene, the usual reflex of politicians, journalists, and even voters is to try to find some version of that unfortunate digit—and some individual culprit. Where is the smoking gun (or thumb)? Who is responsible? And how can they be made to pay? It's an understandable reflex, and of course crime *shouldn't* pay. But all too often, the search for culprits helps to set off new wars or crises—or simply perpetuates existing ones. The launch and persistence of the "war on terror" needed its villains (Osama bin Laden, Saddam Hussein, Mullah Omar) as well as its fall guys back "home" (Joe Biden again). Europe's "fight against migration" needs its evil "mafia" smugglers. The "war on drugs" needs its drug lords and drug-funded rebels, while cold wars old and new need their terrible tyrants. The normal way to proceed, then, is to sift through the wreckage looking for villains and evidence of dastardly intentions. There always seems to be a rich offering to be had on this front, spawning numerous exposés, reports, and book-length investigations. Occasionally, there is a focus on dysfunctional interventions, but these accounts tend to highlight individual "bad apples" whose greed subverts good intentions. Yet such analyses miss a crucial part of the puzzle: the *systematic* ways in which disastrous interventions have tended to reproduce themselves. Indeed, it is often while we are mesmerized by these various villains that the underlying systems wreak their more surreptitious forms of havoc.

In the case of our pizza parlor pyromaniac, finding that burned digit and jailing the down-at-heel restaurateur was all well and good, but that was a case for the courts. For the rest of us—and especially for policymakers, advocates, academics, even journalists—the real challenge tends to reside not so much in "finding the individual responsible" as in examining and hopefully addressing the underlying incentives. To do this, we must learn to become *systems detectives* or, to riff off the title of this book, "wreckonomists." The aim of our crime scene investigation is not so much to uncover individual culpability for the crimes as to highlight the patterns that produce and reproduce them—including the perverse incentives that operate within environments of impunity and secrecy and the systemic features that sustain these dangerous interventions and environments.

This means understanding war and security interventions as *systems*. One definition of a system is a whole that is more than (or different from) the sum of its parts—in other words, an entity whose functions cannot simply be understood by scrutinizing individual mechanisms and elements. As systems detectives, we stress the need to examine how those mechanisms and elements relate to and interact with one another. A clock can't be studied simply by examining each cog, or a traffic system simply by looking at each bus and car and bicycle: we need to understand how *all* these parts relate and interact within a wider environment. Systems tend to exhibit a high degree of *complexity*—a complex series of connections, interdependencies, and relations that is very far from the simple cause-and-effect of, say, pressing the gas pedal to accelerate a car.[13] As we shall see, nonlinear complexity, encompassing cascades and feedback loops among the "games" played by those operating in a systems environment, is a great part of what makes systems so resilient, uncontrollable, and (in the case of our wars and fights) downright frightening.

Wreckonomics is our label for a particular form of perverse systems dynamic in which such complex relations, catalyzed by and combined with a degree of political steer, tend to generate very destructive yet politically and economically profitable consequences. We observe this dynamic especially strongly in interventions concerned with combating threats that are deemed urgent and existential. In the chapters that follow, we map out a variety of failing strategies that have regularly taken the form of a "war" or "fight" on this or that, while being mindful that the pattern we have observed often extends beyond such military and policing interventions. We try to explain not only why wars and fights against a range of threats have failed so badly but also why they have persisted and proliferated. In doing so, we offer a crucial and generally neglected explanation for why they have proven so resilient in the face of failure. And we show how these failing policies have become systemic and self-reinforcing, yielding important benefits for key actors even as huge numbers of people keep losing. Paradoxically, it is precisely by failing that policies frequently make themselves most "useful." Provided that the costs can be played down and carefully distributed to relatively powerless groups, the continuation of a problem routinely offers major payoffs and few costs for those who claim to be addressing it.

★★★

Becoming a good systems detective means looking carefully at the behavior of powerful governments over a long period. It also involves

examining the habits and priorities of institutional actors large and
small within the state—as well as nonstate actors ranging from militias and corporations to a variety of others including journalists, doctors, academics, and humanitarian NGOs. The brevity of this book
prevents a fuller account of all such actors (some of this we do in
other texts), yet crucially shining this kind of "systemic" light allows
us to see how self-defeating political habits are forged amid the vested
interests that have grown up like barnacles around sinking ships. In
this way, we are better able to understand the range of incentives that
make failing policies so difficult to challenge. The underlying interests turn out to be varied, complex, and often surprising. Some are
economic, but many are not. To give one example, those "hijacking"
the war on drugs came to include prominent Mexican politicians
who tried to use the drug-related murders of thousands of women as
a way to reinforce the regressive message that women should stay in
the home.[14]

It may seem anything but tempting to spend our time thinking
through the often cynical gains from misfortune that various wars and
crises have enabled. Given the pressures of daily living, it is hardly surprising that many of us see politics as something that we delegate to
politicians—something that we engage in every few years in the hope
that we will get a better set of leaders to take over, to make things
a little easier, and to deal (however imperfectly) with all the threats
that seem to surround us. Yet today it is becoming all too clear that
our collective penchant for political delegation is just not working.
Amid a range of seemingly intractable crises, we can't rely on our
governments accurately to define the greatest threats—never mind to
provide workable solutions. A general observation: if you outsource
the solution to politicians, they may well end up outsourcing the
problem to you. Threat detection also cannot sensibly be delegated
to those with a vested interest in particular responses, as has been the
case in all the interventions we will look at in *Wreckonomics*. Unless
we take proper responsibility for proper solutions, politics—and insecurity of one kind or another—comes knocking. This is a lesson our

interlocutors in crisis-hit countries have taught us over many years of research on conflict and security, and it is a lesson that inhabitants of privileged liberal democracies now need to learn at speed. The shield of basic security that has kept many people in the West within a rather complacent and naïve political space seems to be radically out of date.

One little caveat, or clarification, before we proceed. Much of the criticism we offer is directed at the political right in Western democracies. This is because the key wars or fights we will consider—those against drugs, migration, and terrorism—have historically been fomented most aggressively by powerful right-wing forces in Western countries, the United States in particular. Yet four points are worth stressing. First, left-wing revolutions have brought their own "wreckonomic" problems, as we discuss a little more in later chapters. Second, the contribution of left- and liberal-leaning governments to the various war and security systems of this book is substantial. Indeed, the idea that complex problems are best tackled through a simple fix has increasingly become something close to a political consensus in a great variety of fields; it is part of the political culture in which we are swimming (and drowning). Third, while the impetus for the interventions we'll discuss has historically come from Western governments, their *systemic* aspects tell us that they are not geographically confined to any one political actor. Once the genie is out of the bottle, the wrecking can continue at the hands of whichever ruthless operative manages to muscle in on the system. Fourth, as the previous points suggest, wreckonomics is about picking up on underlying patterns rather than about "picking sides." Indeed, the reflex to pick a side is often a major part of the problem. Some of these difficulties emerge with particular clarity when we eventually examine the COVID-19 response and the so-called culture wars that have featured prominently in many Western democracies as of late, helping to frame the debate around our various wars and fights.

Of course, moral indignation has its place. But we are also wary of it, especially when it involves the denunciation of all those who are labeled irrational, selfish, ignorant, deplorable, immoral, evil, or some combination thereof. Particularly given the growing influence of social media, denunciation easily extends to those who seem simply to *lack* the necessary moral indignation, so that self-righteousness becomes de rigueur. Intimidation and shaming are sometimes directed at one's own "side" and at those who have somehow failed to demonstrate the necessary zeal or purity.[15] We should not forget here that indignation and intimidation have played key roles in igniting and sustaining some of our most destructive security and military interventions, including the wars on terror, crime, and drugs. If we can remember these dangers, it will help us to avoid being endlessly stuck with waging bad interventions. As we will propose in the final chapters of the book, there are more constructive ways of solving problems. Among the ways forward that we discuss are opening up spaces of dissent, getting to know "the enemy," building (sometimes unlikely) coalitions for genuine protection and harm reduction, and addressing the underlying insecurities that feed so many wars and fights today.

If we are going to get to the point where we can cure our addiction to simple fixes and futile fights, we need to set aside the instinct to denounce and we need to try to get a better understanding of the environments and the incentives in which a wide variety of people—perhaps no better or worse than ourselves from a moral point of view—attempt to make a living and to make sense of the crisis-hit political world in which they find themselves operating. This means understanding the mechanisms that make endless wrecking (or endless war) so persistent and profitable—in short, becoming a good wreckonomist.

The Cases

In the coming chapters, we bring together a wide range of wars and security interventions, putting them into a single framework so as to get a better sense of the mechanisms and logics that perpetuate them. We recognize that we have more specialist knowledge of some of these spheres than others; in particular, we have over many years focused on warfare, peacemaking, the "war on terror," and international migration. But we can also see that, across a wider range of policy spheres, dysfunctional systems of intervention have routinely yielded substantial benefits for key players while distributing costs in ways that renew these systems. These systems are habitually failing in their most loudly expressed goals. Indeed, we find that they are often most successful at renewing themselves precisely when they are failing most egregiously. Failure renews the underlying threat or problem and thereby lends a paradoxical aura of legitimacy to the intervention. Further, failure can be laundered into success through a continuous massaging of the information environment.

A key aim in the book, then, is to look at a range of war and security interventions so as to illuminate who benefits and who loses and by what means. We also investigate the degree to which a "war" framing enables and legitimizes this uneven and unfair distribution of costs and benefits. That is quite a big task for a relatively small book. But we are setting out a framework here, rather than trying to present all the relevant evidence and the vast academic and nonacademic literatures that surround these topics. We put our model through its paces in relation to a wide range of interventions, and we hope that readers, too, will think about how far this framework can help in understanding the systems in which they live and work. At times, our consciously pared-back model runs up against a world that seems stubbornly to resist wreckonomic analysis. Not everything is grist to our mill! In observing some important common patterns, we are also led toward an awareness of *differences*—and the degree to which individual crises and interventions actually depart from our idealized "model." It is our hope that in the friction between model and empirical reality, new insights begin to emerge.

Chapter 2 sets out the model. We have found that, in a great variety of interventions, five systemic mechanisms come together in a peculiarly destructive yet profitable manner. Our first such mechanism is the political *fixation* on a threat and its ostensible solution.

This *war fix* interacts with four other "wreckanisms": the complex *rigging* of both solution and threat by a range of actors; the *export* of the resulting costs; the *cascade* of chaotic consequences that ensues from this distribution of costs and benefits; and the *knowledge-fixing* that misrepresents this destructive process. These elements are not simply sequential, but interact in complex systemic ways—leading to more wrecking in an escalating system. We emphasize that useful and critical insights into this process can be found among those who are "insiders" (in terms of making the intervention) and those who are its "targets." Certainly, this is what we have found in our firsthand research on border control, civil wars, counterterror, and a range of other fields.

Chapter 3 situates our analysis within trends in the study of war and security that emerged, like green shoots, as the Cold War thawed. In one sense, the Cold War was a "pseudo-war": it took the form of a standoff between the two superpowers while also bringing the threat and possibility of truly massive violence between them. But the Cold War was also a foil and a context for a series of *actual* wars (often called "proxy wars") in which the two superpowers were fairly clearly aligned with one of the opposing sides. There was a great amount of *rigging* of the Cold War, and costs and benefits were distributed extremely unevenly. We will see how the Cold War fundamentally helps us to understand—and situate historically—the wars and fights that evolved and accelerated in its long aftermath.

These wars and fights are at the heart of the book. The war on terror (chapter 4) took over where the Cold War left off. As with its precursor, it combined elements of "real" war and pseudo-war. Part of the "pseudo" aspect was implied in the very term "war on terror," for how can you wage war on an emotion? Yet by looking at four real wars that evolved in the context of the war on terror, we can see how the expansionary logic of the "terror" threat allowed for major gaming and benefits-chasing at a proliferating scale—moving from the heart of the global war on terror (Afghanistan) to its fringes (Sri Lanka and Syria) and its long tail (Mali and the Sahel).

Next, in chapter 5, we turn to the "fight against illegal migration" and its winners and losers. Of course, human movement is a very different thing from political violence, yet our aim here is to understand the shared logics of the underlying interventions. On this count, it is disturbing how certain kinds of international migration have increasingly been framed as a threat in recent decades. This "securitization" has triggered cascading consequences. One is the huge growth in the human smuggling market. Another is the increasing opportunity for "partner" states to use migration as a bargaining chip, echoing the systemic relations observed in the war on terror. While nowhere near as large in funding terms as the war on terror, the escalating "fight" (and its associated war on smugglers) has nevertheless ended up creating huge "collateral losses" in political and human terms, including the thousands of deaths along migratory routes and the extensive support for authoritarian regimes that promise cooperation.

Chapter 6 moves back in time to consider the long-standing war on drugs. In some ways, this is a "pseudo-war," but it is striking how extraordinary levels of violence in Mexico, Central America, Colombia, the Philippines, and elsewhere have at times been higher than in "real" war. We can observe complex and often synergistic relationships between the dynamics of the drug trade and the criminalizing and militarized response to it. Moving between the "external" war in poorer countries and the war on drugs and crime in the principal instigating state (the United States), we can throw important light on how addictive the war system becomes once its costs can be successfully exported to those with little or no stake in it.

It is here worth noting one benefit of looking at these war and security systems together: this approach helps us to see how they have been feeding into one another through a series of destructive feedback loops. An early example of this is the way the Vietnam War fed into Nixon's war on drugs—in part from painting peace protesters as drug addicts.[16] A second example is the link from the Cold War's end to other wars. As we will see, Western security structures found a major role—and renewed sources of legitimacy—within an emerging war on terror, a revived war on drugs, and a growing fight against migration (and often among all three put together). When it came to the Cold War's "loser," meanwhile, defeat and a destabilizing process of rapid and oligopolistic privatization fed into Russia's own self-styled war on terror, not least in two terrible wars in Chechnya, besides giving renewed impetus for geopolitical conflict of the kind familiar from the Ukraine invasion.[17] Beyond this, the war on terror has been intimately linked with the war on drugs, notably in Colombia as well as in Afghanistan, where defeating the Taliban and reining in the heroin trade were often presented as part of the same endeavor. The war on terror and its offshoots have also played a very important role in large-scale displacements from countries such as Afghanistan, Iraq, and Syria, feeding into the business of border security, while a significant part of the "securitization" of migration concerns the framing of people on the move as terrorists or drug-runners. In other words, our cases are not self-contained: the "crime scene" we're investigating is complex and systemic, making the task of cutting through this complexity all the more challenging but also all the more urgent.

With these overlaps in mind, chapter 7 examines the distorted information or knowledge environment that has been constructed around all our wars and fights. In this "hall of mirrors," nothing is quite what it seems. Almost any failure can be reflected back as a success. The stronger the fixation on a particular threat, the more pronounced the distortion—and the easier it becomes to mislead the voters who pay for the intervention. Here it is tempting to say that "failure is the new success." We go on to suggest that what is "new" (or new-ish) about this perverse process stems partly from post–Cold War changes to the security environment and partly from increasing market pressures on competing bureaucracies, media organizations, and other key actors. Both these factors are deeply political and deeply tied up in a (post) modern obsession with optics. On a positive note, the chapter suggests that one key opportunity for dismantling disastrous systems of intervention is through changes to the knowledge environment. This is crucial when it comes to establishing clear lines of responsibility for the wreckage.

In chapter 8, we elaborate our discussion of distorted knowledge environments by exploring how far our model applies beyond the more obviously securitized interventions we have considered so far. Our case is the COVID-19 response and what can be learned from both its "laissez-faire" and lockdown incarnations. While often (understandably) treated as opposites, we find that these two extremes both exhibited "wreckonomic" tendencies, albeit to different degrees at different times. In looking at the intersection of COVID-19 responses and the culture wars, we emphasize that a key disadvantage in the various belligerent framings around COVID-19 is that they have narrowed the space for debate and dissent.

Chapter 9 sets out our suggestions for undoing the wreckage of failing systems. Building on the previous two chapters, we suggest that one crucial improvement would be to move from "fixed" to more open knowledge environments. Another way forward centers on the specific ways in which the costs and perverse benefits of the wars can be tracked and contested, including through the creative building of coalitions. There is hope and inspiration to be found here, especially once we comparatively examine how our wars and fights have been challenged in recent years. However, as we seek to dismantle these various war and security systems, we must account for their remarkable resilience. We must also have an eye on the *global* political and economic system in which they have been unfolding and interacting—and in chapter 10 we lift our gaze to consider this. Throughout the book, we emphasize that productive change will elude us unless we understand the mechanisms that make our endless wars and endless wrecking so persistent and profitable. So let us attend, with the dispassionate eyes of the systems detective, to the crime scene investigation with which we began.

2

Wreckonomics 101

How Failure Became the New Success

While academia can be a lonely place where scholars beaver away on their own for years, sometimes, after long periods of study and fieldwork, you find that someone else has been reaching conclusions that are eerily similar to your own. While many scholars live in fear of such an eventuality, we found it to be exciting when we first met at the London School of Economics and then continued the conversation over several years on walks and during college and pub lunches in Oxford. David had been working on disasters, civil wars, and the war on terror, writing books such as *The Benefits of Famine* and *Useful Enemies* and visiting sites of vicious conflict such as Sudan and Sierra Leone from the mid-1980s. Ruben had been working on border security, military intervention, and the political manipulation of fear in Africa and Europe—research that informed his books *Illegality, Inc.* and *No Go World*.[1] Separately, we had developed our own distinct analyses of the persistence of policies that were not achieving their stated ends. When we started working together on this, around the time of Europe's border crisis of 2015, we realized how much our analyses converged. There was something *systematic* going on, with each of these "wars" or "fights" tending to feed off its own disastrous consequences. Disturbed and intrigued by this observation, we plowed on. As we proceeded to join the dots on the war on terror, the war on drugs, and the fight against illegal migration, we came to realize that policies that looked different on the surface shared elements of a deeper logic. We found, in short, *several perversely self-reinforcing systems that fueled the problems they were simultaneously feeding off, a process through which failure emerged as a peculiar kind of success.* Of course, these various crises also differ from one another in important respects, and failure is hardly uniform. But lifting the veil on these underlying similarities and systems logics became our priority.

Systems thinking may seem rather dry—unsurprisingly, perhaps, given that it's usually the domain of scientists writing peer-reviewed papers full of formulas and jargon that most mortals cannot hope or do not care to understand. But bear with us. Coming from a working background in anthropology (Ruben) and history/sociology (David), we are not scientists in the conventional sense. We have no calculators to hand (they are probably lost in a drawer somewhere), no lab coats nor microscopes. Yet what we have found, in strikingly diverse geographical and policy contexts—and going well beyond the three wars or fights that initially caught our attention—is an intriguingly consistent *pattern* that sustains damaging interventions in remarkably diverse fields. We call this "wreckonomics" and we believe that, to beat the wreckers at their own game, we need to become budding "wreckonomists" ourselves. That's why we set about writing this book: a manual of sorts that may give some systems pointers for those who are trying to challenge destructive interventions and the misleading language that tends to surround and legitimize them.

Listen to the Pattern

There are many ways to become a good wreckonomist, and we see more and more of these strange creatures around, even if they haven't labeled themselves as such. Among them are investigative reporters unearthing the costs and benefits of war and damaging interventions; brave activists and NGOs—often in countries on the "front line"—who collate and expose the collateral damage of these various wars at great risk to themselves; and academics who do important field-work or manage to defy the relentless drive toward specialization by actively grappling with the big systemic crises of our moment. In addition, some policy insiders and analysts have charted a path to understanding why perverse systems persist, not least in state bureaucracy and security settings. Their findings will pepper the coming chapters, and more details will appear in endnotes for readers who wish to delve further.

We take inspiration not just from these voices but also, and perhaps more fundamentally, from ordinary people outside or on the margins of these self-reinforcing systems. From civilians in war to migrants in distress, many of those targeted or rendered "collateral damage" have themselves seen through the wars, security interventions, and failing policies that form the subject of this book. We attach more weight to the perspectives of those at the sharp end than to the formulas of systems analysts, economists, and increasingly statistics-obsessed political scientists. Much of our own analysis is an attempt to learn how our various wars, fights, and other interventions look from the point of view of their human "targets." Indeed, our starting point is listening intently to their analyses.

When we have carried out investigations on these lines, we have found not only an acute critique of the vested interests of war but also an opening toward change. When David was in Sierra Leone to research the 1990s civil war, he was struck by how well informed many ordinary citizens were about politics even when they were coping with terrible situations. In large part, this seemed to reflect the way politics had come knocking on the door of ordinary people in the form of outright war, extreme violence, and widespread population displacement. Knowing something about politics was part of surviving. One thing that many civilians had learned was that the civil war was not a straightforward contest between two sides (as most of us are accustomed to seeing a civil war) but rather a kind of fixed sporting contest—a "sell-game," as some called it—in which outright battles were usually avoided and government soldiers were frequently and profitably cooperating with the very rebels they claimed to be opposing (see Figure 1).[2] By questioning the assumption that rebels were uniquely responsible for tearing the country apart, it became possible to see that the trumpeted solution (the counterinsurgency) was actually an integral part of the problem. Civilians saw how rebellion had offered a huge opportunity to powerful players with diverse economic and political goals, not least those within the army. One practical implication of this kind of analysis was the pressing need for better pay, conditions, and training in the army—and moves to do this were an important part of the country's peace process.

When Ruben first arrived in Senegal some years later to work on migration to Europe, he was struck by a related analysis among those targeted by border security. In one of Europe's earliest "migration crises," some thirty thousand West African migrants had arrived at the Spanish Canary Islands in wooden fishing boats in 2006, sparking a large-scale deportation campaign and the rollout of a "fight against illegal migration" along the Atlantic shoreline. On the outskirts of the Senegalese capital, Dakar, some of the deportees now confronted

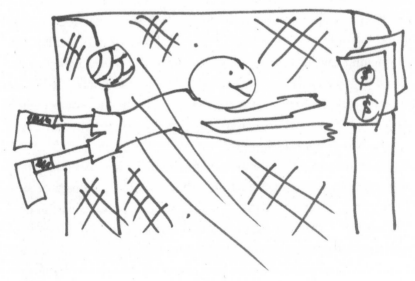

Figure 1 The "sell-game" of civil war. Illustration by David Keen.

Ruben with an uncomfortable realization: as an academic studying migration, he was in their view part of a profitable system that was living off the migrants' misery. "There's lots of money in illegal migration," said a deportee leader while pointing out, day after day on long walks through his seaside neighborhood, all those who fed off this system. These were not just academics but also reporters, NGOs, and European and Senegalese maritime forces on the horizon just beyond this fishing community. The vessels would stop patrolling the coast the moment a bribe appeared, deportees kept saying. Beneficiaries also included Senegal's president, Abdoulaye Wade, who was reported to be financing his reelection campaign with Spanish aid money designed to secure Senegal's collaboration in deportations and border patrols.[3] As Ruben was able to observe, the border experiment in West Africa was a pilot project of sorts for a much wider system in which major "partners" in European immigration control—from Libya to Turkey and Sudan—have wielded threats and/or leveraged their promised cooperation not just for a windfall of aid but also for valuable impunity and wider strategic and economic ends.

We had thus in our own quite separate ways developed an analysis of the "political economy" of war and of security operations—asking the old question "Who gains?" (*cui bono*) as well as "In whose wider interests are the operations staged?" In this, we had both tried to listen to the analysis of ordinary civilians on the "front line," building an analytical framework in dialogue with their perspectives. This process of "listening to the pattern" also involved listening to security operatives themselves. When Ruben initially went to Spain and West Africa to study the business of bordering Europe, for instance, his assumption was that the border guards and police would be dour and difficult folk; patrolling seas and fences, they were part of a machinery that had led to the deaths of thousands (while being seen by migrants, as we heard, as corrupt). Yet the more he talked to them, the more he found *internal* criticism, with at least some border operatives suggesting they were "not the solution" or acknowledging the damage their operations caused. Looking across our various crises and interventions, from counternarcotics to the wars on terror and crime, there has been no shortage of such internal critique. It would be foolish to ignore it.

As we plied our own respective trades over the years, we had in this fashion—and quite unbeknownst to ourselves—started to become budding wreckonomists. As we worked on this book, and on articles and reports leading up to it, it became clearer that what we were aiming for was a kind of *political systems analysis* that allowed for spotting the similarities and even shared logics between rather different areas of policy wreckage. The way to start building this analysis, we found, was by listening closely to those most affected by a given system of intervention, whether as insiders, targets, or "collateral damage." From there, we could start joining dots higher up these systems, observing interactions among distinct crises and policy interventions.

When it comes to our role as "systems detectives," we should recognize that the *academic* system today tends to discourage the wider view. While we will look at this a little more closely in chapter 7, we note here that a competitive academic marketplace has encouraged a high degree of specialization. The positivist trend in political science and elsewhere has been putting more and more store in hypothesis-testing combined with quantitative data-gathering, with a focus on topics and questions where such data is available. Within the qualitative disciplines, meanwhile, researchers have often felt a strong pressure to specialize on some very narrow topic on which they can establish their expertise.[4] While specialization has its virtues, there is a danger of not seeing the wood for the trees. We need to lift our view, the better to spot wider patterns and logics. This is what *Wreckonomics* sets out to offer. By listening to the analyses at the sharp end of the wars and to our fellow systems analysts inside and outside academia, we have been able to identify some significant shared patterns (amid the still significant differences). And we have tried to abstract and specify the shared logics in the war and security settings that we are analyzing. These logics, insofar as we can identify them, imply that some deeper underlying process may be in operation.

Political Systems Analysis: From Conspiracy and Complexity to Co-creation

This may all seem rather abstract. While we will soon have occasion to flesh out our model, let us first return to the wider analytical move that this book is offering as we seek to answer a simple question: Why do disastrous interventions so frequently persist and grow?

Of course, there are many possible explanations, but it's helpful to look first at two contrasting camps—which we call "conspiracy" and "complexity"—before we outline our own approach, which centers on the co-creation of damaging systems by diverse actors.

While *conspiracy* may be a value-laden word, we still find it to be a useful shorthand for explanations that emphasize the role of powerful vested interests in planning and sustaining disastrous interventions. It should hardly need saying that profiting from disaster has been a rather central theme in human history—not least when predatory European colonialism inflicted enduring disaster on vast swaths of the world.[5] Indeed, the history of empires and capital has set the context for the global inequalities and tensions that underpin the wars and fights considered in this book (a point we return to in chapter 10 in particular).[6]

Supplementing this longer view, prominent left-wing critics such as Noam Chomsky have documented a range of specific political and economic gains from destructive wars and security systems in more recent decades, often emphasizing the disproportionate power and greed of the United States. In an explicitly Marxist analysis, the geographer David Harvey stresses that capitalism has generated a huge problem of underconsumption (as billions of poor people cannot afford to buy capitalism's ever-expanding output), which in turn has encouraged a destructive marriage of profit and violence. In what Harvey sees as a modern version of Marx's "primitive accumulation," private capital moves increasingly into the arms industry and into foreign wars and "reconstruction," while also taking over many of the security functions previously carried out by the state.[7] Some analysts have highlighted that "free market" ideology may proceed alongside—and even depend upon—very high state spending on prisons, defense, border security, policing, and so on.[8]

Besides radical academics, many of those who stress the role of powerful interests in sustaining wars and other security systems are journalists and activists, reaching from antiarmaments groups to civil rights advocates and high-profile investigative reporters. Such analysts go well beyond the search for individual culprits that was exemplified in our "burned thumb" example in chapter 1. Instead, they tend to emphasize that there is something *systemic* joining together seemingly disparate dots, usually involving some combination of corporate and geopolitical power.

When it comes to a specific focus on the profits of disasters, the best known work in recent years is probably that of Naomi Klein. Coining the term "disaster capitalism" in *The Shock Doctrine*, Klein suggested that wars and major disasters have been treated as an opportunity to push through privatization and other forms of economic liberalization, as powerful vested interests take advantage of the "shock" and disorientation that surround these disasters. Her book includes detailed analyses of the botched but highly profitable US-led reconstruction in Iraq, of the oligarchs' manipulation of rushed privatization in Russia, and of how Hurricane Katrina was used to push through privatization and the destruction of public housing in Louisiana. If capitalism is the main culprit in Klein's account, the finger of blame is also pointed firmly at the "Chicago School" of economists, who were influential in promoting privatization around the world and who sometimes admitted that they saw crisis and disorder as an opportunity to push this agenda. In related work, Antony Loewenstein's book *Disaster Capitalism* shows how the post-2007 financial crisis in Greece, for example, was used for such ends. Loewenstein is one among many prominent journalists, activists, and academics to have cataloged the profiteering from mass detention and incarceration in the United States and elsewhere, including in the context of wars and fights against crime, drugs, and migration. In such analyses, the gun is definitely smoking, yet instead of a single villain, we end up with a systemic set of aligned interests centering on powerful capitals and capitalists who are "making a killing out of catastrophe."[9]

These investigative exposés are an important resource; indeed, having once trained as journalists ourselves, we want to emphasize the value of learning from and collaborating with our fellow "systems detectives" in the media and in popular writing. All too often, academics have taken such findings too lightly. Yet if we focus on what we might call a "hard conspiracy" approach, there are also some significant problems. One is the difficulty of proving intention. Smoking guns are rare, and those exploiting crisis tend not to advertise what they are doing. Relatedly, once you think you have *found* a smoking gun, there may be a temptation to exaggerate its importance.

Another problem with the idea of a grand capitalist or Washington-led conspiracy is that local agency may be dangerously downplayed. When it comes to postindependence Latin America, Héctor Hoyos is critical of Klein's focus on the power of Washington (and Chicago), and he stresses the *domestic* forces pushing toward liberalization as well as repression.[10] Postcolonial scholars such as Dipesh Chakrabarty have also offered an analysis that takes local agency very seriously, as have path-breaking investigative journalists such as P. Sainath in his powerful reportage from rural India, *Everybody Loves a Good Drought.*[11] Going back to colonialism, we should note that even colonizers needed collaborators, particularly where the former were trying to establish systems of government (as opposed to simple killing and pillage). Many scholars have shown that when colonialism's "collaborators" presented themselves as cooperating, this was sometimes part of an elaborate balancing act that allowed them to attract external support as well as internal followers—a maneuver we will consider further in the next chapter's discussion of Cold War conflict.[12]

Standing in contrast to authors emphasizing some kind of conspiracy are those who stress *complexity.* Within this framework, the smoking gun virtually disappears; indeed, sometimes it seems that no one is in charge and that the global political economy has an intractable life of its own. Those who emphasize complexity tend to find at least some degree of predictability. At the same time, the very complexity of political-economic systems is usually taken to mean that attempts to interfere will not play out as intended.

A helpful and humorous guide to complexity thinking is a slim book from the 1970s, John Gall's *Systemantics: How Systems Work and Especially How They Fail*. Concerned with understanding the complex laws governing the behavior of complex organizations, the book is a veritable candy store for systems detectives such as ourselves. "Systems are like babies," Gall tells us. "Once you get one, you have it. They don't go away. On the contrary, they display the most remarkable persistence. They not only persist: they grow. And as they grow, they encroach." Rather than simply addressing the problems they were set up to deal with, Gall argues, systems tend to strengthen themselves by generating *new* problems—in part to justify their continued existence.[13]

Of course, we don't need to go all the way with Gall and anthropomorphize "the system," as if systems somehow had their own desire and will. The important point is that an emerging system tends to bring all kinds of new problems, all kinds of perverse incentives for growth and buy-in, and all kinds of cascading effects—and that all of these tend to push toward further growth.

To take an example rather far from our wars and fights, we can see some of these systems dynamics at work in our own professional corner of academia. In the United Kingdom, for example, a rather relentless growth of student numbers has been matched by escalating fees and competition over ranking. In this world of proliferating targets centering on revenue, excellence, impact, satisfaction, and so on, successes are routinely registered and publicized. But the complex demands within such a system have tended to undermine some of the fundamental aims of universities, notably knowledge production. Both staff and students often seem too busy to read and too busy to think. A key factor here is the climate of increasing assessment and surveillance ostensibly aimed at efficiency and ensuring "value for money" and, ironically, "satisfaction." Something similar is happening in many ordinary workplaces where "target culture" has taken hold: in the name of efficiency, as many readers will be aware to their cost, you end up not doing what you should be doing.

We engage Gall here because he foreshadows how systems theorists have tended to analyze complexity in more recent years. His *Systemantics* epitomizes the emphasis on "natural complexity" as an explanation for dysfunctions, an explanation that clearly does not depend on the existence of a conspiracy or even of bad intentions. He also reminds us that there may be nothing specific about our wars and security operations; they are simply examples of a much wider pattern in which systems feed on themselves—a phenomenon that is all too frequently ignored. We revisit this wider picture at later points in the book. However, while perverse systems dynamics affect many spheres beyond our core wars and fights, the framework of "war" or "security" seems to turbocharge the self-reinforcing tendencies of failing-yet-succeeding interventions. When we look closely at our five wreckonomics mechanisms at the end of this chapter, we will get a better sense of why this is so.

If systems so frequently reinforce themselves while undermining their own objectives, then we also need to be extremely humble in any attempts to address systemic problems. In Gall's view, "The fundamental problem does not lie in any particular system but rather in systems *as such*"; given the resilience of such systems, there is no "easy fix" but rather an obligation to understand them better.[14] And systems thinkers of a more recent pedigree would tend to agree.

To take an example from the humanitarian field, Ben Rangalingam and Harry Jones have argued that complex systems may appear random but nevertheless tend to be characterized by an underlying order and even a degree of predictability.[15] That would seem to create at least the *possibility* of a helpful intervention. But these authors also emphasize that interventions can easily become part of the problem— particularly when they fail to engage with complex social realities in a holistic and systemic way.[16] When organizations are confronted with the complex mess of reality, they often "carve off" a part of this reality and try to "put this right" while ignoring links to other dimensions of the mess.[17] We will see this tendency of fixating on one aspect of a complex reality in all our wars and fights, along with a tendency for the intervention to grow once the initial "fix" does not work.

Robert Jervis's *System Effects,* the most influential attempt to bring systems thinking into the study of international relations and diplomacy, exhibits even greater skepticism when it comes to making effective interventions. Moving freely between ecological and political systems (as do many of our complexity thinkers), Jervis emphasizes that a small change in one part of a complex system can have multiple knock-on effects. Contingencies and patterns that can be fully detected only on a systems level frequently outwit the best (or worst) of intentions. In this context, policies and regulations—whether in the pursuit of security or raising taxes or something else—will tend to fail in their stated aims. Jervis makes an eloquent plea for modesty: we should not imagine that we can tinker with complex systems and expect to know what will happen.

All of these insights are relevant for *Wreckonomics*. But just as we have noted significant dangers with an emphasis on conspiracy, we should also note significant drawbacks with an emphasis on complexity. Systems thinkers tend to convey relatively little sense of what kind of interests might be driving the complex systems that they are examining. "One of the critiques levelled at complexity science," as Ramalingam and Jones observe, "is that there is no real way of dealing with power."[18]

Here, it's helpful to draw on work by the anthropologist and security scholar Mark Duffield, who has been a significant inspiration for both of us. Over many years, Duffield has himself pursued a kind of systems thinking, analyzing the deep political and historical dimensions of wars, security, and development, especially in the Horn of Africa. With a number of others, he has highlighted how in the "political economy" of war, disasters, and security, there are a number of vested interests that frequently ensure that things *go wrong in the right way*. For example, projects of "humanitarianism" and "development" often go badly wrong but still may be seen as serving a function in "containing" what Duffield calls the world's "uninsured" populations. In his 2018 book *Post-humanitarianism*, Duffield took his analysis a step further and showed how *depoliticized* versions of systems thinking—increasingly influential in international interventions—can actually be a neat and dangerous way to evade responsibility for one's actions: once everything is sufficiently "complex" and "systemic" (and once a sufficient number of decisions are being made by computers), there is no one left to blame for the wreckage. Duffield wisely warns that power does not like to analyze itself, and he suggests that a focus on complexity can conveniently sideline political and historical analysis of how the system has come to be and who is manipulating it for what purposes.[19] Once "target populations" are treated as mere parts of an abstract system, their history and humanity tend to recede from view. Yet we desperately need history—and what academics like to call "structure and agency"—in the picture.[20]

So where does all this leave us when it comes to our wars and fights? Are we facing, to put it crudely, a Grand Conspiracy or a Systems Cock-Up? Social scientists very often emphasize the *contingency* of events—the extreme difficulty of predicting what will happen—and we have considerable sympathy with this reflex. However, it remains important to highlight any underlying patterns and predictabilities: history is not just "one damned event after another." While distancing ourselves from "hard conspiracy" and the idea of a Grand Master Plan, we are nevertheless uncomfortable with versions of "complexity theory" that take humans radically out of the picture. Our own approach emphasizes human agency and the *co-creation* of events. Put plainly, a whole host of factors and actors will generally need to come together for a particular intervention to become established and dominant. Co-creation is a highly unequal dance of instigation, implementation, and reaction, which frequently reflects longer colonial legacies and deeply entrenched power imbalances. This is partly why we speak

of a *systemic* crime scene. However, we emphasize that it is not sufficient for someone "at the top" to will an intervention into existence
and assume that all else will smoothly follow. Nor can our war and
security systems be usefully dismissed as irredeemably complex, un-
changeable, and unpredictable. It is true that, at any given moment, a
particular "solution" (perhaps a system of heavily securitized borders
or a system of Mutually Assured Destruction) may come to seem both
natural and inevitable. But such systems have a particular *genealogy* (to
use a term favored by Michel Foucault); we need to understand the
conditions that made them possible. As part of this, we also need to
understand the complex array of interests that support—and benefit
from—a given "solution." Focusing on the particular confluence of
agendas and contingencies that underpins any system of intervention
helps us to move away from the sense of pessimism and intractability
that both "complexity" and "conspiracy" frameworks tend to bring.
We begin to see better how change is possible.

Here, we find ourselves rather in sympathy with analysts such as
Nafeez Ahmed and Adam Tooze, who have pointed to the existence
of multiple overlapping crises that feed damagingly into one another.[21] These crises may yield substantial benefits for economic elites
and for a range of political and security actors. And some of these
actors may feed opportunistically on the very crises they have helped
to produce. But this doesn't mean that everything has been carefully
planned in advance, that the relevant interests are closely coordinating
with each other, or that they have it "all under control." We emphasize that the system as a whole tends to acquire a certain resilience
and longevity from the complex interests that have grown up around
it. Correspondingly, change becomes possible when these interests—
including the implementers of our various wars and fights—begin to
push (or are coaxed) in another direction.

In dealing with systematically disastrous political interventions,
then, we must take seriously *both* the claims of the "conspiracy" camp
around how vested interests are driving these interventions forward
and the "complexity" camp's emphasis on unpredictable system effects.

We want to suggest a form of political systems analysis that joins a political economy approach with systems thinking, and that moves across different scales of intervention without presuming that any one level of explanation will be sufficient.[22]

A good starting point in any political systems analysis is not to treat systems as unmovable monoliths. We must avoid what scholars like to call "reification," reinforcing the power of the "thing" we are seeking to criticize. Instead, we approach our systems as always in tension and always in the making.[23]

However complex a system is, it is likely to have been given a strong *steer.* Just as ecologists recognize that humankind has disproportionate influence on ecological systems, we also need to recognize that some individuals and groups have disproportionate influence on the complex systems surrounding and partially derailing policy interventions. Part of the steer, as we see it, centers on the manner in which the negative "side effects" (or system effects) of a benevolent-sounding policy have frequently been ignored, neglected, massaged, or actively hijacked. Such negative effects are not necessarily "unintended" even at the outset, as a more naïve kind of systems theorist may assume; they might be intended, or they might simply be considered insufficiently important to prevent the initial intervention. In exploring why failing systems persist, we will look at systems (and actors within systems) that cannibalize their own mistakes for complex but to a large extent identifiable purposes. Some interventions are so strongly characterized by this process of hijacking and cannibalizing that talking about "mistakes" becomes increasingly meaningless.[24] In circumstances where the relevant policy is maintained in the face of growing evidence about these negative effects, it becomes particularly difficult to sustain the claim that these effects are "unintended."

Moving further down the scale of intervention, we approach our frequently spectacular wars and fights as workplaces. As such, they are in hock as much to "office politics" as to geopolitics. In "listening to the pattern" in these admittedly peculiar workplaces, our political systems analysis emphasizes the interplay between complicity, subversion, and perverse incentives—an interplay that may be familiar to us from any workplace. This interplay can of course be conspiratorial, complex, and contingent all at once. Once a system of workplace targets has been put in place, we can be sure that some workers and bosses will start gaming it to their advantage while perhaps others are grumpily resisting the New Order. Sometimes we will find elements of *engineered complicity,* where instigators of an intervention can be seen to bring an increasingly complex system into being through encouraging buy-ins—a "soft" version of the "conspiracy" outlined above. Yet at other times, such complicity can be undermined by the counteractions of "partners," not to mention by the actions of "target groups" themselves.

In short, we find that power within our war and security systems— and indeed a great many workplaces more widely—cannot realistically be seen simply as located "at the top" but is actually distributed much more widely through complex networks and relationships, including those that are geared toward tackling the relevant "threats."[25] As these various systems adapt to the disasters that they are ostensibly confronting (and often helping to reproduce), they also tend to reproduce themselves, mutating, consolidating, reorganizing, and moving further from the original intentions of those who played a key role in designing or initiating them.

Perhaps, as our "war bus" swerves around hairpin turns with precipitous drops on either side, it is less than reassuring to think that it is being steered not by a single driver but by a selection of its most influential passengers, each with their own agendas and their own ideas about where the bus should be heading and even what the bus is actually *for.* In these circumstances, there tends to be no simple way of turning back. But we believe that recognizing our current predicament—and putting the brakes on its systemic drivers and devious "fixes"—is a pretty good start.

Following from that, we must also recognize that the bus can be steered *elsewhere.* Indeed, our emphasis on what we may call "distributed agency" suggests that such complex systems can be changed and even dismantled—and part of the point of *Wreckonomics* is to identify the opportunities that do exist for challenging destructive systems. We discuss this further in the final chapters of the book. Systems of intervention are not all in hock to perverse incentives and self-interest; there are usually countervailing factors at work (like democratic control and pressure for fairness and accountability) within taxpayer-funded systems.[26] Part of the way forward is to notice and give credit in those situations where creativity, selfless professionalism, and intelligent kindness have been allowed to emerge. It means noticing moments and spaces of resistance, including among the very warfighters or security actors whose workplace is somewhere on the "front line."

The economic and political interests vested in war or security *can* be dismantled, as our interlocutors reminded us in Sierra Leone's war and Senegal's border control landscape. What has once been constructed as a threat may be reverse-engineered into something else. As former migrants and their families remarked during fieldwork in Senegal and neighboring Mali, legal pathways for mobility existed between West Africa and Europe in the postwar years when willing workers did not need to embark on unseaworthy boats and no government contemplated erecting walls against them. The fight against migration and the "war on smugglers" are fairly recent historical inventions with specific causes and functions, and there is nothing inevitable about the current way of doing things. A little further south, in Sierra Leone, many civilians understood that peace would depend, in part, on addressing the "sell-game" of the war and reforming the counterinsurgency. Neither Sierra Leonean political actors nor their international counterparts were *permanently* stuck in the mode of reproducing rebels through dysfunctional counterinsurgency. Similar green shoots of hope have started to appear in the "war on terror" and its various proliferating variations. Instigating countries have begun to lose faith in the project, and, correspondingly, the advantages of cooperating (or appearing to cooperate) show signs of diminishing.

The point is that perversely self-serving interventions are far from set in stone. Systems are not all the same; resignation to them and their "complexity" is itself part of the systemic picture and part of the perverse resilience that we must dismantle, as the politics of climate change also reminds us. Building on such examples, we hope that some "systems sleuthing" and attention to vital clues will help us to clamber out from under the wreckage of war and crisis that besets our collective present and future.

Wreckanisms: Four "Fixes" (and One Great Unfix)

We have emphasized the importance of pattern-spotting. But what exactly is this pattern that we have observed? What are the shared logics in our wars and fights? And how does our wreckonomics framework help to explain the persistence of bad interventions? We can break the pattern down into five discrete mechanisms. As if by magic (but these things take work!), the headings of the mechanisms correspond to the W.R.E.C.K. in wreckonomics.

W is for the "war fix." All of our dysfunctional interventions— whether these are wars or fights or some other kind of struggle or policy endeavor—begin with a very basic and hazardous maneuver: *they transform a complex, systemic issue into a simple threat that urgently needs to be combated.* Generally, this threat is highlighted at the cost of marginalizing other considerations, something that tends to exaggerate and expand the threat over time, often out of all proportion. The "fixation" on a singular threat (see how we just dodged the bullet of "*Freckonomics*"!) is usually accompanied by the fixation on an equally singular "solution" or magic bullet. Fixation has been addressed by security scholars via the term "securitization," which will make appearances in later chapters; suffice to say for now that we believe the pattern of fixation goes beyond security interventions in the strict sense.[27] It is usually driven by governments, though not always: state officials and supranational organizations have provided key impetus to the war on terror, the war on drugs, and the fight against migration; defense contractors and other commercial actors have played a large role behind the scenes in all our wars and fights; and ordinary voters, interest groups, media outlets, and even NGOs have regularly fed into their buildup and momentum. At an extreme, the fixation results in what psychoanalysts would label "fetishization," or an unhealthy obsession with something out of all proportion to its real importance. In general, fixation does away with a complex understanding of complex problems; it generates affective buy-in among voters and institutional buy-in among security actors; and it tends, as a result, to wreck the possibilities for a proportionate, rational, and democratically scrutinized response to a given problem.

R is for the rigging or fixing of the "game" that ensues. It refers to the ways in which the objective of defeating an enemy or a threat cohabits with a set of emerging subsidiary games that may work at loggerheads with the official aim even while strengthening the overall system of intervention. Again, this may apply to wars and fights but also to situations that have little or nothing to do with war. Wars tend to bring about the conditions (including secrecy, suppression of dissent, and the need for victory) in which rigging can flourish. But wherever there is a loudly trumpeted commitment to winning or reining in some kind of threat, significant opportunities for rigging are likely to arise. The underlying solution (perhaps a "war" or a "fight" or simply a strong policy push) may itself be a gamble of the most reckless kind—frequently fueling the problem it claims to address. Nevertheless, a growing group of players may be pretty sure of big wins within this floundering intervention thanks to the various subsidiary games that have grown up around the overarching or original game. Such rigging may take the form of a "double game" with covert winners subverting their own loudly expressed cooperation in a particular endeavor. This double gaming may involve actors looking the other way instead of enforcing whatever overt policy they are tasked with implementing. At the extreme, it involves the actors' active collusion in the phenomenon they claim to be combating. In both cases, *the very phenomenon that key actors claim to be opposing is also, surprisingly often, the phenomenon that is helping them the most.*

E is for export. Alongside the gaming of the *benefits* of intervention there is generally an export or "externalization" of its costs. To continue our own fixation on "fixing," we can also call this "fixing the fallout." In general, we find that *the costs of intervention tend to be perversely distributed so as to minimize negative impacts on the powerful.* The costs of fighting the reviled but reproduced phenomenon tend to be subtly but systematically redistributed so that the instigators of failing policies are protected from the worst effects while the most significant suffering is passed down the line to those with little political power or "skin in the game." In other words, unwinnable fights tend to generate what economists call "negative externalities," costs that are off the books and that someone else has to deal with. The starkest examples often come in the context of wars and "fights" of different kinds—indeed, this offloading of costs and consequences helps greatly in explaining why the wars persist despite the wreckage they generate. But again, there are many interventions other than war where externalizing the costs is a key feature of the system, a point we will return to intermittently.

C is for cascade. Our first three "fixes" suggest that manipulation, corruption, and self-interest are key to wreckonomics, which wouldn't be wrong. Coming back to our political systems discussion, there are many fixers and small-c conspiracies or collusions to find amid the wreckage. Yet our cascade mechanism is in many ways the Great Unfix: it points directly at the *complexity* of the systems of intervention that we are investigating. A cascade refers to the process by which shocks within a system build up in "nonlinear" fashion through complex interactions. Such shocks may swiftly take on system-wide characteristics the way an avalanche builds from the smallest movements of snow on a mountainside. More specifically in the context of our interventions, we approach the cascade as *the process by which our wars and fights begin to spiral out of control owing to* *complex systems dynamics.* While other analysts (notably Jervis) would proceed to typologize different "system effects," we limit ourselves here to distinguishing between two dimensions of this dynamic runaway process. First, there is the *cascade of costs* as the intervention impacts "target groups" and the wider society. As we will see, our wars and fights are notable in how frequently "blowbacks" and reactions from targets (migrants, smugglers, insurgents) and wider populations contribute to runaway change. Second, there is a related *cascade of games.* The intervention itself tends to undergo runaway proliferation, partly in reaction to the blowbacks but also partly due to its own systemic momentum, as more actors instigate or "game" their own versions of it. To make this yet more complex, such cascades interact across different interventions in a context where our various wars and fights have frequently fueled one another. These interventions cannot be understood simply by looking at vested interests among instigators and implementers—we must bring to the picture an account of systems dynamics to understand why wrecking things has become such a runaway enterprise.

K is for the knowledge fix. By this we mean the habit of fixing the facts to oversimplify the problem and to retain a grip on the whole cascade of escalating policy failure. All the various systems that we will discuss are prone to distortion of the knowledge environment around the threat and the professed "solution." This in turn distorts the emotive environment while constraining decision-making. It may be a truism that the first casualty of war is truth, yet the extent to which the information environment is distorted in our wars and security interventions is nevertheless astounding, frequently leaving the wider public with a "through-the-looking-glass" view of what's really going on while minimizing the scope for genuine questioning and dissent. The knowledge fix is integral to our other four mechanisms—starting with the war fix, which distorts the rationale for "war," and continuing through to the cascading costs, failures, and illicit gains of war, all of which routinely disappear from public, policy, and even academic debate. Where costs are mentioned, they tend to be treated—if at all—as unrelated to the intervention itself. Those who try to highlight the hidden costs of a particular way of doing things are likely to be marginalized or vilified (or even, in a twist to the knowledge fix, to have their interventions labeled "disinformation" or "misinformation"). Here, the war framework comes into its own as a tool for suppressing dissenting views. In short, we can say that *the knowledge environment is to a large extent shaped in such a way that threats are inflated, failure is erased, responsibility is outsourced, and spaces for dissent and debate are greatly diminished*, setting the conditions for further cascades. This distortion of the information environment is often overt, yet, in keeping with our political systems analysis, it can also (and simultaneously) be systemic in origin, as part of the wider dynamic ecology of the intervention.

We can imagine our "wreckanisms" interacting in a chain of events, as we have tried to illustrate in Figure 2: the fixation on threats and solutions is followed by rigged games and exported costs, both of which cascade and so feed the problem—in a process that is regularly "knowledge-fixed" in such a way that the systemic causes of the growing problem are underplayed. However, while the idea of a cycle

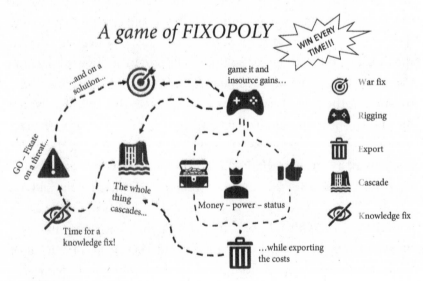

Figure 2 Wreckonomics as a cycle.

is helpful in getting a grip on the process, let us note three things. First, while we have presented the mechanisms in neat sequence, they actually interact in complex and nonchronological ways. Gaming and rigging frequently precede fixation, while their benefits develop in parallel to the exportation of the costs, and so forth. We are, in other words, faced with a complex process in which one round of wreckage feeds into further wrecking and fixing. Second, while all mechanisms are "required" if an intervention is to be truly "wreckonomic," they may also occur in other combinations. Third, and most important, what *is* particular to wreckonomics is a *peculiar combination of chaos and stability,* or proliferation and persistence, in the systemic process we have identified.

Let us offer a more abstract rendering of the complex relationships among our mechanisms (Figure 3). To the left, around the "war fix," we find the stable pole of the system: a rather self-contained machinery exporting its costs and insourcing its benefits while justifying itself ad infinitum through the distorted "mirror" of the knowledge fix. To the right, around the "cascade," we find the unstable pole where runaway change occurs through the proliferation and escalation of costs and

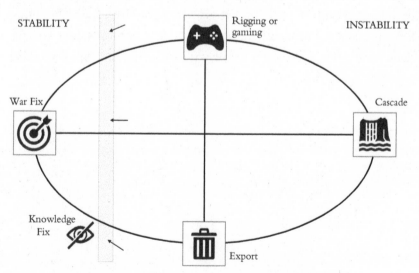

Figure 3 Complexity of interactions among "wreckanisms."

games. Together, the dynamic interaction between these poles helps explain how disaster-producing systems may sustain themselves, legitimize themselves, and proliferate over time.

Within our five "wreckanisms," we may observe several different kinds of "fix." First, there is a fixation on a single solution to a single problem (as in our "war fix"). Second, this project may itself offer an easy fix for complex and intractable problems, not least through its role as a distraction. Then there is the fixing of the game in which the extraction of selfish benefits may be more important than actually winning (or, to put it another way, redefining what it means to win). When it comes to the costs, there is a fixing of the fallout. In the knowledge environment, there is a fixing of the facts. Finally, and again perversely, this wreckonomic cycle is also a "fix" in the sense that it is *addictive:* it's a habit that is damaging both to ourselves and to others and to which politicians, interveners, and voters alike seem to be compulsively returning.

One way of summing up this habit of wreck-and-fix is the old saying "If you have a hammer, everything looks like a nail." Yet the more our politicians and security actors hammer away, the more cracks are starting to show. Crucially, those delivering the blows rarely have to deal with the resulting wreckage themselves. By highlighting hidden costs and hidden benefits, we become not just better systems detectives. More important, we may start peering through the cracks and spot a way out.

3

Cold War Games

When War Is a Self-Licking Ice-Cream Cone

What is the aim in a war? In many ways, the answer would seem to be obvious. The aim is to win. Yet war often provides military cover for a variety of aims and practices which have very little to do with winning, and which may sometimes *impede* victory—or make us fundamentally question what winning looks like in the first place. The Cold War, as a strange kind of pseudo-war that embraced many complex games and many real wars, is an ideal place to start asking such questions—offering clues to the wider pattern in *Wreckonomics*.

In the first section, we see how the long demise of the Cold War proved to be a time when scholars of war and security could see the diversity of aims in war with particular clarity. Some of this diversity was revealed at the geopolitical margins. A further clue came when those who were benefiting from the Cold War proved reluctant to let it go and when a series of transnational security threats—sometimes real, often exaggerated—served to justify further war and security investment. In the second and third sections, we focus quite selectively on some of the games that were pursued in the context of the Cold War itself, which allows us further to interrogate the notions of war and victory. At both macro and micro levels, we find that profit and institutional power-plays were very important, that actions predictably strengthening or inflating the threat or enemy were commonplace, and that the image of success was sometimes more important than the reality. Macro-level gaming included the channeling of huge resources toward defense contractors and the Pentagon within the United States, which interacted with its Soviet counterpart in the "arms race." We illustrate microlevel gaming by revisiting the Vietnam War. Whether in "hot wars" like Vietnam or in the wider Cold War military standoff, winning in the conventional sense was rather far from being the overriding preoccupation of the diverse coalitions who said they were signing up to the global conflict.

In making this argument, we are not trying to say that gaming or "rigging" war for political or economic profit—and pursuing the image rather than the reality of success—represented the whole story, whether during the Cold War or in its aftermath. Far from it. The Cold War was certainly not a "phony war" for the millions of people whose lives it destroyed. It involved countless vicious "proxy wars" in Central America, Africa, and East Asia and fed into a number of genocides and politicides from Guatemala to Indonesia. On one level, the Cold War can plausibly be seen as a struggle for strategic dominance by the superpowers. The clash of powerful state interests highlighted in the international relations "realism" school was all too real. Conversely, the Cold War's ruthless competition for influence was (in this and many other ways) "a continuation of colonialism through slightly different means," in the words of historian Odd Arne Westad.[1] Indeed, leaders of newly independent countries had very good reason to take heed from the violent removal of Congo's Lumumba or Indonesia's Sukarno, to take but two prominent examples. As the international relations scholar Mohammed Ayoob has argued, "security" looked very much like insecurity for those at the sharp end of the superpower quest for global dominance.[2]

Yet a political systems analysis complicates the picture in interesting and constructive ways. First of all, it encourages us to build a picture of aims, relations, and reactions across different scales and levels of analysis. Even in Washington and Moscow, the determination to "win" was complicated by a number of factors. One of these was the determination to put a good gloss on any setbacks. We saw this with the numerous claims of "success" in Vietnam as well as in Soviet-occupied Afghanistan—claims that were eventually contradicted by ignominious withdrawals. Further, political systems analysis emphasizes *agency,* including among those at the sharpest end. Every global war is fought with local co-operation. Yet, as in the preceding colonial period, those who are conceptualized in Washington or London or Paris or Moscow as a *means* turn out to have *goals of their own*, goals which substantially shape the direction of the project that appears to have been agreed upon. As in colonialism proper, the influence of (ostensible) "allies" on the overall direction of Cold War conflicts is often underestimated. We explore this widely distributed agency further in our discussion of the Vietnam War. Conflicts in what was then widely referred to as the "Third World" had a life and dynamic of their own, which often predated the Cold War. Decolonization processes, a key part of this, were often infiltrated and brutalized by Cold War rivalries.[3] Although some writers have stressed sharp distinctions between warfare in the Cold War and post–Cold War eras, the continuities—as Mats Berdal has argued—are in many ways more striking.[4] While proclaiming one's allegiance to the United States or to the Soviet Union was certainly an integral part of the Cold War, this did not mean that defeating Communism or capitalism was always the overriding aim of local "allies" who looked for support for a wide range of political and economic agendas. Separating these out from "winning" is always complicated, and Berdal points out that even a military faction dedicated to victory may need to raise money through economic predation.[5] When we come to look at our various wars and fights against terror, migration, crime, and drugs, we will find variations of the Cold War (and colonial) reliance on local "allies" who turn out—surprise!—to have complex agendas of their own. As during the Cold War, these local agendas—including winning, but certainly not limited to it—have interacted with similarly complex agendas among dominant powers in frequently disturbing ways. To see this in some detail, let us look to one of the more neglected corners of the Cold War chessboard: Sudan in the 1980s.

War and Security Rethought

In the dying days of the Cold War, a human disaster was unfolding in Sudan, where hunger was being systematically used as a weapon by the Sudanese regime. Yet as with the campaign for famine-stricken Ethiopia next door—most notably via the Live Aid concert and its calls to "feed the world"—the political manipulation of starvation and relief received very little coverage while famine was unfolding. In the case of Sudan, the silence around famine creation and manipulation was shared by Western governments. This was partly because the violence and starvation in Sudan's civil war were taking place in the context of Cold War geopolitics, with its perceived need to cement Sudan's loyalty as a buffer between Libya and Ethiopia.[6] There was a temptation for Western actors to see a friendly government pitted against "Communist" rebels, and this combined damagingly with a more bureaucratic impulse to paint failing relief operations as a *success*.[7] In David's research among aid workers and ordinary Sudanese citizens, moreover, it soon became clear that economic motivations—and political strategies like divide-and-rule—were of rather fundamental importance in driving the violence, alongside the attempt to "starve out" rebel supporters. Profitable systems were growing up around and shaping the conflict and the famine. Some centered on price movements—a boon for those selling high-priced grain, buying low-priced livestock, and employing forced labor. Some of the potential benefits centered on ejecting populations from oil-rich areas, where civilians were accused of having sympathy for the rebels. At the same time, attacks on these civilians were also creating recruits for the rebels, helping to spread the rebellion.

As with Sierra Leone's "sell-game" and its collusion between the counterinsurgency and insurgents, war in Sudan was quite different from what we think. Again, this was not exactly or exclusively a war-to-win, but an evolving system of exploitation in which even the reproduction of the enemy could serve a function in legitimizing extraction and repression.

David's early work on Sudan's conflict, resulting in his book *The Benefits of Famine,* was part of a wider shift in the study of war and peace amid the winding-down of the Cold War. Both war and the functions of war were being rather radically rethought, and a range of voices—our colleagues Mark Duffield, Alex de Waal, Mats Berdal, and Mary Kaldor among them—sought to identify the various interests served by war that were often obscured by labels such as "ethnic conflict" and "superpower rivalry" as well as by the loudly expressed aim of winning.[8] Looking at the "new wars" or dirty, transnational civil wars of this time—wars that involved the widespread targeting of civilians, seemingly "irrational" violence, and multiple criminal or armed factions—such authors started pinpointing how crude political and economic interests (as well as complicated identity politics) had congregated around seemingly "unwinnable" wars. While there were substantial disagreements over the "newness" of targeting civilians (for example), a political-economy approach to war was coming strongly onto the radar screen. Recognizing that neither politics nor "winning" had disappeared, such writers nevertheless wanted to highlight that war was not simply a contest-to-win or even the pursuit of Carl von Clausewitz's "politics by other means": sometimes, for example, it included the pursuit of "economics by other means." In any event, there was a process of rethinking what war actually *is.*

The end of the Cold War further stimulated the interest in complex local drivers of conflict that some had already begun to explore during the Cold War itself. The most "obvious" explanation for civil wars around the world—that they had been stoked by the strategic rivalries of the two superpowers—was now largely removed from the table. It was increasingly clear that other motivations needed to be brought into the picture.

Apart from the intellectual opportunities, the Cold War's demise also presented *political* opportunities. But some of the most important ones were spurned. With the fall of the Berlin Wall and the collapse of Communism in the former Soviet Union and Eastern Europe, there was a chance to move toward a radically different world order in which war—and planning for war—was much less prominent. For generations who had grown up with the threat of nuclear war, it was a moment of great relief as well as great promise. The end of war was an obvious opportunity to dismantle the expensive and destructive apparatus of violence that had been deemed necessary in order to win that war. On the cards was a potentially massive "peace dividend" that would allow tackling underlying social problems on both sides of the Cold War divide and beyond.

Yet in the 1990s, this promise was not fulfilled. Military spending did come down a little in the United States and in Western Europe. But the resources allocated to war preparations remained remarkably high. A key claim in the United States was that the government needed enough weapons and troops to fight *two major global wars simultaneously*.[9] Meanwhile, even as the perceived threat from Communism receded, a wide array of menaces—from terrorism to drugs and even migration—was increasingly said to be threatening Western countries. While there were potentially positive elements to the broadening of the concept of security (as in UN calls for "human security"), the gaming of the wider security environment was soon rampant. In the face of public pressure for major budget cuts, endangered bureaucracies discovered a series of new, newish, or revived security threats—both real and imagined. Once the "war on terror" unfolded in the 2000s, levels of US military spending rose dramatically (see Figure 4).[10] The US-based Project on Defense Alternatives noted in 2010 that "US defense spending is now stabilizing at levels significantly above Cold War *peaks* (adjusted for inflation) and far above the Cold War average, in real terms."[11] By their count, spending peaked at $696.5 billion in 2008 (adjusted for 2010 dollars), compared with an average of $517 billion during the Reagan years.[12] It seemed to be a case of "The Cold War is over. Long live war itself!"

In this context, not only was war being rethought in academia, but so was security. According to the body of work on "securitization" that emerged as the Cold War thawed, security and insecurity were not simply a given or a fact but *actively constructed*. Some international

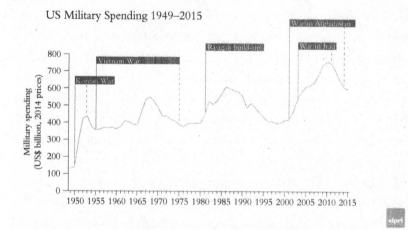

US Military Spending 1949–2015

Figure 4 US defense budgets since World War II. Source: Stockholm Peace Research Institute.

relations scholars suggested that certain political problems become "securitized" through political "speech acts." Such problems are framed as somehow outside the realm of normal political deliberation and as in need of a robust response that may end up breaching democratic norms and legal safeguards. Particularly in its original formulation, securitization theory emphasized *how* certain issues were being securitized rather than spelling out the interests that were driving this process. These interests were addressed more thoroughly by academics plowing a political economy furrow similar to that of our war scholars above. Among them, Didier Bigo emphasized the active participation of security professionals in shaping and benefiting from emergent security threats, while other authors, including Peter Andreas, highlighted the deep vested interests in the emerging security environment around drugs and borders in the United States. The result, parallel to our war debate, was an opening up of what *security* is and whose interests are served by invoking it.[13]

As noted, among the issues becoming heavily "securitized" from the 1990s was migration, or rather, certain *kinds* of it, specifically lower-skilled migration from "South" to "North." As the Berlin Wall came down, the first border barriers were rising up on both sides of the North Atlantic—in a reinvention of security that, in the US case, went as far as repurposing military helicopter landing mats used in Vietnam as part of the fencing on the border with Mexico.[14] When Ruben investigated this world of border security some years later, he saw first-hand how the "securitization" of migration was not simply being propelled by political rhetoric from the top down; border agencies and front-line officers were also contributing in various ways to inflating the migratory threat in their daily work. Joining a growing body of scholarship that treated security as a workplace and as a practice, he examined the deep vested interests that were shaping this border security industry. From defense contractors to border agencies, from politicians looking for votes to NGOs and academics looking for funding, the fight against migration was the gift that kept on giving.[15]

In our political systems analysis, we must bring together the rethinking of war and of security. Securitization theory showed that once a problem had been "securitized," this facilitated a number of measures that benefited some actors even when these measures did not actually reduce the named "threat." *Fixating* on a threat, in our broader terminology, has frequently allowed an emergency mentality to take hold in which accountability can easily vanish and abuses mount, paving the way for the various underhand "games" played out in our wars and fights.[16] Similarly, political economy analyses started revealing how any war, or war-like security intervention, has a very particular distribution of costs and benefits, which is often hidden by this fixation on the enemy (and on the idea of war as a contest). Some people bear the brunt, while others enjoy impunity and escape the costs; a lucky few will reap the rewards. Understanding this perverse distribution of costs and benefits is of fundamental importance if we want to challenge the dominance of war and security fixes.

Of course, you might expect some kind of "antiwar" analysis from academia (though other opinions are available, as perhaps best illustrated by Edward Luttwak's 1999 article, "Give War a Chance").[17] Yet in our research, we have found that some of the most devastating critiques of war and security systems come from those who are charged with implementing them. Indeed, listening to some hard-boiled generals, we find that our theorists of the 1990s were in some ways latecomers to the critical political economy of war.

As long ago as 1935, a former US general, Smedley Butler, published a pamphlet called *War Is a Racket*. He, if anyone, was in a position to know: his record of service included the Philippine-America War, the Mexican Revolution, and the First World War. As it happened, his screed offers one of the most trenchant criticisms of war's skewed distribution of costs and benefits. War "is possibly the oldest, easily the most profitable, surely the most vicious" of rackets, he began. "It is the only one international in scope. It is the only one in which the profits are reckoned in dollars and the losses in lives." He noted that the war racket was "conducted for the benefit of the very few, at the expense of the very many" while asserting that thousands of new millionaires had been created in the United States as a result of the First World War—a war that would surely lead to "back-breaking taxation for generations." How many of these millionaires had "shouldered a rifle," Butler wanted to know, or "knew what it meant to go hungry in a rat-infested dug-out?"[18]

To General Butler, as to our academics a few generations later, the very nature of war was in question. Yet his "war as a racket" isn't quite the full picture either. One thing that Butler, as much as our war analysts of the 1990s, also pointed to was that we must examine war through the complex relations and interactions that it generates, which in turn help to create, sustain, and regenerate it. That is, it is helpful to move from studying wars to studying *systems,* whether we label those "war systems," "security systems," or "systems of violence," as the case may be. This systemic understanding offers a window onto how wars and security interventions evolve and consolidate, how they frequently reinvent themselves even when an enemy has been defeated, and how winners as well as losers emerge from this process. Moreover, they let us glimpse how various layers of objectives and interests may coexist within a war or security system, sometimes to the point of developing symbiotic relationships or "agreeing to agree" on self-serving versions of reality. With these systemic glasses on, let us now do some detective work on a prominent hot war within the Cold War: Vietnam.

Orchestrating War "at the Appropriate Level"

Seen as a whole, the Cold War involved a very particular—and very skewed—distribution of costs. Most obviously (and some things are so obvious that we may forget to notice them), the Cold War saw a lack of direct confrontation between its two main rivals. The main reason for this was also pretty obvious (in terms of the desire to avoid a nuclear conflagration). But that element of *nonconfrontation* has also been an important element in many other wars, including the civil war in Sierra Leone that we briefly discussed in the previous chapter. A key aim in any war is to stay alive. While the financial costs of the Cold War were heavy for US taxpayers and while Soviet citizens and Eastern Europeans paid a heavy price in freedom, nevertheless a very large proportion of the costs in terms of actual conflict were in effect exported to significantly poorer countries and former colonies outside Europe and North America—countries such as Guatemala, El Salvador, Indonesia, Vietnam, Malaya, Laos, Cambodia, Ethiopia, Angola, and Mozambique, to name but a few, in which Cold War rivalries (as well as other national and regional tensions) were played out.

When it comes to the hot conflicts of the Cold War, then, many of Butler's contentions prove rather applicable. The profits were reckoned in dollars and the losses in lives—but, seen from Washington, DC, those lives were by and large the lives of *others*. The organization of violence in the proxy wars had, in this sense, quite a lot in common with the colonial-era outsourcing of warfare, and in this, it exhibited a cost-distribution template that is with us to this day.[19]

Vietnam illustrates this skewed cost distribution even though the costs for the United States, as an active party to the armed conflict,

were unusually high. Almost sixty thousand US servicemen died in
the theater of war. Vietnamese casualties were hugely higher, with
estimates ranging from one to three million war deaths, the majority
civilians.[20] Within this devastating picture, the Vietnam War offered
significant political and military opportunities for *rigging the war and
fixing the fallout.* When it comes to these less well-known costs and
benefits, an insightful guide is a second US military general, one
William Corson. Reading General Corson's 1968 account of the
Vietnam War, *The Betrayed,* we get a strong sense of the political
economy that helped to shape the conflict.

Corson stressed that American interests in Vietnam went well beyond winning the war and involved both personal (career) and institutional priorities. He noted, for example, "Peacekeepers may be
blessed but war makers get promoted. . . . Each of the military services has seen in Vietnam an opportunity to 'get theirs,'" a point to
which we will return.[21] While the Vietnam War was normally discussed in terms of American tactics and Cold War strategies, Corson
also showed how the South Vietnamese authorities were able to pursue a number of highly profitable activities—and to forestall pressures
for democracy—in the context of large-scale American aid aimed at
"defeating Communism":

> After twenty years of fighting, war has become a way of life for the lead-
> ership of the ARVN [South Vietnamese Army]. They are in no hurry
> to pursue the enemy, for from their point of view the goal is not to de-
> feat the enemy, but to maintain their position, receive promotions, and
> enhance their personal fortunes. Combat, at best, is an extra-curricular
> activity to be engaged in as a last resort.[22]

Importantly, this is not just a description of people deviating from the
norms of behavior that we might expect in a war. Echoing Butler's
analysis of the First World War and the pattern we observed in Sierra
Leone and Sudan, it is a description of what war actually *is* or, at least,
has the potential of swiftly becoming.

The point is not simply that people sometimes deviate from the
aim of winning but that they may actually have several aims, of which

winning (and fighting) is only one—and sometimes quite far down the list. Coming back to our systems perspective: there is no contradiction between arguing, in a realist vein, that US geostrategic interests provided a rationale for the pushback of Communism in Vietnam and showing how, once unleashed, the war started to develop "games" large and small that kept it going and expanding in the service of various individual, institutional, and political interests.

Part of the ARVN's money-making system was siphoning off US aid; part of it was taking bribes to release captured Viet Cong rebels; and another part was pocketing the salaries of soldiers who had been killed or who had deserted, with these "ghost soldiers" providing a perverse incentive for keeping military units undermanned. Army officers would sometimes pay good money for especially profitable military assignments.[23] In this context, the US *fixation* on the Communist Viet Cong was a problem for the war effort as well as an opportunity for the South Vietnamese "partners" involved in it. For one thing, it was difficult or impossible to rein in corruption in a context where the Viet Cong were presented as a kind of embodiment of evil, so that anyone who could claim to be part of the coalition opposing them had an enormous amount of leeway. Aid was never made substantially conditional on human rights observance or reining in corruption.[24]

If winning was often low on the list of priorities for South Vietnamese soldiers, it was in some ways actively *threatening*. As Corson put it:

> [O]ne thing the GVN [government of South Vietnam] seeks to avoid [is] the end of the war and the withdrawal of US forces. . . . The GVN's power is based on the US presence, and since that in turn is based on the level of violence it is to their advantage to orchestrate the war at the appropriate level.[25]

Meanwhile, many of Saigon's military tactics—like those of the Americans—had the predictable effect of reinforcing an enemy that made political capital out of endemic corruption. A variation of that story from the past two decades is—or should be—familiar from the revival of the Taliban amid aid-supported corruption in Afghanistan.

In sum, Butler and Corson would both surely agree that "regular" war—whether the First World War or the Vietnam War—adhered quite closely to our second mechanism, the fixing or rigging of the game. We can add that, once an enemy has been *fixated* upon as an existential threat, the scope for such gaming grows immensely, while accountability and a clear view of the mounting costs and counter-productive consequences of the war tend to disappear from view.

In this way, Vietnam also illustrates rather well our mechanism of the "knowledge fix." As with the security interventions we will look at in detail in coming chapters, a concern with *image* often trumped a concern with actually winning, certainly as far as US government officials were concerned. As Hannah Arendt noted, "[W]hen all signs pointed to defeat in the war of attrition, the goal was no longer one of avoiding humiliating defeat but of finding ways and means to avoid admitting it and 'save face.'"[26] General Corson himself wrote:

> The [US] politicians saw in Vietnam, or so they thought at the time, a chance to pull off a cheap victory against the Communists. When their initial judgments about Vietnam were found to be in error, there was no way to confess their error without risking defeat at the polls.[27]

This concern with image and appearance found a "scientific" mirage in what came to be known as the "McNamara fallacy" after US defense secretary Robert McNamara, whose obsession with the metric of enemy body counts encouraged him to believe the war was winnable. When a retired chief of staff of a key field command, Douglas Kinnard, later surveyed two-thirds of all US Army generals serving in the war between 1965 and 1973, he found that only 2 percent of them saw the "body count" as a valid measure of progress. "A fake—totally worthless," said one respondent; "often blatant lies," said another.[28] Yet this did not stop the metric from changing the nature of the war for the worse. Tragically, McNamara's concern with image—and with gruesome metrics in lieu of genuine "wins"—extended right down the line, where such concerns shaped the escalating catastrophe. In Nick Turse's reckoning with the war, *Kill Everything That Moves,* one US infantry captain put the matter simply and chillingly: "Your success was measured by your body count. It came down through the channels."[29] Michael Bernhardt, a US soldier who declined to participate in (and later helped expose) the My Lai massacre, described the perverse incentives that prevailed: essentially, whether you killed a Vietnamese person who was a threat or one who wasn't a threat, it counted just the same.[30]

Meanwhile, South Vietnamese officers, as conflict specialist Stathis Kalyvas observed, "saw artillery shelling as an easy way to show that they were aggressive without running the risks of actual 'search and destroy' operations."[31] Yet the costs of such "image-friendly" military decisions by US and South Vietnamese soldiers alike were borne by civilians, largely out of view in the official accounting of the war.

This takes us (back) to the industrial-scale *export* of costs, which, as we are seeing, was deeply entangled with the fixes both of the game and of the information environment. A key feature of this war system—and of so many of the systems we are analyzing in this book—was that the risk of being subjected to harm/violence was in effect being passed down the chain of power and privilege, while most of the benefits were simultaneously being passed *up* that chain. That is, the fallout was also being fixed. Corson highlighted the perverse distribution of risk very clearly when he noted that the South Vietnamese government soldier

> has a lot to complain about—he has been drafted under a law which enables the sons of the rich to escape the draft indefinitely, his term of service is indefinite, his pay irregular. . . . Because of this and many other inequities, the ARVN soldier takes his resentment and anger out on the people. He rapes, loots and pillages in the manner of a conqueror rather than a protector. . . . [T]his kind of behavior . . . has made the Vietnam War unwinnable.[32]

The underlying resentment resonates with some of what we know about US conscripts. Many of these two sets of combatants were drawn into egregious abuses. This reflected in part the distribution of risks, which were borne acutely by the "grunts," or those on the ground. As Susan Faludi put it, based on an insightful interview with the My Lai whistleblower Bernhardt, "The way that vast numbers of GIs came to see it, the invisible men in the control ships had left the troops to die on the ground while they buzzed back for hot showers, martinis and movies in their air-conditioned suites at base camp." Often, these troops "were meant to be the ambushable 'bait,' put there to attract enemy fire so that the air force could swoop down and claim a fat body count."[33]

In Vietnam, not only were costs being passed down, but this process was spiraling out of control in a *cascade* of violent consequences. These included reproducing—and widening the category of—the enemy. All the while, the body count rose, suggesting the war was in fact being "won"—until one day, as in Afghanistan some decades later, it was lost.

In this emblematic "hot" war within the Cold War, we have discovered several of the important mechanisms that help inform our framework. Specifically, in the context of a *war fix* and the relentless rhetoric about the imperative of defeating Communism, we have found strong elements of *rigging* the system, *exporting* the costs, *cascades* of violence as the gaming and exporting generate blowback and self-reinforcing cycles of predation on civilians, and *knowledge fixing* that creates misleading impressions of "success" that incentivize further such violence. In other words, our very brief excursion to the Vietnam War has given us a baseline view of the W.R.E.C.K. in wreckonomics.

At the same time, this excursion has rendered the picture more complex—for example, in suggesting that each mechanism may interact with others, often creating destructive feedback loops. Footsoldiers' frustrations with the Vietnam War "games" of their superiors fed into abuses, which in turn fed back into the difficulty of winning the overarching game (the war itself) for the US forces, who played their part in seeding a particularly blinkered knowledge environment as this situation worsened (while pushing costs down to front-line Vietnamese combatants and civilians, and so on). From a systems perspective, these relations and feedback loops contributed to the war system's remarkable resilience, helping to explain how it could persist and grow even as suffering and failure proliferated.

Mutually Assured Construction

In our political systems analysis, we have suggested looking at war not simply as an abstract system but as a workplace. Vietnam was a case in point. In this strange and often deadly workplace, "agency" was widely distributed, with the South Vietnamese leaders, officials, and even ordinary soldiers finding ways to rig smaller games in ways that did not always fit squarely into the overarching war-to-win of the superpower. Cold War scholarship suggests that, rather than being an anomaly, this feature was endemic not just in "hot" proxy wars and armed conflicts but also in the systematic atrocities that took place under the cover of "containment." Westad is among the Cold War historians emphasizing this point: he stresses "the key role local elites played in abetting and facilitating these superpower interventions." Such elites, he adds, tended to pursue *their own goals*—whether in the form of anticolonial struggles or "extreme forms of violence" against the poor peasantry in times of sweeping political and economic transformations.[34]

Besides local or national elites, other actors were also busy building their own subsidiary games on the back of a larger one. In the United States, war had turned into a vast bureaucracy, as the obsession with metrics such as "body counts" suggested. Bureaucratic priorities did not always coincide with "winning." Published in 1974, as the Vietnam War was drawing to a close, Morton Halperin's influential *Bureaucratic Politics and Foreign Policy* showed how competition in Washington, DC (over budgets, power, status) was encouraging each bureaucracy to present its own performance in the best possible light.[35] We find an irony here in that, despite that apparent confrontation between "big government" and "market-based systems" during the Cold War, state bureaucracies were competing fiercely for resources even on the side that was supposedly pushing *against* big government. In fact, conditions of "war"—or at least "cold" war—represented a near-ideal environment in which the departments and forces charged with providing "security" were able to promote their own importance and expand their own budgets, generally at the expense of other departments and to the detriment of spending on domestic infrastructure and services. Even on the "free market" side, the Cold War proved a paradoxically fruitful environment for large-scale state spending and pork-barrel politics: at a very basic level, if you could make a halfway plausible claim that some resource allocation was necessary in order to defeat the evil of Communism, then it was hard to say no. The United States has seen intense bureaucratic battles both between the Defense Department and other departments as well as within the armed services. In terms of the latter, William Shawcross's book *Sideshow* suggested that the US Air Force seized on the strategic bombing of Vietnam as a way of underlining its own importance and guaranteeing its independence from the army.[36]

We will return to these underhand institutional "gamings" of war. Yet for now, let us move up the scale and consider the wider economic and political gains to be had from gaming the Cold War's macro dimensions.

For politicians across several decades (especially in the United States), the Cold War offered a useful card to play at election time. On this political level, the "war fix"—the W in our wreckonomics—was fundamental to the mutual escalation that ensued. On both sides, we can observe a simplification and magnification of the geopolitical threat (essentially the *other* superpower) and an obsessive fixation on arms buildups that this engendered. Crucially, whether the enemy was conceived as Communism or capitalism, this arms race was largely self-justifying. It was generated by fear, and it perversely generated further fear—through the arms buildup it involved on either side of the Cold War divide and through the active inculcation of popular anxiety.[37] And following closely in fear's footsteps was a major dose of self-interest for the politicians who stood to gain electorally as well as for the defense contractors standing to gain commercially. Through its escalations and growing benefits, the wider Cold War system was developing a strongly self-sustaining quality.

Paranoia was a friend here. Amid the drumming up of anti-Communist sentiment under the Truman and Eisenhower administrations, yet another freethinking US general, Douglas MacArthur, observed in 1957:

> Our government has kept us in a perpetual state of fear ... with the cry of a national emergency. Always there has been some terrible evil at home or some monstrous foreign power that was going to gobble us up if we did not blindly rally behind it by furnishing the exorbitant funds demanded.[38]

James Carroll's *House of War* conveys the fearful tone of these years. In a chapter titled "Self-Fulfilling Paranoia," he notes that at a 1956 Senate hearing, a group of US Air Force generals "testified that the Soviets were on the verge of surpassing the United States in both the number and quality of medium- and long-range bombers. It was a complete fantasy, but it worked, and the Air Force got the [budget] increases it wanted." Running against John F. Kennedy for the Democratic nomination in 1960 was former Air Force secretary Samuel Symington, who said the Soviet intercontinental ballistic missile (ICBM) force would soon total *three thousand*—while in reality the number of operational Soviet ICBMs at the start of 1960 was *four*.[39]

Of course, the Russians were indeed building up their nuclear capabilities—and they were themselves pointing to the *American* buildup as justification. Reflecting in part a wider and long-standing hyping of industrial production of all kinds, Soviet premier Nikita Khrushchev claimed to be manufacturing missiles "like sausages."[40] In the Cold War, as happens so often, an important part of this knowledge-fixing involved not just fixing the metrics (whether of bodies or bombers) but also fixing the time frame. By focusing on *future* threats and on enemy weapons capacities that were proclaimed to be rapidly increasing, it was possible to justify one's own military spending. What went missing—and this is a major theme in our wars and security interventions more generally—was *how one's own behavior was shaping the system in which one was operating.* This is a vital part of systems thinking, but one that is habitually neglected when the problem is seen as somehow "out there." While systems-oriented international relations scholars may treat this situation as a "security dilemma," from another point of view it is also a security opportunity.[41] The time of mutual assured destruction (MAD), which promised "rational deterrence" via the annihilation of both sides in the event of a nuclear launch, was in this sense also a time of mutual assured *construction,* where the Soviets could be assured the Americans would continue escalating and vice versa, thus creating a system that proved mutually beneficial to powerful actors yet constantly risked outrunning either side's capacity to rein in expenditure, Cold War proxy wars, or indeed the missiles themselves.[42]

In the 1960 Democratic primaries, Kennedy ended up outdoing Symington in the rhetoric of fear, before going on to use that alleged "missile gap" when he ran against the Republican incumbent, Eisenhower.[43] Kennedy's fixation on Soviet missiles was another example of threat inflation that served short-term commercial, institutional, and political interests.[44] Claiming in his famous 1961 presidential inauguration speech to be engaging in a heroic struggle against war itself,[45] Kennedy nevertheless ramped up Cold War tensions, and in October 1962 the Cuban Missile Crisis brought a severe risk of nuclear annihilation. Amid widespread talk within the American military establishment of not only missile gaps but also "bomber gaps" (and with some generals recklessly stressing the value of a "first strike" in a nuclear confrontation), the US government had not only accelerated its military buildup under Kennedy but had also moved nuclear missiles into Italy and Turkey.[46] At this point, Russia began constructing its nuclear missile sites in Cuba, while Kennedy added to the brinksmanship with an eye on impending congressional elections.[47] The system had reached its ultimate cascading point, yet there was still enough sense left in the MAD world to pull back from the brink.

Another notable period of crisis came when Ronald Reagan was US president between 1981 and 1989. This was a time when senior US officials were insisting that a "limited nuclear war" within Europe was both feasible and winnable—and that a "first strike" with nuclear weapons was a defensible strategy under certain circumstances. This was also a "golden era" for the military-industrial complex, with huge expenditure on B-1 bombers, fighter jets, and more.[48] Throughout all these periods, the "war fix" was providing important *political* benefits domestically while interacting synergistically with the fixations of the other superpower. This political escalation went hand in hand with a *commercial* fix for a hugely powerful industry with a close ear in Washington (and a revolving door for high officials). Let us look at this next.

The Self-Licking Ice-Cream Cone

When we try to explain why extremely large amounts of scarce resources are devoted to making systems that are designed to kill other human beings, it is difficult to separate vested interests from strategic interests, as well as from real fears around security, particularly since all of these are interacting in complex ways. But sometimes the real world will remove or significantly diminish what statisticians would call "a variable," so that things become a little clearer. One such instance was the sharp demise of Communism in the Soviet Union and Eastern Europe, with the Berlin Wall coming down and Western governments declaring victory in the Cold War. Would this lead to the dismantling of the military-industrial complex in the West? The answer, as noted, was no. Even as "political economy" analysts of civil war were beginning to suggest that violence and security structures tended to persist when peace was declared, on the international stage something rather similar was looming ominously into view.

In 1993, defense industry grandees had attended what came to be known as the Last Supper, where the US deputy defense secretary warned that budget cuts would bring consolidation to the sector, putting some of those attending out of business. Consolidation did follow, with defense conglomerates gobbling up smaller rivals. So that was one adaptation to the "crisis." But soon a range of new or newish threats had been found and highlighted, bringing new opportunities and pushing budgets back up.[49] Noting this process was a group of academics and investigative journalists, including Andrew Cockburn, who had spent many years reporting on the military-industrial complex. In his 2021 book *Spoils of War*, Cockburn echoes Corson and Halperin as he remarks, "Outsiders generally find it hard to grasp an essential truth about the US military machine, which is that war-fighting efficiency has a low priority by comparison with considerations of personal and internal bureaucratic advantage." Going back to the 1950s and the Korean war, Cockburn notes that half the US casualties in the first winter of the conflict were due to frostbite and a lack of decent cold-weather boots. He observes that "the aerospace industry, as aircraft manufacturers had sleekly renamed themselves, was infinitely more powerful and demanding than the bootmakers, and so that was where the money went." Large-scale funding went into B-47 strategic nuclear bombers and fighters designed to intercept such bombers, both of precious little use in the Korean theater.[50]

As the geostrategic threat receded, the "baroque arsenal" of the Cold War—to use Kaldor's term—was looking ever more unfit for purpose.[51] Already in 1997, economics professor Ann Markusen noted in *The American Prospect*:

> [W]hen pressed to identify the enemy, the military establishment invokes the specter of rogue states and terrorists—despite the fact that threats from such quarters could not possibly be responded to with Cold War equipment. . . . Precisely because we don't know who our

enemies are, this logic goes, we need to spend more defending ourselves against their surprise emergence.[52]

This kind of logic eventually went into overdrive after the terror attacks of September 2001, which we return to in the next chapter. Meanwhile, the so-called Iron Triangle (consisting of defense contractors, the Pentagon, and Congress) continued to underpin vast defense spending, benefiting from "its immunity to the kind of public scrutiny to which other government institutions are subjected."[53]

In this context, some insiders dismissively referred to the phenomenon of the "self-licking ice-cream cone." A term that appeared in the immediate post–Cold War period, a "SLICC" (in line with the military penchant for acronyms) is any program that "appears to exist in order to justify its existence and produces irrelevant indicators of success."[54] Initially used to refer to the first Gulf War (as well as to NASA programming) and subsequently applied to our cases of arms racing and the Vietnam War, the term helpfully points a finger at how the putative solution to any large threat can be "gamed" beyond recognition, a move that yields benefits for the players but that also pushes huge costs onto those further down the system—including taxpayers and civilians turned into "body counts" or "enemies." As this book proceeds, we will see that many SLICC systems—across a great variety of fields—perpetuate themselves precisely by reproducing the very problem they are supposedly set up to deal with, all the while producing self-serving justifications for their existence and their actions.

In the post–Cold War years, the bureaucratic-commercial SLICC games were being reinforced by *political* games in a complex two-way relationship. We saw this not just in the mobilization around new threats but also in the recycling of old ones, specifically the old superpower conflict. NATO had been set up in 1949 in response to the perceived threat of the Soviet Union, and its founding treaty committed member states to treat an attack on one of them as an attack on them all. But rather than being dismantled with the West's declared victory in the Cold War, NATO was now eyeing eastern expansion. Within the United States, a powerful set of political, bureaucratic, and commercial interests was lining up behind this expansion. President Bill Clinton sought to appease parts of the electorate, and America's huge military-industrial complex was eager to find valuable new markets. Aware of the importance of the Polish American vote in the US Midwest in particular, Clinton chose Detroit to announce in 1996 that NATO would admit its first new members (Poland, the Czech Republic, and Hungary) by 1999.[55]

Many Russians saw this expansion of NATO as alarming, and Moscow was particularly sensitive about any suggestion that Ukraine would join NATO. Now it's clear that the more militaristic tendencies within Russia—which are today wreaking such appalling destruction on the people of Ukraine—are fueled by complex factors and cannot be explained or excused as simply the consequence of Western machinations or NATO expansion. Nevertheless, the dangers of mutual escalation carried over from the Cold War itself. Already in 1997, the very architect of the US policy of Cold War containment, George Kennan, had cautioned that expanding NATO would be "the most fateful error" since it would inflame "the anti-Western and militaristic tendency" within Russia.[56]

Yet what looked like an "error" from one point of view looked suspiciously like "success" from another. Cockburn is not alone in calling the expansion of NATO a "mutually profitable partnership" with Russia.[57] Many large and small actors have been able to keep benefiting from the escalation of (post–)Cold War tensions over many years, from generals purveying variations of the old "missile gap" theory[58] to "borderline euphoric" defense lobbyists being told by lawmakers of rising threats amid Russia's invasion of Crimea.[59] If we move from commercial to political gains, perhaps the largest beneficiary was Vladimir Putin himself. Now that he is locked in a reckless and unwinnable war with echoes of Vietnam and Soviet Afghanistan, Putin's strategy may be running up against its limits. But in the context of a widespread emotional attachment to Russia's great power status, Putin successfully used high-profile aggression in the near-abroad to compensate for dwindling domestic legitimacy; he also used foreign enemies to justify internal repression.[60]

Adopting our systemic lens, we may say that Putin has taken to an extreme a phenomenon observable, at various points, on both sides of what used to be called the Iron Curtain: the construction of political capital out of enmity within a tense overall geopolitical context that has essentially been co-created.

Complicity, Atrocity, Strategy

This admittedly all too condensed and partial story of the Cold War sets the tone for the coming chapters' wars and fights in various important respects. First, it shows how our basic "wreckanisms" apply across scale, from the games in "hot wars" such as Vietnam to those of the wider political "war fix." Second, it adds to our emphasis on the co-creation of war and security systems, as well as to our emphasis on the escalation (or *cascade*) that such co-creation tends to entail. Third, the chapter highlights how aspects of this co-creation have strong echoes and continuities across colonial, Cold War, and post–Cold War periods, notably in the significant leeway that "partner states" enjoy when it comes to shifting the goalposts or simply setting up their own.

We have emphasized how the Cold War was hijacked by all sorts of agendas and subsidiary games. In Washington and Moscow, politicians regularly inflated the threat of the adversary for domestic or foreign policy ends. This was especially the case on the side of the United States, whose notable economic and military superiority in a sense "required" a formidable foe if there was to be sufficient popular alarm. In the defense sector, the fixation on an endlessly escalating threat (a variation of our *war fix*) provided a chance to game the Cold War for great commercial profit. To large parts of the state apparatus on both sides of the Iron Curtain, here was a chance greatly to bolster institutional power and funding. Meanwhile, elites in the "Global South" frequently mobilized tacit or direct superpower support for their own political-economic agendas. At the extreme, as we saw in Vietnam, a Cold War–style conflict could prop up an undemocratic regime through the influx of military support. The crossed cables of these subsidiary games made the Cold War increasingly like a runaway train. Insofar as there was an overarching goal, it was not so much the goal of "winning" (for either side) as the persistence and growth of the system itself.[61]

★★★

Our investigation into the evils and rackets of the Cold War adds up to a pretty complex and disturbing "crime scene" of the kind alluded to at the beginning of the book. Surveying this scene, our systems detectives may feel they have at least cracked some elements of the terrible case at hand. Allowing themselves a flat pint of Oxford ale, perhaps, they may even feel a little smug. But wait! It's just at this moment that a third detective, somehow even more crumpled than ourselves, turns around with one eyebrow raised in familiar fashion.

"Oh, there's one more thing," he says, and we realize this is the famous TV sleuth Columbo.

"You say winning is not everything," he notes with that character-istic slur. "But defeating Communism was a real and persistent goal. And the Cold War was actually *won*. Even before that, the United States very successfully projected its economic and political power in the second half of the twentieth century."

We are just recovering from Columbo's unexpected foray from crime into politics when our disheveled hero reminds us of one of Robert Jervis's insightful points: while the Cold War's various "hot wars" and proxy wars were often individually disastrous, cumulative "system effects" meant that the Soviet opponent was actually worn down over a period of time before eventually collapsing.[62]

Of course, there is some truth in all this. In the Cold War, the superpowers' quest for geopolitical dominance was all too real, and international relations' focus on grand strategy and the geopolitical balance of power cannot sensibly be pushed to one side. Whether in relation to civil wars or global wars and fights, we are not trying to suggest that winning is irrelevant. Indeed, not just "realists" but also critical scholars of war have emphasized the continued importance of

"traditional" strategic and ideological considerations even in contexts
that were coming to be seen as emblematic of criminal and economic
interests in war, for instance in the former Yugoslavia.[63] It remains the
case, however, that in a variety of Cold War and post–Cold War conflicts we are confronted by a proliferation of actions that were geared
more toward gaming than winning; we are confronted by a fairly
systematic massaging of the truth; and we are confronted by many
actions that predictably *strengthened* the enemy.

How can we resolve the intellectual tension here? And what exactly
is this enterprise of winning-but-losing?

Our first attempt at a resolution is that, as with many of the "wars"
and "fights" we consider in this book, the costs of the Cold War were
outsourced while the benefits were *insourced*. This was a war fought "in
other people's countries"—and most commonly without US troops.
Of course, the Vietnam War was costly in terms of American lives, but
as noted it was far more costly for the Vietnamese. We know too that
Moscow also tried to outsource the costs, though these costs eventually hit home with the Soviet casualties and huge expense of a conspicuously failing war in Afghanistan.

A second observation on winning-but-losing—which we will explore in different contexts as the book progresses—is that even conspicuously failing wars may serve a wider purpose. Even though the
United States eventually "lost" in Vietnam, the ruthless pursuit of
this war did send a *signal* to America's allies and enemies around the
world—a signal that they were dealing with something formidable.
Certainly, US cold warriors frequently referred to the importance
of sending such signals in the context of their own blinkered version of systems thinking represented by containment strategy.[64] Later,
Washington's failing wars in Afghanistan and Iraq were also signals
that American power was to be taken seriously by countless regimes
in the Middle East and elsewhere. As noted, such signals also bring
domestic political benefits, as they allow politicians to appear "tough."

Importantly, the floundering war in Vietnam did not prevent wider
strategic gains in less "spectacular" theaters that received a great deal less
coverage in the international media. "Hot wars" such as Vietnam—and

indeed the spectacular arms race—may have usefully distracted from such gains at various points of the Cold War. One crisis under the radar in the mid-1960s was Indonesia, which saw a genocidal scale of violence against Communist Party members and suspected or conveniently assumed sympathizers. Though much about the role of Washington (including the CIA) remains unclear, recent investigative accounts detail chilling complicity with the killing campaigns while also making clear that the military leader General Suharto had a great degree of leverage and freedom of maneuver. One recent book suggests that the "Jakarta method" of orchestrated mass killings turned what had once been a key nonaligned country, with crucial natural resources and the world's largest Muslim population, into an ally—and it did so silently, away from the spotlights.[65] That was one of the "successes" of the Cold War, a maneuver with massive human costs "elsewhere."

As with the other "wars" and "fights" that we consider in this book, the Cold War system was an arena in which diverse and proliferating goals from many different parties played themselves out. Again, winning was one important goal for many parties, but there were also many others. And winning meant different things to different actors: it was quite possible to "lose" in Vietnam and yet register a series of strategic and diplomatic "wins" in Indonesia, Guatemala, Brazil, and Sudan. Part of what we need to appreciate is that there were many ways of "winning" that disappeared under the radar of media coverage and much political analysis—ways that did not actually involve a military victory over a named opponent. In any policy intervention, we need to trace how a variety of aims interact, a task that becomes particularly urgent, and also particularly difficult, when the intervention is some kind of "war" or "fight." Sometimes these various aims clash with one another, and sometimes they act in concert; an example of the latter is when there is a shared interest in keeping a war going.

The proliferation of aims—and the co-creation of damaging systems—becomes even clearer when we step away from interstate or superpower conflict in the Cold War and examine how transnational "threats" have been combated under the cover of war or security. We address this in our next three chapters.

4

A Life of Its Own

The "War on Terror" as Frankenstein's Monster

One September day, as we were struggling with the complexities of wreckonomics, a cacophony came raucously to our attention, rattling its way across Oxford's dreaming spires. We realized that this was St. Giles' Fair, which every year flashes and drums itself into one of Oxford's most decorative streets, injecting a rush of cotton candy and adrenaline into young blood and ancient cloisters. Wild rides whiz past the windows of St. John's College—waking port-addled dons from their evening slumber, perhaps, and setting hearts aflutter with a very un-Oxford like slogan: "Scream if you want to go faster!"

Heads still in the book, we found the funfair suggestive as an analogy of how our war and security systems operate. It might seem odd at first, but bear with us. One thought was that security, in its many forms, had in the post–Cold War years become a funfair-style marketplace where political and commercial entrepreneurs sold a set of wild rides and gambles to (often gullible) voters and (often repressive) governments. New post-9/11 outfits such as the burgeoning US Department of Homeland Security were part of this, bringing border policing, counternarcotics, and counterterror increasingly under one umbrella while catalyzing all sorts of scrambles for funds, "synergies," and new security markets.[1] We ourselves have sometimes had the chance to visit the security fairs (or "expos") where security companies set up their stalls and ask state investors to "roll up!" and invest in the latest unmanned aerial vehicle system, border technology, AI-guided risk profiling, or surveillance apparatuses—products that have frequently been tested on real people.

A second thought was that, like the funfair or traveling carnival (its US equivalent), security markets are in the business of selling *emotion*. They sell fear and the relief that comes from fear's release. They also sell a shared escape into fantasy. Funfair operators use tried-and-trusted tricks to manipulate our emotions: the big prize prominently displayed, the peer pressure for scary rides, the titillating House of Horrors. In our wars and fights, strong emotions have also effectively been stirred up and manipulated by political and security actors. This emotive investment goes some way toward explaining why we rarely see proper, dry audits of the costs and benefits of our wars and fights. These belligerent projects are somewhat set aside from normal political and economic life, with its checks and balances. In many ways, they take us to a make-believe land, a magical world where almost anything goes and where buyers are routinely "taken for a ride." Yet somehow we keep coming back for more. The voters funding the various wars are in a fundamental sense *being played* by a system that is, quite rationally, getting more and more adept at giving (fleeting) satisfactions and manipulating emotions.

These two features of our war and security systems—their market logic and the scope for manipulation—make them particularly impervious to challenge. These features also make them prone to a staggering degree of proliferation and expansion, as we shall see in the coming three chapters. We start by visiting the house of horrors that has for many years been the central attraction of our grotesque funfair: the war on terror. Staring the monsters in the face, we get a better understanding of the runaway dynamics that arose when terrorism was fixated upon as an existential threat. In the next chapter, we move to a smaller yet increasingly significant security system, "the fight against illegal migration," which further illuminates how such systems have been gamed for a variety of political and economic ends. If we may continue with our analogy, this process evokes the unequal inter-action between seasoned fairground operators and their frequently naïve customers. Finally, we visit the generally losing gamble of the wars on drugs and crime. Here, we explore the addiction to a failing war in which the "highs" and "hits" from conspicuous but fleeting "successes" have been allowed to outweigh longer-term costs—not least because these costs have been effectively outsourced to others.

Enemy Wanted

It is worth remembering that the war on terror was the monstrous offspring of the Cold War, with the CIA-supported insurgency against the Soviet occupation spawning the jihadist networks that would eventually mutate into al Qaeda. At one level, this was dis-astrous "blowback." Yet in the dying days of the Cold War, US neo-conservatives and the military-industrial complex were also *seeking* an expansive new enemy.

In George Orwell's *1984*, Oceania switches allies and enemies right in the middle of Hate Week so that posters have to be rapidly pulled down and replaced while the rationales for hating are rapidly rein-vented. In what is sometimes rather loosely called "the real world," the pace of change is rarely this quick, but shifts in the working definition of the enemy at times feel similarly disorienting.[2] One moment, the West was busy denouncing the evils of Communism. Then suddenly we heard that the Cold War was over. Then it quickly became clear that this was not a time for relaxation; on the contrary, it was impera-tive to wage a range of existential wars which themselves seemed to succeed one another with dizzying speed. And terrorism was soon to become, from one point of view, "the perfect enemy."

In the 1990s, you could already see the signs of that hunger for enemies—and sometimes these were actual signs. In the Pentagon in the latter part of this decade, a mock "personals" ad had been taped to a wall:"ENEMY WANTED. Mature North American Superpower seeks hostile partner for arms-racing, Third World conflicts, and general antagonism. Must be sufficiently menacing to convince Congress of military financial requirements."[3] In the same period, neoconservatives penned an influential article urging the US administration "to go abroad in search of new monsters to destroy."[4] These new monsters were increasingly seen as being *nonstate* threats, as emphasized by Robert Kaplan, whose dystopian article on a "coming anarchy" of transborder criminality, terrorism, and displacement found eager ears in the Clinton White House.[5] Importantly, the turn toward nonstate threats (including migration, drugs, crime, and terror) was a rather bipartisan affair—even if, as we shall see, the US right was key to its most macabre manifestation in the war on terror.

If the rigging or gaming around the terror threat was already under way in the 1990s, it took the terrible attack of 9/11 for the crosshairs finally to fixate on the new global enemy. The US-led war on terror began in earnest with the attack on Afghanistan in 2001. Defended on the grounds that Osama bin Laden had been operating from Afghan soil, the invasion nevertheless represented a remarkable and reckless expansion in the working definition of the enemy beyond the (mostly Saudi) perpetrators of 9/11. After the Taliban had been deposed in Afghanistan, the focus of the war on terror shifted to Iraq, which was invaded in 2003 despite having no weapons of mass destruction and no connection to the 9/11 attacks. From there, the global war on terror spread across the world, moving further and further from any plausible claim to be addressing the crimes that lay at its origin. Caught up in this escalating war system was a wide range of countries, including Somalia, Kenya, Mali, Mauritania, Algeria, Pakistan, Sri Lanka, Syria, Libya, Yemen, the Philippines, and even China. In all of them, national security actors used the threat of terrorism for their own violent ends, including in the brutal mass detention and targeting of civilian Uyghurs by Beijing.

We can already see here that the war on terror exhibits an extreme version of our cascade of "wreckanism." Part of what we want to explain in this chapter, through our political systems analysis, is how it expanded so hugely. Looking at the *cascade of games* requires examining its troubling relation with the *cascade of costs*. The "war" enabled a vast range of games by instigators, implementers, and "enemy combatants" alike—and all these games generated huge costs and risks to civilians. As we shall see, these costs grew greater once governments that were in some way marginal to the US-instigated global war on terror started replicating (and complicating) its games and fixations.

It's notable that terrorism, as a tactic of political violence, has one eye on the systems in which it operates, frequently seeking to generate a heavy-handed state security response which is then used to attract more recruits and supporters.[6] Provocation was part of the thinking behind the 9/11 attacks themselves. At a time when al Qaeda was losing support in key countries such as Egypt, key strategists were looking to replace the "near enemy" (various national governments) with a "far enemy" (the United States). As Fawaz Gerges shows in his excellent book *The Far Enemy*, a key idea was that the United States would come to fulfill—through its retaliation for 9/11—the role of aggressor that extremist elements had cast for it.[7] Provoking a heavy-handed response, significantly, has also been part of the strategy of other terrorist elements—for example, ISIS in Syria, al-Shabaab in Somalia, and a combination of al Qaeda and ISIS affiliates in Mali.[8] Here lies one key to the mutually reinforcing cascades of costs and games in the war on terror. In the context of a repressive state, terrorist tactics become more politically attractive, and when such terror tactics proliferate, state repression itself becomes more tempting.

Positioned at the heart of the war on terror, Afghanistan and Iraq were beset by large numbers of terrorist attacks *after* the respective US-led military interventions—yet the attacks were often taken as justification for further war efforts. As with al Qaeda's violence and the retaliation it induced, this process of responding to US-led violence again illustrated the way that violence may create legitimacy for itself. In 2004 John Kerry, then the Democratic candidate for the US presidency, put this well when debating with George W. Bush:

"The President just talked about Iraq as a center of the war on terror. Iraq was not even close to the center of the war on terror before the President invaded it."[9]

The trend inside Iraq mirrors a global pattern over the heaviest years of the war on terror. In the face of a massive counterterrorism effort (and the associated invasions) since September 2001, the number of terrorist attacks in the world increased very rapidly—from around 3,300 in 2000 to almost 30,000 by 2015. Meanwhile, the number of fighters in Islamist-inspired terrorist organizations more than tripled, from around 32,000 in 2000 to more than 110,000 thirteen years later, while deaths climbed (with a very uneven geographical spread; see Figure 5).[10] Numbers have fallen since, alongside a diminution of the war on terror's intensity. While correlation does not of course equate to causation, these figures at the very least suggest that the war on terror has been—in many crucial respects—a story of failure.

So what exactly propelled this floundering endeavor? One factor, often neglected, was the huge military machinery that was left potentially in limbo at the end of the Cold War—a case, perhaps, of "all dressed up and no one to shoot." More than this, we suggest that the war on terror was fueled and sustained by a wide range of benefits—in terms of power, profit, legitimacy, and impunity—that it

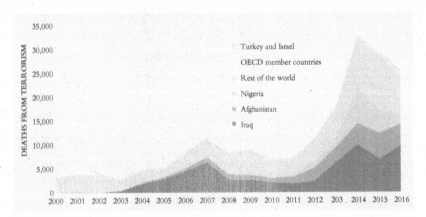

Figure 5 Global deaths from terrorism, 2000–2015. Source: Institute for Economics and Peace (2017).

promised and frequently provided for a wide range of political and institutional actors. This included, of course, major beneficiaries within
the war-instigating US state machinery and among its key Western
allies; in both cases political and military leaders and institutions found
various payoffs from endless war even as it was floundering. Crucially,
beneficiaries also included many abusive and repressive actors in "cooperating" countries, including countries on the fringes of the global
war. Claiming to be collaborating in the self-consciously righteous
global fight against a widely denounced evil, many national and sub-
national actors have tended to use this collaboration to further their
own agendas. Moreover, this sometimes *reinforced* the very enemies
they were purportedly opposing—through repressive actions and
even sometimes through acts of assistance and coordination. While
not all of this reinforcement was intentional, we can nevertheless observe the emergence of a system in which failure in the declared
project of a war on terror disguised success in a variety of *undeclared*
projects at various levels. When this failure reproduced terrorism, this
frequently helped to legitimize abuse while abetting the continued
expansion of the war system in ways that benefited key instigators and
implementers.

In the rest of this chapter, we will examine the phenomenal expansion of the war on terror by moving from its historical heart in
Afghanistan to two of its fringes (Sri Lanka and Syria), and on to one
important site within the war's long tail (Mali). In each case, we can
see how the mechanisms of wreckonomics have fed a runaway monster to the point where it eventually escaped, to a large extent, the
control of its creator.

Afghanistan: Expanding the Enemy

When Kabul fell to the Taliban in the summer of 2021, a set of explanations for this ignominious "end" were swiftly offered up. Common
explanations included a "lack of political will" on the part of the

United States as well as the idea that the Taliban had benefited from portraying themselves as the latest in a series of Afghan movements resisting non-Muslim invaders. Fingers were also pointed at Western hubris in launching an ambitious "democracy-building" project in a country the interveners had dramatically failed to understand.[11] There was some truth in all of these arguments. But a crucial explanation for the failure, as we shall see, can be found in our various "wreckanisms" and the perverse "successes" embedded within them.

As with Iraq in later years, Afghanistan proved to be a highly lucrative system of intervention. The system of benefits extended to numerous international actors who were able to project an image of success amid the reality of endemic failure—not least by trumpeting the number of "terrorists" who were said to have been killed or captured. Benefits also extended to a large and growing number of national actors who came to be involved, in one way or another, in the war. Crucial here was a process of hijacking the original "anti-terror" agenda, a process that routinely went under the radar. For example, the claimed "elimination" of terrorists was appropriated by local actors for a range of economic and political purposes, with a number of important Western actors fairly systematically colluding for reasons of their own.

Consider, by way of example, the events that unfolded in 2003 in Helmand province, southern Afghanistan. Helmand at this point was a key theater in the war on terror. Yet here US government–linked militias such as the 93rd Division were regularly stoking popular grievances and anger, not least by accusing non-Taliban Afghans of being Taliban. Counterproductive in terms of gaining civilian support, this practice nevertheless created identifiable payoffs for a diverse coalition of actors who claimed to oppose the Taliban. All manner of local disputes and economic rivalries could be "settled" by accusing someone of a rebel affiliation.[12] One example came when the 93rd Division labeled Hajji Bismillah—the Karzai government's transportation director for the city of Gereshk—as Taliban. This man had been responsible for collecting tolls in the city, which was a key hub for transport in the province. With him out of the way, the Division was able to monopolize toll revenues.

That same year, US soldiers went to the governor in Helmand, a brother of US-favored warlord Amir Dado, to discuss refurbishing a health clinic and a school. On leaving, the soldiers' convoy came under fire and two American soldiers were killed, the first US combat fatalities in Helmand. US personnel suspected the attack was the work of Dado rather than the Taliban, adding that this suspicion was confirmed by one of Dado's former commanders (who said Dado arranged the attack in order to keep the Americans reliant on him). Yet Dado's forces quickly seized a Taliban conscript called Mullah Jalil, claiming *he* was the true assassin, and the Americans promptly sent Jalil to Guantánamo in Cuba. Anand Gopal, commenting on this episode, writes, "Unaccountably, this happened despite the fact that, according to Jalil's classified Guantanamo file, U.S. officials knew that Jalil had been fingered merely to 'cover for' the fact that Dado's forces had been 'involved with the ambush.'"[13] Neither these killings nor the atrocities committed against many of those arrested had the effect of undermining Dado's close relationship with US Special Forces, since the latter (in Gopal's words) "deemed him too valuable in serving up 'terrorists.'"[14]

Dado's men and US Special Forces were now patrolling together, helping the US military to register favorable metrics in the "war on terror" even as this endeavor was drastically manipulated in the service of avarice, the pursuit of political power, and the furtherance of local vendettas. As such perverse processes became commonplace across Afghanistan, counterproductive effects multiplied. Studies at the time noted that the excesses of occupying forces—and of those who were gaming the insurgency—were pushing many civilians toward the Taliban.[15]

Variations of Dado's "double gaming" were widespread across notionally different sides of the conflict.[16] Such processes tell us a lot about the failing war on terror—and a lot about the dubious and damaging practice of extracting "success" from the jaws of systematic failure. Already beginning in 2001, when the US-led coalition got behind the warlords of the Northern Alliance, a great deal of violence was consolidated by bringing some very abusive characters into the newly established government, including one Abdul Rashid Dostum, who had developed an almost uncanny ability to switch sides to his maximum political advantage during Afghanistan's many war-ravaged years. Within the US-led coalition, the "evil" of the Taliban was seen as justifying and necessitating more or less unconditional support for those who claimed to oppose them. Yet the agendas of such actors were often remarkably exploitative—and frequently quite consistent with alienating civilians and killing or arresting people who had little or no connection to any active Taliban rebellion. Meanwhile, the Americans in particular were extracting their own brand of success from this systemic failure to confront the violence. They were point-ing proudly to all the "terrorists" who had been killed or arrested, and they were operating on the assumption—tried, trusted, and ultimately found wanting in Vietnam—that there existed a limited number of "bad guys" whose progressive elimination would make everyone safer (a fixation to which we return below). This was not simply a delusion but an alternative reality that was willfully embraced and purpose-fully propagated for identifiable—and on the whole self-interested—reasons.[17] Richard Holbrooke, former US special representative to Afghanistan and Pakistan, had (in)famously suggested that "we may be fighting the wrong enemy in the wrong country."[18] Yet here was an enemy that seemed endlessly expandable and very frequently useful, with counterinsurgency actors fomenting a cascade of further enmity and insurgency.

Another part of the gaming of the enemy concerned poppy pro-duction. The popular image in the years after the invasion, conveyed by the international media, was of a Western-backed government that was trying to rein in the Taliban rebels/terrorists and to constrain the drugs economy that was helping to sustain this rogue group. On this model, success depended on how the wars on terror and drugs re-inforced one another: vigorous counternarcotics operations alongside large-scale injections of troops were of the essence, alongside sufficient international aid to "win hearts and minds" (a.k.a. WHAM, with apologies to George Michael and Andrew Ridgely). But when you look at the conflict through a wreckonomic lens, you get a far less optimistic assessment of the likely effects of pumping in aid while simultaneously escalating military intervention and seeking to eliminate poppy production. Amid US-instigated counternarcotics operations, posts as police chiefs in poppy-growing areas were being sold to the highest bidder at a cost of as much as $100,000 for a six-month appointment. Since the monthly salary was $60, one quickly gets an idea of the profits involved.[19] Corruption, perversely abetted by counternarcotics, frequently and predictably pushed civilians toward the insurgency.[20] Crucially, local warlords allied with the United States retained a strong interest in drug production as well as in various kinds of violence that allowed them to feather their own nests even as conflict continued.

This highlighted a larger quandary for the occupiers: many of their collaborators did not *want* a strong or developmental Afghan state that would rein in their autonomy. A "shadow state" in effect lurked on the fringes of state institutions, often undermining them while still trying to game resources from the state and the international community.[21] In many respects, the relationship between warlords and the Taliban was not one of simple opposition. Indeed, collusion was often as notable as conflict. Through collusion and alienating civilians, the behavior of key warlords very often strengthened the Taliban in ways that should have been predictable.

This big mess did not necessarily represent "failure"—either for Afghan officials, for local warlords, or indeed for the international coalition waging a war on terror. All these groups were able to point to statistics suggesting that they had been doing an excellent job, whether this was the acreage of poppy crops that had been eliminated or the number of Taliban terrorists killed or arrested. But this was essentially a *distortion*, a mirage of success that hovered uneasily over the reality of endemic corruption, widespread official and semi-official violence, and a Taliban movement growing increasingly strong on the back of precisely this violence, corruption, and foreign intervention.

★★★

Let's take a step back. If Hannah Arendt detected in Vietnam some important early signs that image management was beginning to rival (or even to take over from) the priority of winning, the murky arts of information management have become considerably more sophisticated since then. A "rosy picture" may emerge, in part, from the involvement of a diverse range of organizations, consultants, and private operators in a wide-ranging and mutating project of counterinsurgency-cum-state-building.

A crucial aspect of this systemic gaming and distortion, which we discuss further in chapter 7, concerned the distribution of aid. The figures are staggering, with some $100 billion spent by the United States on nonmilitary assistance in Afghanistan between 2002 and 2013 (and significantly more since then), besides the billions expended by other donors and multilateral organizations. Yet despite some positive noises about improvements to education and sanitation (from a very low base), it was clear that the aid programming was beset by huge mismanagement. Hillary Clinton, upon assuming her role as secretary of state, agreed. "There is very little credibility for what was invested," she said. "It's heart-breaking."[22] Yet the scandals kept coming both in military and civilian aid. Nonsensical infrastructure proliferated on the back of US funding, as we noted at the beginning of this book. One study of the "monstrous failure" in Afghanistan quotes the US special inspector general's office (SIGAR):

> [F]or the 2012 and 2013 fiscal years, the United States has been providing Afghanistan, practically the most corrupt nation on earth, with $1.1 billion in fuel for the Afghan military—even though the US has made no effort to determine how much fuel the military actually requires. When SIGAR looked, it found that the Afghan military was counting trailers and other non-motorized conveyances in its list of vehicles needing fuel. What's more, it had destroyed all records of fuel dispersals.[23]

The Taliban were gaining substantial funds from their ability to disrupt and instrumentalize development projects. UN Special Representative Peter Galbraith was prompted to remark, "The U.S. spends hundreds of millions on Afghan security companies who use the proceeds to pay off the Taliban not to attack, or, in some cases, to stage attacks so as to enable the local warlord (a.k.a. security contractor) to hire more men at higher prices."[24] A 2010 US House of Representatives report noted that many of the Taliban attacks on security firms "are really negotiations over the fee." A task force assembled by US general David Petraeus estimated that $360 million of US taxpayers' money had ended up with the Taliban, with criminals, or with powerbrokers who had ties to both of these groups.[25]

Meanwhile, by reinforcing a sense of insecurity, warlords who advertised themselves as "anti-Taliban" were able to underline how essential they themselves were to successful counterinsurgency. In effect, they were able to extract large amounts of aid and government funding—and impunity for their own human rights abuses—by claiming to oppose the Taliban even as they engaged in the kind of corruption and abuse that brought new recruits and supporters to the Taliban.

"Afghanistan in many ways is sort of a perfect case study of how not to give aid," said Human Rights Watch's longtime representative in Afghanistan.[26] The founder of Afghanistan's first independent policy research institution, Andrew Wilder, found that international aid, far from "winning hearts and minds," had tended to fuel corruption as well as resentment about uneven aid distribution. Analysts have often mentioned the need for aid as a "peace dividend" that would consolidate conflict resolution. But with much of the aid following the violence and drugs into the south and southwest of Afghanistan, there was instead a kind of "peace penalty" for relatively peaceful parts of the country which lost out on aid—providing, in effect, another perverse incentive to stoke violence.[27] Meanwhile, by not delivering aid to Taliban areas, the US-backed government encouraged the Taliban to see the UN and NGOs as stooges for Washington, greatly adding to the danger that aid workers faced.

We can begin to see some of the ways in which the war on terror and the invasion and occupation were leading to a "Great Game" of sorts in Afghanistan. We could continue by examining, for instance, the disturbing dynamics of drone campaigns on the Afghan-Pakistan borders or by considering how, through withdrawing into their bunkers, the "internationals" increasingly managed to retreat into a make-believe world while leaving the disastrous, corrupt reality of the war outside the gates.[28] However, to prevent this account from proliferating any further, let us rein it back by returning to our "wreckanisms" of distortion, fixation, and the cascade.

In Afghanistan as in Vietnam, *distortion* played a major role in the "success" of the failing war and occupation. Accountability over the diverted and mismanaged multibillion-dollar aid program was slow in coming. Even slower was accountability for the violence, as when the label of "military-age males" was used to legitimize fatalities from drone strikes.[29] Distortion helped in presenting failing operations as political successes, whether this misleading picture was painted by the US occupier, its Afghan counterparts, or both.

The distorted lens also helped expand the enemy. Once there had been a *fixation* on the enemy as "jihadi terrorists"—with the United States playing a key role here and other countries joining in enthusiastically—then a wide range of actors benefited from this fixation. Gaming the emerging "war on terror," these self-styled "counterinsurgency" actors were even able to conjure new enemies while positioning themselves beyond criticism. We have seen how this game had an escalating and runaway quality, with the label "terrorist" becoming useful for a range of local and national agendas. In this process, the enemy was to some extent coming "unfixed" as a *cascade* of enemies, aims, and projects proliferated.

Alarmingly, this process was replicated internationally. There were two aspects to this, the first of which was Washington's expansion of the war on terror to new theaters, including into Iraq and Somalia. With this expansion came a very particular kind of systemic "learning" across the proliferating theaters, cascading the violence still further.

One such example comes from the latter years of the Iraq occupation where, as in Afghanistan, US Special Forces had been heavily involved in what some of them took to calling "a game of whack-a-mole." Here, as in Afghanistan, Joint Special Operations Command (JSOC) was launching a war within a war against ostensible insurgents. This war—like the wider one—was becoming self-propelling. With each set of kills, more names were added to the "kill list." And as each name was ticked off, more people joined the ranks of the insurgency. The high level of indiscriminate violence was helping to turn local society against the invaders, creating more "bad guys" in the process— which in turn made the whole business harder to stop, especially as no-one was keeping tabs on the process. Freed from both host-state and US congressional oversight, JSOC was left free to "game"—and spread—its particularly violent version of the war to an astounding degree. One US Ranger, while praising the leader of the campaign, General Stanley McChrystal, saw the dangers of the working model as it spread outward from Afghanistan and Iraq. "You have an em- powered executive branch that more or less has license to wage war wherever it determines it needs to, worldwide," he said. "You've got this great hammer, and, you know, why not go hammer some nails?"[30] The hammers and nails had certainly established a remarkable sym- biosis. The enemy *and* the war machine were proliferating together as the game of whack-a-mole went global (see Figure 6).

In addition to Washington's expansion of the target, a second de- structive aspect of the "globalizing" war on terror was that various *external* games were cascading on the back of the original war. Well beyond Afghanistan and Iraq, other states increasingly saw fit to pos- ition their own violence within a global framework that conferred a degree of "legitimacy" on it—while often helping to secure a great deal of aid and other resources. In many ways, this echoed dynamics in the Cold War. Crucially, the primary aim of key state actors in the war on terror was very often not to defeat terrorism: they were routinely aiming to stay in power, to eliminate local rivals, to make money, to launder their image (whether nationally or internationally), or some

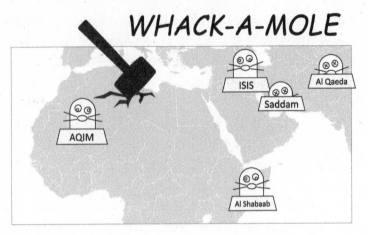

Figure 6 "Whack-a-mole" in the war on terror.

combination of these. In these circumstances, the continued existence of terrorist groups (while clearly a threat at some level) began to fulfill complex purposes. Indeed, even an *increase* in the power of terrorist or rebel groups could begin to serve important functions. We will look at this external proliferation or cascade next, visiting Sri Lanka and Syria in turn. We are aware that we will have to skim over major historical and political complexities of each country's conflict as we do so.[31] But our purpose is a simpler one: to examine how the global war on terror, through adaptations and mutations, came to take on a life of its own.

Shark-Infested Waters: Sri Lanka's Conflict

Of course, there's no shortage of villains within profitable war systems, as we have already seen in relation to Afghanistan. If we consider Sri Lanka during the humanitarian disaster unfolding in 2008–9, we actually get two villains for the price of one. First there is the sinister figure of Mahinda Rajapaksa, president when more than forty thousand Tamil civilians were massacred by government troops after being coerced into areas that the government itself had declared to be "safe."[32] Then there is Mahinda's brother, Gotabaya, defense minister at the time, who resembled a Bond villain to the extent of keeping a tank full of sharks at the bottom of his garden. Asked later about the ruthless counterinsurgency that he had helped to mastermind, Gotabaya was also quizzed about those sharks and how he could afford them on a public official's salary. He responded by asking, "[H]ow many people have fish tanks in their houses. . . . What's the difference between a shark tank and a goldfish tank?" Gotabaya went on to invite sympathy for his heavy workload by reference to the sharks: "That was the only relaxation I had those days. . . . Various people can say various things, but I proudly say that I managed to end the 30-year war."[33]

While the shamelessness of such individuals is important to understand (we are talking about the politicians, not the sharks), our interest in systems suggests a rather different focus. What we see in Sri Lanka—far from the principal sites of the US-led war on terror—are local systems of violence, corruption, and predatory politics that were intersecting very damagingly with a global war system.

Tension between Tamil and Sinhalese communities (much of it going back to British colonial divide-and-rule) was exacerbated by the 2004 tsunami, responses to which were often seen as favoring Tamil areas. Ethnic tensions were seized on and exacerbated by Mahinda Rajapaksa when he propelled himself to the presidency in 2005 on a pro-war, pro-Sinhalese platform. By the late 2000s, Mahinda and his brother were increasingly legitimizing the conflict with the Tamils, and the state violence this involved, by reference to the global war on terror. This helped the Rajapaksas to portray a wide range of dissenting actors—both globally and domestically—as either "terrorists" or "terrorist sympathizers." At the height of the humanitarian disaster in 2008–9, even aid agencies were routinely tarred with this brush, as when UNICEF was accused of sustaining the rebels with its nutritional biscuits and turning "Tamil Tiger" fighters into "Supertigers."[34]

The fixation on a globally recognizable "terrorist" enemy lent substantial impunity to the regime.[35] Given the indefinite internment of "unlawful enemy combatants" in Cuba's Guantánamo Bay, it was perhaps difficult for the United States and its allies to criticize the indefinite internment of hundreds of thousands of Tamil civilians in euphemistically named "welfare centers." And given the increasingly popular refrain in the West that liberty must be weighed against security (with even some leading North American lawyers and liberals speaking up for torture or "coercive interrogation"),[36] it was perhaps difficult to raise objections to the "balance" that the Sri Lankan government was itself striking (a "balance" that included taking away suspects and dissidents to be tortured). In a twist, the Sri Lankan government was also able to game *criticisms* arising from the US-led war on terror. For example, Western media outcries over abuses in the camps were met with the response that these same media outlets had played a key role in justifying the invasion of Iraq.[37] As a war leader, Mahinda Rajapaksa courted support from China, Pakistan, Iran, and other countries, quite successfully playing them off against the West. He liked to criticize what he called "foreign countries unnecessarily intervening in our internal affairs" while also praising China in particular for being more respectful of national sovereignty.[38]

While we have emphasized that the gaming of wars may sometimes take precedence over *winning*, Sri Lanka was clearly a case where the government not only wanted to win but was prepared ruthlessly to manipulate information and the humanitarian community in the service of this goal.[39] Part of this was the positioning of its own counterinsurgency within the framework of the "global war on terror." Government forces did achieve a crushing military victory in 2009. Yet wars and emergencies, in our experience, rarely disappear the instant that victory is declared.

The end of Sri Lanka's outright war presented a series of opportunities for gaming the "postconflict" phase and for exploiting a continuing state of emergency, in a manner that in some ways echoed the nonending of the Cold War. "Emergency" helped many members of the Rajapaksa family to engage in forcible corporate takeovers.[40] By 2012, the Rajapaksa family also reportedly controlled around 70 percent of the government budget via various ministries and was profiting greatly from "reconstruction" in the north and east.[41] Of course, the corruption and patronage politics that played an important role in sustaining the family's on-and-off rule until 2022 was nothing particularly novel. Yet war and a continuing sense of emergency were making a big difference, adding to the impunity, abuse, and exploitation by actors linked to the government.

Gains within the military were notable too. Toward the end of the vicious government counterinsurgency, David talked with a young government soldier at one of the "welfare centers" in the northern town of Vavuniya—essentially a camp in which Tamil civilians were forcibly detained behind barbed wire while government officials combed the captive population for "terrorists," who were sometimes taken away and killed or tortured. The war would soon be over, David suggested, and the soldier and his colleagues would perhaps get to go home and enjoy conditions of relative peace. "Oh no!" the soldier replied without hesitation. "There is still a lot of work to do—many pockets of resistance, and we have to prevent terrorism!" He added the number of troops would not be diminishing any time soon, and he was right. Shortly after victory over the Tamil Tiger rebels was declared, the government announced an *increase* in the size of the army—by fifty thousand.

When the size of an army is increased just as a war is ending, that may tell us quite a lot about war—and quite a lot about wreckonomics. Jobs and salaries in the army had to be protected. The army had long served as a kind of social safety valve, absorbing large numbers of young Sinhalese, often from poorer areas and with relatively meager prospects outside the military, as Rajesh Venugopal's important work shows.[42] Large kickbacks had been pocketed from a flourishing arms trade, and these kickbacks continued. The war mindset was also continuously useful in suppressing dissent. One think-tank report from 2009 had noted that "both conflict as well as the assumption of extraordinary powers and measures by the State have become normalised as a part of everyday life."[43] Widespread detention using antiterrorist powers persisted into the "postconflict" phase. Almost four years after the Tamil Tigers had been crushed, Human Rights Watch reported that the Rajapaksas "continued the trend of recent years to accumulate power at the expense of democratic institutions," while the government "targeted civil society through threats and surveillance."[44] As one observer noted in 2011, "In the absence of an overly inquisitive press, an effective investigative police force, an independent judiciary or the meaningful scrutiny of parliament, the war and its aftermath provided an ideal opportunity to loot the country's coffers."[45]

There were still further developments in the long and sorry tale of terror politics in Sri Lanka. While the civil war had seen the Sri Lankan government hijacking the global war on terror for the oppression of the Tamils,[46] in 2011 some Sinhalese nationalists began attacking mosques and Muslim properties in the name of targeting Islamic extremism.[47]

After anti-Muslim riots in Kandy district in March 2018, a radical Salafi preacher, M. C. M. Zaharan, posted a video calling for attacks on non-Muslims and on the police as well as threatening retaliation for violent attacks on Muslims by Sinhalese Buddhist militants.[48] In 2019, the terrible Easter bombings hit Colombo. Organized by a group of home-grown radical Islamists, including Zaharan himself, the attacks killed more than 250 people and injured many more. In the atmosphere of fear after the bombings, Gotabaya Rajapaksa was elected president on a platform of enhancing public security.[49] Yet as so often in the war on terror, the perceived need for a "tough" response was squeezing out careful analysis of causes as well as functions. One observer stated that Gotabaya Rajapaksa's "role in whipping up and condoning anti-Muslim violence in the recent past, the context that precipitated the Easter plot to begin with, was overridden by a narrative of national unity."[50] Hundreds of Muslims were subsequently arrested, often on flimsy evidence and facilitated by the long-standing Prevention of Terrorism Act, and the Muslim minority was subject to further antiminority violence under Gotabaya's 2019–22 administration.[51]

Of course, we are not pretending that a short section can do justice to the complexity of Sri Lanka's history of political violence, and we are not arguing that the war on terror framework was uniquely to blame for the country's predicament. Rather, we suggest that, once such a global "war" had been unleashed, it presented profitable opportunities for reframing existing violent state projects—and for rigging them too. The global war on terror offered additional impunity, additional legitimacy, and additional political and economic opportunities for extending violence—just as the Cold War had done in a wide range of countries.

A more hopeful ending to this story arrived in 2022 when, as the country faced deep economic crisis, the Rajapaksas were forced from power amid widespread protests against their misrule. The protest movement among other things sought to commemorate atrocities, to address community divisions, and to find some accountability. While Gotabaya's hand-picked replacement soon launched crackdowns, one activist remained upbeat: "People stood up against monsters and gave them the finger. . . . We managed to send Gotabaya home. If people could send him fleeing, and hiding in [army] camps and on islands, there's no stepping back from that."[52]

Given that the Rajapaksas have already returned once from the wilderness, we have to be cautious. But at least there is hope. In Syria, by contrast, an abusive president has relentlessly consolidated his power. We will suggest some surprising ways in which this was done.

Runaway Terror: Syria's Long War

In some ways, Syria's civil war has seen a classically ruthless counterinsurgency with the government not hesitating to use extreme violence against civilians and even deploying starvation as a weapon.[53] But there was more to it than that. We would naturally assume that governments try to prevent rebellions and are especially hostile to the more extreme elements within an uprising. Yet in many ways the brutal regime of Bashar al-Assad actively *provoked and bolstered* armed rebellion in Syria, and it gave particular support to some of the most violent fundamentalist elements within the emerging rebellion even as it deprived many rebel-held areas of relief. Several methods were important here. With the passing of time, a protest that had broad national and international legitimacy was pushed not only into armed revolt but also, sometimes, toward criminality and even terrorism.[54] In these evolving circumstances, significant parts of the international community began to wonder if Assad might be some kind of "lesser evil" in relation to the emerging threat from ISIS in particular.[55] This contributed to Assad's room for maneuver in pursuing a ruthless war strategy that included starving out areas of rebel strength until they capitulated. Quite how much of the evolution of the rebellion was specifically intended is not yet clear. No doubt the intentions were complex; as usual in such situations, they were shrouded in secrecy. But government-rebel interactions in Syria do seem in many ways a striking example of what Arendt once called "action as propaganda." By this she meant using violent action to help make initially implausible propaganda (in this case, about one's enemies) appear more and more true as time goes by and as the effect of one's actions takes hold.[56]

An astounding range of Syrian government actions had the effect of encouraging violence and extremism. Wittingly or unwittingly, the Assad regime helped to precipitate rebellion through its vicious recriminations against protesters and through subsequent torture, arbitrary imprisonment, and predation.[57] Behind the scenes, it selectively released violent fundamentalists from prison, boosting these elements and thereby helping its claim to be waging war on violent jihadis.[58] The Syrian regime whipped up sectarian sentiments through selective attacks and divisive language; in particular, groups with links to Shi'ism were stirred into fear of Sunni factions and Sunni extremists.[59] The regime seems to have actively colluded with some terrorist attacks, inflating the fear of terrorism,[60] while also sometimes cooperating economically with rebel groups.[61] It promoted scarcity in rebel-held areas (partly by blocking aid), which not only created incentives to capitulate but also helped extremist groups such as ISIS that were offering an "alternative government" to a regime that was offering neither protection nor assistance.[62] Finally, the regime at times offered partial immunity from its own attacks to ISIS in particular, while focusing much of its violence on alternative—and nonfundamentalist— local government structures.[63] This was a very particular and peculiar "counterinsurgency."

You may recall that in chapter 2 we gave a summary of our second mechanism of gaming, saying that *the very phenomenon that key actors claim to be opposing is also, surprisingly often, the phenomenon that is helping them the most.* Assad's apparent encouraging of the terror threat in Syria fits this model rather closely; without it, the war could well have seen a different outcome.

The gaming of Syria's conflict extended to the many external actors congregating around the "civil war," all with their own complex agendas. Let us focus on one key actor, Russia, instigator of its own "wars on terror" in the form of two destructive wars in Chechnya in the 1990s. In September 2015, Moscow intervened militarily in Syria (siding with Assad and Iran), citing the global war on terror. At this point, the Assad regime was struggling militarily and rebel forces had been spotted only eight kilometers from the presidential palace in Damascus. In this fraught context, Russia's intervention helped to revive the Assad regime. Like Assad, while claiming to be targeting ISIS, Russia focused most of its attacks on opposition groups that were less extreme than ISIS and that were especially threatening to Assad.[64] Having been alarmed by regime change in Libya following NATO's military intervention, Moscow did not want to see Western-backed regime change in Syria. The Russian government also appears to have been looking to exert leverage on Western governments via its intervention—and in particular to reduce the diplomatic isolation that had arisen, in large part, from Russia's 2014 aggression in

Ukraine.[65] So, again, this was very far from the simple "counterterror" operation that Moscow claimed.

Russia was rightly condemned—not least by US officials—for participating (along with Iranian and Syrian government forces) in the devastating attacks on Aleppo in November and December 2016, which resulted in horrific civilian casualties. What often disappeared from view is that in July 2016 the US and Russian governments were for a brief period *jointly* planning air strikes on jihadist elements of the rebellion (al-Nusra and ISIS). Significantly, this included strikes in "areas where the opposition is dominant, with some possible Nusra presence," as the US State Department put it.[66] Moreover, the United States was carrying out its own air strikes with significant civilian casualties,[67] and the US government even announced in September 2016 that non-Nusra opposition forces in Aleppo would be targeted if they failed to separate themselves physically from Nusra by the time US and Russian forces were ready to strike.[68] Amid opposition fears that the United States was being drawn closer to Russian definitions of legitimate targets, Secretary of State John Kerry referred to the Jaysh al-Islam and Ahrar al-Sham (two groups within the armed opposition) as "subgroups" of ISIS and Nusra.[69] In the run-up to its devastating attacks on Aleppo, Russia was publicly talking about a plan to fight together with the United States in the city, and US officials declined to issue a denial.[70] Notwithstanding US officials' revulsion over Aleppo, the geostrategic context of a shared war on terror narrative proved in many ways to be a permissive environment for the Russian attacks, including those on Aleppo itself.[71]

Across a range of countries, including Syria, there has been a tendency for targets to expand, in practice, from those who were said to be perpetrating acts of terrorism to a much wider group that includes assorted rebels as well as civilians caught in the vicinity of these various factions. In Syria as well as in Sri Lanka, this dangerous expansion was intimately linked with the gaming of the war on terror and the wider failure to rein in those who claimed to be waging such a war.

Mutation and Proliferation: Mali and the Sahel

As a disturbing coda, let us bring in one further case: the ongoing insecurity in Mali and the wider sub-Saharan Sahel. In the past decade, the project of fighting terror has proliferated in this region alongside a proliferation of insurgent groups themselves, drawing in more and more actors in ways that have generated both large benefits and costs—the latter concentrated among local civilians targeted in the violence.

To state the obvious, the insecurity and armed conflict across this impoverished region cannot be traced back to the war on terror alone, any more than in Syria or Sri Lanka. However, our concern here is limited to understanding how both official and insurgent "games" (and the associated costs) started cascading off the back of the terror threat.

The active US extension of the war on terror was key to this story. After 9/11, US Africa Command was soon seeking to extend its footprint into the continent. The threat of jihadist insurgency in the arid Sahel-Sahara belt, reaching from Mauritania and Senegal in the west to Somalia in the east, was its key justification. In May 2003, one US general summed up the perceived stakes: "We might wish to have more presence in the southern rim of the Mediterranean, where there are a certain number of countries that can be destabilized in the near future, large ungoverned areas across Africa that are clearly the new routes of narco trafficking, terrorist training and hotbeds of instability."[72] Even more so than in Afghanistan, the threat that was being fixated upon was sufficiently vague to encompass narcotics and irregular migration. Yet the fights against these threats were to contribute to the further proliferation and mutation of the war on terror in coming years.

Washington was not going it alone in its threat fixation (and conjuration). France retained a keen and anxious eye on its former colonies in the Sahel, and as in Syria and Sri Lanka, there was also an opportunity here for regional powers to play into the war on terror for their own political ends. Among them was Algeria, whose military regime had waged a "dirty war" against Islamist groups in the 1990s and which now started driving jihadists south into Mali. Some authors, notably the anthropologist Jeremy Keenan, have argued that Algiers was seeking to insert itself into the global war on terror to curry favor in Washington, DC. Others contest this idea, citing regional and local dynamics. While the degree of intention behind this "export" of jihadism is contested, it's clear that it contributed to the emergence of the various jihadist factions that were soon to rise to prominence, among them Al Qaeda in the Islamic Maghreb (AQIM), earlier known in Algeria as the Salafist Group for Preaching and Combat.[73]

In Mali, a ransom economy developed in which high-profile kidnappings filled jihadist coffers with Malian state complicity, including through hostage negotiations. As one report stated:

> The alliance between the Malian leadership and local notables based on organized crime also applied to AQIM's kidnapping for ransom business. These arrangements go a long way to explain why the Malian security apparatus by and large stopped short of confronting AQIM and its practice of using northern Mali as a safe haven for its hostage cases.[74]

Seasoned Mali observers noted how the president at the time, Amadou Toumani Touré (known as ATT), "accepted millions of dollars of US military aid, which was supposed to be used to drive out al-Qaida in the Islamic Maghreb, but he never actually went after the group's encampments." Meanwhile, "[t]he military itself was racked by nepotism, and officers often skimmed off their soldiers' ammunition and pay."[75]

A complex series of cascading games proliferated in the early 2010s, drawing in France as well as the European Union and eventually the UN machinery. Let us focus briefly on one key event: the 2012 separatist rebellion in Mali's north. While not the first in the country's postindependence history, the uprising swiftly came to be entangled with the existing jihadist threat, with the Malian security "market-place," and with the wider geopolitical security environment.

First, government corruption was fueling the anger in the desert north, where perceived state complicity with jihadist groups and the drug trade added significant kindling.[76] Second, the uprising had received a crucial spark from the return of northern Tuareg fighters from Libya following the NATO intervention and subsequent implosion of that country. Third, jihadist groups were ready to jump on the separatist bandwagon. Soon these groups (some of whose figureheads, such as the notorious Iyad Ag Ghaly, showed a deft maneuvering similar to that of Afghanistan's warlords) elbowed the Tuareg separatists aside and gained control over key northern cities. From there, they launched spectacular attacks designed for maximum exposure, desecrating Timbuktu's ancient shrines, staging executions, and applying a brutal version of sharia law.

Some in the Malian establishment were quick to blame Western states and their cascading wars. As one military officer told Ruben in 2014, "It's NATO which went along and did all that in Libya, and it's Europe which has let all these terrorists lose." He pointed a finger at the TV in his office, which showed the advances of ISIS in Iraq, as his voice rose: "It's you! It's you!"

The cascading violence in the north soon triggered a cascade of political consequences. Soldier casualties at the hands of separatists stirred discontent and helped to precipitate a coup d'état. Insurgents and jihadists were able to move south in the ensuing chaos. Amid national and international alarm at the jihadist advance, the French military intervened in early 2013. This in turn was followed by a UN peacekeeping mission, MINUSMA, pushed by Paris at the Security Council. Added to the mix was additional EU "support" for policing migration through the desert amid the 2015 crisis in the Mediterranean. The international presence had established itself on a range of fronts, with the French military operation morphing into a longer-running counterterror mission named Barkhane. By this time, Mali had started to be called "Africa's Afghanistan," a moniker that was still in place some seven years later when the Kabul debacle fed fresh concern in Western capitals about the fate of Mali and the wider Sahel.[77]

By the time of Ruben's fieldwork in 2014, Mali was becoming a complex laboratory for security and insecurity which actively imported personnel and practices from the Afghan "experience," a connection hinted at by a private security contractor at Bamako's Senou airport in 2014, whose T-shirt bore the imprint "May the last person to leave Afghanistan turn off the lights." But lessons from Afghanistan had not been learned. Part of the problem was the sheer *number* of overlapping security interventions. French and US counterterror operations jostled with EU military trainers, European antimigration policing initiatives, and the sprawling UN peacekeeping mission. The proliferation of security aims in Mali was going well beyond the "war on terror" proper, yet in doing so it showed the significant capacity for the "war fix" to proliferate and mutate. While the "war on terror" was increasingly out of favor as a term, at the core of the international intervention in Mali was French-led counterterrorism, with the United States looking on from the sidelines, combined with another key European concern: containing and controlling irregular migration.

These operations were hugely extendable and soon covered vast expanses of the wider Sahel. The extension of warfighting included US drone bases in Niger and French collaborations with national forces across the region under its Barkhane umbrella, headquartered in the capital of its key regional ally, Chad. Before the Mali intervention, as we saw, it had been clear that leaders of countries on the front line (such as Mali's ATT) had stood to gain significantly from simultaneously abetting and fighting the jihadist threat. With the very significant largesse of the transnational counterterror operations, huge incentives were being continuously created for national political and military partners to keep the pressure "right." Here, the proliferation of aims (fighting migration, terror, drugs, instability) allowed national leaders to mobilize threats on a wide palette. In late 2017, to take one example, Mali's then president, Ibrahim Boubacar Keïta, was asked by journalists how he would respond to those French voters who thought France's counterterror operation Barkhane was too expensive. He responded, "Mali is a dam and if this dam breaks, Europe will be flooded." Indispensable "partner forces," especially those of Chad's strongman Idriss Déby, were equally becoming dependent on indefinitely cracking down on insurgency across the Sahel, obtaining political and economic support in return for their favors. Within Mali and soon also in its neighbors Burkina Faso and Niger, military forces were able to gain substantial impunity, leverage, and control through their militarization of territory and their selective targeting of insurgents.[78]

In this situation, it was perhaps no surprise that the "enemy" kept proliferating into an ever-metamorphosing range of jihadist and insurgent factions. Various constellations loosely related to ISIS and al Qaeda clashed, competed, mingled, and sometimes overlapped with militia groups as well as with smuggling operations for contraband, arms, and people. Notably, many of these drew their sustenance from ostensibly offering "self-defense" against state or state-backed militia violence.[79] The result was a spiral of violence that has spread across the Sahel and shows little sign of abating. By early 2022, the UN High Commissioner for Refugees (UNHCR) said some 2.5 million people had fled their homes in Mali, Niger, and Burkina Faso in the past decade.[80]

In the early days of France's military intervention in 2013, *tricoleurs* had fluttered in Timbuktu and the jihadists seemed to have been "pushed back" with the Malian people's approval. Yet barely a year later, it was amply clear that the systemic incentive to fixate on the "terror" threat was contributing to a cascade of costs and games that echoed what we have observed in our other conflicts. In particular, the parallel with Afghanistan is notable. However, the interventions in Mali and the wider Sahel are different in several important respects. For a start, the region's conflicts were themselves in large part a *cascade of costs*, as the Malian military officer had suggested to Ruben in

Bamako. The larger war on terror had motivated jihadist groups to mobilize and escalate their presence in the desert (as a new mujahideen) while the NATO intervention in Libya (itself not unrelated to the post-Iraq interventionism of Western powers) had helped spark Mali's fateful separatist uprising. Further, the "security" and counterterror interventions on Sahelian soil were showing a rather extreme *cascade of games* as external interveners increasingly sought to combine fighting terror with containing migration and drugs while drawing multilateral organizations into the picture (and leaving increasing scope for Sahelian security actors to set their own agendas within the wider "fix"). Further, these cascades were combining to deadly effect as violence and displacement spread radically outward into neighboring countries despite the escalating security interventions, which frequently added fuel to the fire. There was a further twist here. Back in Mali, as violence and popular discontent proliferated and coup followed coup, the relationship between the ruling junta and the French soured to such an extent that Bamako bid its former colonizer farewell and invited Russia's Wagner mercenaries to help establish "security" on its territory.[81] Yet through all these dramatic shifts, there is a stable point: the gainful fixation on terrorism and its related "threats," which are now being fought under partly "new management."

Ways Out of the Franken-war

Much of the criticism of the war on terror has rightly been focused on Washington, DC. In popular protests against the invasions of Iraq and Afghanistan, the politics of resources (oil and gas) and the rapaciousness of big companies (Halliburton, Unocal) played a big role. While these are important areas of critique—as highlighted, not least, in Naomi Klein's compelling work[82]—we have in this chapter uncovered a view of war's gains that is more complex and perhaps even more disturbing. In looking at one high-profile case within the war on terror and three more "marginal" ones, we have been able to highlight, first, the remarkable extent to which this sprawling project has been *gamed* not only by international but also by national and local actors of various kinds; second, the tremendous expansion of the enemy enabled by *fixation* on the terrorist threat; and third, the *cascading* dynamic of this self-propelling war framework in terms of both games launched and costs incurred. We have stressed just how actively counterproductive the war on terror has been in terms of reproducing rather than curtailing terrorism, and we have drawn attention to the substantial benefits that have been extracted from this "failing" enterprise at a great variety of levels. What we were able to detect in Afghanistan, above all, is not so much a contest as a system—a system that was highly dysfunctional (when it came to the livelihoods and security of Afghans in particular) but also highly *functional* for diverse actors who were shaping and maintaining it. In Sri Lanka, Syria, and perhaps especially in the Sahel, we saw how the war system has transformed and mutated over time. In this process, we can discern how the global war on terror lurched beyond the control of its creator—mutating, proliferating, and to a large extent enduring despite its many well-documented failings.

If we were back at the fairground's House of Horrors, we would at this point be confronted by Frankenstein's monster, a creature that takes on a life of its own and eventually seeks revenge on its human creator. The analogy with the monstrous growth of the war on terror was not lost on the Iraqi novelist Ahmed Saadawi, whose *Frankenstein in Baghdad* has a junk dealer sew together the body parts of blown-up victims of the violence accompanying the Iraqi occupation.[83] Brought alive, the monster is soon outrunning its creator, acquiring further body parts from the junk dealer as it embarks on a rampage of killings in the capital. In Saadawi's haunting creation, we find an eerie metaphor not only for the devastation besetting Baghdad amid occupation but also for the *global* war on terror in its escalating, out-of-control aspects that have been so central to this chapter, and to our political systems analysis overall.

The Franken-quality of the war system scaled from the international level down to local dynamics and individual operations.

Whether it was Assad in Syria, the Rajapaksa brothers in Sri Lanka, or the shifting coalitions claiming to sign up to "counterterror" in Afghanistan and Mali, the war on terror has proven remarkably consistent in conjuring up a ghoulish array of Frankenstein's monsters with relatively little regard either for the priorities of the war on terror's initial "creator" or for the civilians they exploit and control in the name of counterterrorism.

For a wider view on this process, let us turn to the rigorous—and tireless—work of the London-based NGO Saferworld, with whom we have collaborated on several occasions. Saferworld has over the years examined conflicts in a wide range of countries affected by the war on terror. In a 2022 report distilling lessons from more than twenty individual studies, Saferworld emphasizes that state corruption and state violence tend to feed various "proscribed groups" (often explicitly labeled terrorists), while state actors very frequently reap political and economic benefits from the continued existence and even growth of precisely these rogue groups. Such conflicts have tended to be billed as a "war on terror" both internationally and by national governments in the countries concerned. But to a large extent, they have also been struggles over governance in which state corruption is a major "losing card" in terms of popular support—a dynamic that proved decisive in Afghanistan, for example. "Many states nurture or inflate the 'terror' threat to acquire [the] benefits of fighting it," the report concludes. "Many states use the benefits attained by participating in 'war on terror' for other ends. . . . [It is] a self-reinforcing system, which typically resists attempts to transform it" (Figure 7).[84]

In the context of a variety of armed conflicts around the world, a key consideration for interveners is avoiding a trap that has sometimes been laid by extremist groups. In analysis that chimes with experience in Afghanistan and many other countries, Saferworld's report notes that proscribed groups "have surprising potential to outlast and exhaust their military opponents, and undermine any statebuilding efforts that exclude them, sometimes over decades."[85] The lesson is ignored at everyone's peril.

A self-reinforcing system

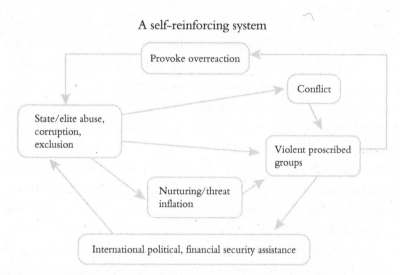

Figure 7 A self-reinforcing system of violence, as depicted by Attree and Street (2022) for Saferworld.

The short-sighted gaming of the war on terror goes a long way toward explaining why long-running wars have failed to end while new wars on terror have proliferated. In Sri Lanka and Syria, we have looked at countries not subject to a direct occupation but nevertheless subject to different kinds of violence associated with the war on terror. We find that the framework of a global war on terror has set up some remarkably perverse incentives for governments that claim to be collaborating in this ostensibly righteous endeavor. This has allowed them to legitimize massive abuse against civilians while enjoying significant international support. It has legitimized corruption on a major scale. And it has routinely created incentives (most notably, perhaps, in Syria) for nurturing the very problem of terrorism that "collaborating" governments claim to be addressing.[86] In Mali and the wider Sahel, we have seen the war on terror transform in complex new directions while leaving Western interveners staring into another Afghanistan-style failure on a regional scale, a fear compounded by Niger's 2023 coup.

Yet we must add a final word of caution, and at least a partial qualification to the self-perpetuating model that we are putting forward. Many of the state actors we have considered—in Washington, Moscow, Damascus, and Colombo—can cynically claim their wars have been "won." The US "homeland" has not actually seen any large-scale jihadist terrorist attacks since 2001. Moscow has gained strategic advantage in Syria. Assad stayed in power via his ruthless machinations, and the Rajapaksas won on the battlefield and later returned to power. In addition, and coming back to a crucial overarching containment game in the Cold War, the global war on terror and its offshoots can plausibly be seen as sending an intimidating message to a variety of governments while expanding key players' strategic footprint into regions such as Central Asia and the Sahel. All this may make us wonder whether we are really telling stories of failure in the strategic game. Any sound judgment here will depend on the timescale and on which costs are taken into account (points we return to in chapter 7). We should reiterate that the "wins" in Afghanistan and Mali did not last, that Sri Lanka ejected the Rajapaksas, and that even such victories as did accrue were built on the proliferation of insecurity and the mass suffering of civilians. This perverse balance of costs and benefits rather precisely mirrors the Cold War. Coming back to the war on terror, we can say that while "success" is claimed among the instigators (and sometimes at least partially *achieved* within particular zones and timescales and on the basis of wider strategic games), "failure" is exported (perhaps to others, perhaps to the future). The costs remained to a considerable extent off the books—but it's hard to banish them forever. Notably, when the war on terror brought a cascade of disastrous invasions and support for abusive regimes that claimed to cooperate, this significantly eroded the legitimacy on which the United States has relied when marshaling allies on the global stage.

We will have occasion to return to the issues of timelines and of exported costs as we proceed to the other wars and fights that we encountered in the Sahel and in Afghanistan—interventions targeting migration and drugs.

5

Double Games

Fear and Fraud in the Fight against Migration

In the previous chapter, we visited the House of Horrors to get some clues to the runaway quality of a fearsome system for combating terrorism. With our systems glasses on, we started to see some of the ways in which extreme fixation on a threat has led to a cascade of consequences and subsidiary security games. Perhaps it's tempting to leave the funfair behind at this point. But it turns out that we have more to learn there.

Blink as you emerge from the House of Horrors and look closely for a moment at what's happening over at our fairground attractions and carnival stalls. Observe the excitement and naïveté of the visitors as they move aimlessly among the stalls and rides, rummaging for their wallets! Next, look at the stallholders and you may soon figure out that the game being played here is tilted in their favor. The locals visit the fair only once a year, whereas the workers keep accumulating more expertise with each passing day. The market that results from this imbalance is to some extent *rigged,* which means that any unscrupulous traders can effectively manipulate the ignorance and complacency of their customers. There are stories galore of manipulated games: wheels of fortune can be weighted to stop in particular positions, stuffed animals fail to be knocked over, prize balloons are deflated so they are harder to pop, and so on. Magician-turned-policeman Dave Goldenberg some years ago had this to say:

> [T]he word "mark," meaning a sucker, came from the carnival. Years ago, when a crooked operator found someone who was gullible enough to fall for his scam, he would literally mark the person with some chalk by clapping him on the back when the sucker finished playing the game. Other dishonest operators on the lot would look for people with the chalk marks and entice them to play their games.[1]

Systems detectives as we are, we must ask: in our various wars, do the instigating states resemble the carnival "suckers"?

In some ways, yes. It's true that there are major power inequalities between richer instigating states (often former colonial powers) and poorer implementing states (often former colonies). But before we assume that the former are simply the "makers" of global wars and interventions, with the rest reduced to the passive role of "takers," we should consider some *other* asymmetries—most notably, the asymmetry of information.

The authors of these various wars have the money, military muscle, and political influence to back up not only the wars they are waging but also their claim to be setting the rules. But what most people tend to miss—and this includes many Western politicians themselves, as well as many leftist critics of various forms of "imperialism"—is that prominent political actors are not just playing; they, too, are *being played*.[2] And they are being played by actors (like our stallholder entrepreneurs) who have seen it all before.

A range of canny operators, often living rather near the sharp end of our various wars, have seen a number of international interventions come and go. They know that Western obsessions and bogeymen shift over time—perhaps Communists in the 1960s, 1970s, and 1980s; drug lords in the 1990s; terrorists from 2001 on; and more recently human smugglers. These national and local actors understand very well how to manipulate such obsessions and how to turn them into political power or economic gold. And they know that many foreign officials will be happy as long as their "partners" can assure them (perhaps quite erroneously) that a key problem has been tackled. Partner-state actors also tend to understand the ignorance and the arrogance of these temporary visitors (who today may not visit at all but instead send drones or cameras while subcontracting most of the work to locals or algorithms).[3] Partner-state actors tend also to be sensitive to the way that racism and postimperial fantasies inform the hubris of those who assume themselves to be in charge, turning this to remarkable advantage.

This imbalance—which we have illustrated through our fairground—is a familiar feature of what economists call the "principal-agent problem." In a classic principal-agent problem, the agent (our implementer) exploits information asymmetries to pursue goals different from those of the principal (our instigator), thereby undermining the principal's project. A good portion of our analysis in *Wreckonomics* falls rather squarely within this framework: in particular, a whole series of "wars" and "fights" by various principals have been radically undermined when the implementing agents have exploited information asymmetries and have followed agendas of their own. Such dynamics are relevant in the fairground too, and we should note that principal-agent problems have been applied to information asymmetries *in the market* (with the buyer cast in the role of principal and the seller often concealing important information in the role of agent). In our fairground example, the seller has far superior information and may use this to take advantage of the buyer. We have seen this pattern already in the war on terror, and will shortly see it at work in border security.

In the political systems analysis in *Wreckonomics* we also *depart* from the classic "principal-agent" problem—notably when it comes to "moral hazard." Classically, moral hazard kicks in when the agent uses information asymmetries to engage in detrimental behavior in the belief that the costs will be passed on to the principal (for example, driving badly because a company has granted you accident insurance, or making risky loans because you believe your bank will be bailed out by the government). Certainly, this mechanism is relevant to international peace and security, for example, if a national government stirs up grievances or even rebellions while believing it will be protected from their consequences by international backers, or if "partner states" in counterterror or migration controls start feeding a given problem in the hope of international support. However, a more fundamental and generally neglected moral hazard is that *the principal* may engage in risky and often predictably counterproductive behavior in the (mostly well-founded) belief that costs can be passed on to others—to the agent, perhaps, as well as to other groups and individuals (including those the agent is trying to instrumentalize and exploit). Thus, when it comes to moral hazard, we may be tempted to turn the principal-agent problem on its head. As the chapter progresses, we'll see plentiful examples of reckless behavior from the "principal"—to the point where the principal-agent problem, as normally conceptualized, ceases meaningfully to explain what is going wrong.

For now, we will see gaming and double gaming in full swing as we visit the "fight against illegal migration" and occasional "war" on smugglers playing out in the United States, Europe, Australia, and increasingly elsewhere too. Global border security is dwarfed by the staggering war on terror investment. Yet like its counterterror counterpart, the fight against migration has proliferated worldwide. Also like the war on terror, it has given rise to—and been sustained by—an intricate kind of game among instigators, "partners," target groups, and voters. In particular, the uneven relationship between those who inhabit a particular world (our stallholders or "agents") and those who visit for a short while (the customers or "principals") can help us to think about other rather unbalanced relationships that shape our systems of wreckonomics.

"Fighting the Illegals": Europe's Outsourced Border-Builders

In the windblown port town of Nouadhibou, coated in desert dust and lapped by the open Atlantic, something strange was happening in 2005. Migrants were leaving its Atlantic shoreline by the thousands in brightly painted wooden fishing boats, setting out on a hazardous crossing to the Spanish Canary Islands, which had by this time become one of the far-flung outposts of Europe's still incipient battle against irregular migration. Nouadhibou, in the north of the sparsely populated country of Mauritania straddling the Maghreb and West Africa, had long been a magnet for migrant workers in its own right: Senegalese traders, fishermen, and willing jobseekers for the mining and hospitality industries frequently crossed the country's southern borders with little trouble, joining a thriving informal economy. But now, the migrants' sights appeared to be set on the European Union, rattling politicians in Madrid and Brussels. What was going on?

As it happens, the way in which Nouadhibou suddenly turned into a crossroads for unwanted migration was symptomatic of the larger failures of Europe's fight against illegal migration—and of the perverse gains arising from it, both monetary and political.

First of all, routes had shifted: that very year, 2005, saw one of the largest migration "crises" at the borders of Europe since the Schengen agreement had greatly facilitated movement within the EU, effectively creating an external border for the EU as a whole. Hundreds of undocumented Africans had made their way to the fences of Spain's enclaves of Ceuta and Melilla along the northern Moroccan coast. In the scramble to climb their way into Spain, some of them had been killed by security forces while others had been expelled into the desert.[4]

After the crisis at the fences, heavily magnified by the media and politicians, came the reinforcement. Spain was making good on its earlier promise to extend the fences (news of which—ironically—had motivated the migrants to stage the entry attempt in the first place). Spain was also leaning on Morocco to police its northern territories with a heavy hand. Routes had shifted to evade the obstacle, turning toward the Canary Islands. The situation was ripe for Europe's next migration crisis to play out in 2006 in this tourist archipelago, with faraway Mauritania finding itself the latest stopover on the deadly global roadshow of fighting migration.

This kind of "cat-and-mouse game," with increasingly dramatic entry attempts, had been well known for years from the US-Mexico border. Mexican migrants had staged "kamikaze runs" across the San Diego border in the 1990s, motivating fence-building that subsequently pushed routes into inhospitable terrain.[5] European officials failed to learn from this experience. Meanwhile, it soon became clear that Mauritania had skin in the game. In that very year of rising boat departures, 2005, disgruntled military officers had staged the latest in the country's long line of coups since independence from France. Yet instead of using this militarization of the territory for the purpose of blocking migration exits, as the Europeans would have wanted, the junta conveniently looked the other way. And so, with an open door to the Canaries thanks in no small part to the Mauritanian authorities' inaction, West African workers took their chance. The regime had found an ideal bargaining chip in its relations with Europe, whose leaders now had to recognize and engage with the coup leaders. A beautiful relationship was born.[6]

In the coming years, Mauritania became a testing ground for the "fight" that the Europeans would later go on to expand across the West African Sahel, West Asia, and far beyond in an attempt at *externalizing* migration controls, as far away from the European borders as possible. Again, this push to externalize mirrored what the United States had already been pursuing together with its Mexican and Central American neighbors.[7] In both cases, the externalization of controls came to overlap with the wars on drugs and terror in terms of the authorities involved and in terms of the tendency to displace the problem. In more recent years, the Spaniards' machinations in a West African desert state have been used as a template for European externalization in countries ranging from Niger to Azerbaijan.[8]

Following the Mauritanians' successful bargaining with migration, the model had nevertheless seemed a success for the "principal" in Madrid (and Brussels). In interviews, Spanish officials boasted of their innovations and of their close work with their new partners. The collaboration involved building a migrant "reception center" on the

outskirts of Nouadhibou with the help of Spanish aid. It quickly got
dubbed "Guantanamito," or little Guantánamo, and essentially worked
as a kind of "expulsion roundabout" while Spanish Red Cross and
Mauritanian Red Crescent workers, managing the center, provided
some useful humanitarian branding. The junta, meanwhile, received
diplomatic recognition and new rounds of European aid. Its security
forces were equipped via European funds and patrolled the coast together with Spanish Civil Guards. With the help of such political and
financial largesse, the Nouadhibou route died down, to Spanish de-
light. What was not to like?

For Mauritania's junta, the decrease in departures was a mixed
blessing. The lucrative status of crossroads was being taken away. In
the event, the authorities found a way of cooking the books and
restirring the threat. By the time of Ruben's research on Mauritania's
borders in 2010, the flow of expelled migrants remained steady, but
those now being sent down to the Senegalese and Malian borders were not necessarily on their way to Europe. Instead, Ruben
kept hearing (and stock-taking reports, including by the Spanish
Red Cross itself, corroborated these accounts) how migrants living
and working in Nouadhibou were now likely to be stopped on
the streets, bundled into Guantanamito, and added to the tally of
clandestins (illegals).[9] The Mauritanian forces had found a perfect
racket: the manna of unwanted migration could be conjured out
of thin air, much like the ghost insurgents of the war on terror.
Anyone, after all, may be presumed to have the *intention* of traveling to Spain. This game took on disturbing racial overtones, all the
worse given Mauritania's difficult colonial and postcolonial history
of race relations, with anyone "black" (including, in many documented cases, Mauritanian citizens) being potentially liable to detention and even expulsion. As one Senegalese policeman, enrolled
into fighting Europe's migration problem in a Spanish-provided car
and with Spanish pay, put it during a patrol on his side of the border,
"It's very difficult to detect the clandestine migrant. . . . Just like that,
he becomes a boatman, or else he appears as a simple traveler. . . .

They don't exhibit their illegality in Senegal, it's something that you can't detect." Alarmingly, Mauritanian forces and law enforcement were sometimes "detecting" it by simply reading it off people's skin. At the time of writing, they remain handsomely rewarded for their racially charged battle against migration.[10]

In short, the Mauritanians and Spaniards had colluded in creating a market—or a club—for fighting migration on their own terms. The Spaniards were all too happy with this arrangement, despite the Mauritanian double-gaming. Following the 2006 "boat crisis," Spain had suddenly opened embassies and rolled out an ambitious "development" plan across the whole West African region, all with the intention of convincing poor regional states to participate in migration controls. The "fight against the illegals," as the officer in charge of Senegal's navy operation put the task at hand in an interview, was going swimmingly. Yet there was no time to rest. Spanish Civil Guards insisted that patrolling operations should not be drawn down or else the migratory threat would come roaring back, and they kept extolling (in public, at least) their even-handed "collaboration" with the West African forces. "We help them to fight migration," one senior Spanish border official insisted in an interview. In the longer perspective, however, this was rather far from a happy win-win—as the Europeans were about to find out.

Escalating the Fights, Escalating the Demands

The Mauritanians had hardly been the first to realize gains on the migration-fighting market. Across the Atlantic, Mexico had long been amply rewarded for its role in fighting migration on its northern neighbor's behalf, including through crackdowns on Central American migrants crossing its own southern border.[11] As for the Mediterranean situation, by the early 2000s Libya's Colonel Muammar Gaddafi had already discovered that he sat on a prize possession. During the international embargo, the "Brotherly Leader" had turned his eyes to his African neighbors: sleeping in a great Bedouin tent in New York in time for the UN General Assembly was all of a piece with his newfound role as chief spokesman for downtrodden African nations breaking free from old colonial shackles. He had established close business links with states in the Sahel and invited African workers into Libya's labor-hungry economy. As Italy and its northern neighbors anxiously began eyeing the Mediterranean for signs of migrant boats, however, Gaddafi started seeing his country's African workers as a double asset. On the one hand, workers could still be exploited; on the other, they could be "weaponized." Soon enough, pacts were being struck between Gaddafi and Italy's Silvio Berlusconi to the tune of billions of dollars. Even so, the Brotherly Leader, fully grown into his Reagan caricature of "mad dog of the Middle East," escalated the rhetoric and threatened that Europe would "turn black" unless more favors were forthcoming. And come they did: Libya emerged from the international cold thanks in no small part to Gaddafi's migration maneuvers. Simultaneously, he also succeeded in presenting himself as someone who could help in the war on terror—not least because of his role in *stirring up* terror.

Then came war. Amid the Arab Spring, NATO and assorted Middle Eastern countries intervened militarily in Libya's scramble for power. The violent removal of Gaddafi and the conflict that followed led to a *cascade* of displacement and migration (including into Mali, as we have seen); it also, and very much relatedly, escalated the gaming and brinkmanship. As NATO missiles put a stop to his previously cozy relationship with European leaders, Gaddafi did not give up on his threats and cajoling—quite the opposite. Europe would be "invaded" by migrants, he said, unless NATO backed down; his troops tried to make good on his threat, forcing African workers to board unseaworthy vessels at gunpoint. In the following years, assorted warlords have kept up this tradition by simultaneously "combating" and facilitating migration, taking handsome rewards with both hands as smugglers-cum-guards while threatening Europe with further "invasions."[12] In one notable episode, one militia leader in Zawiya, known as Al Bija, was found by journalists to be managing the smuggling market by taking a substantial cut from any departing boats before promptly "rescuing" those who had not paid, towing them back to brutal detention centers run by his own tribe.[13] The double game, once played on a small scale by Mauritania, was by the time of Libya's conflict a high-stakes geopolitical game that was deeply infused with moral hazard.

The stakes were to rise higher still. In 2015, Turkey's Recep Tayyip Erdoğan was in a tight spot: he had called snap elections and was accosted from all sides. Like Gaddafi and the Mauritanian junta, Erdoğan held the trump card: migration. Though the details remain murky, and Ankara denies everything in usual order, it is clear that Turkish border guards and police looked the other way, opening the gates to the Syrians stranded within its territory as well as to Afghans, Iraqis, and others from further afield. (Questions still remain over Russia's role in fomenting the crisis as part of its Syria maneuvers.) The move would strengthen Erdoğan's grip on power as he extracted promises from the EU—only partially met, but that did not particularly matter for electoral purposes—on visa-free travel and on financial rewards running into the billions.[14]

Selling oneself as an unreliable bulwark against migration had by 2015 become big business. "Weapons of mass migration" is how one scholar, Kelly Greenhill, has labeled this use of migrants as a geopolitical plaything. Whatever we call this gaming of migration and forced displacement, it is a remarkably effective way for relatively powerless states to exert pressure on their stronger counterparts.[15] One further example comes from Morocco, which in 2022 managed finally to shift Spain's policy on occupied Western Sahara in its favor in exchange for further migration enforcement—halting, at least temporarily, the brinkmanship that had fomented politically motivated "border crises" at Ceuta, Melilla, and the Strait of Gibraltar over at least two decades. The costs of this bargaining were regularly borne by migrants; for instance, in June 2023 at least twenty-three migrants died between the

Spanish and Moroccan fences at Melilla, where they had been trapped and tear-gassed in a security operation subsequently covered up by both sides.[16]

In her study, Greenhill goes so far as to argue that the "softer" features of liberal democracies—including respect for rights and for open democratic debate—make them particularly vulnerable to "weaponization."[17] However, this fails to account for the evident *lack* of respect for rights, as we saw in the border violence at Melilla. What is also missing from her picture is the systemic feedback loop that is so central to the escalating fight against migration, just as it is to the war on terror. Once fighting migration has been *fixated* upon as a paramount political objective in destination states, and once huge resources are being spent on this endeavor, "partner" actors will spot vulnerabilities and opportunities to play on this ostensible existential threat, selectively closing and opening the gates.[18]

As we noted at the start of this chapter, both instigators and implementers can benefit from the fight by insourcing the gains while exporting the costs. The unevenness of global refugee hosting responsibilities is part of this picture. UNHCR figures as of 2023 confirm a broader trend: some 83 percent of refugees worldwide are hosted by low- and middle-income countries, and 72 percent by countries neighboring conflict zones. Turkey, topping the list of global refugee hosts, can reasonably argue that it has done its "fair share" in hosting nearly 3.8 million refugees, mostly from neighboring Syria. From this viewpoint, when larger refugee hosts "weaponize" migration and displacement, they are in many respects using the "weapons of the weak" against a more powerful counterpart, to use anthropologist James Scott's term. While border security has spectacularly failed to address international migration in the round (and has generated a raft of destructive consequences), it has nevertheless "succeeded" in keeping refugees away from the protection that might have been provided by the richest states in the global system. Yet this is far from the only "gain" for the instigators. Another comes via the potent politics of distraction and drama that bordering provides, as we will now see.

Globalized Border Security and Its Winners

It is worth backtracking here to recall how swiftly borders became bulwarks against unwanted migration, as even a cursory glance into history shows. The end of the Cold War once promised, to optimistic liberal voices, a "borderless world"; instead, it gifted us an increasingly globalized border business. The *cascade of games* that we identified in the war on terror also applies strongly in the field of border security. Not only are more and more "partner states" being enrolled in border security (fomenting "internal" games), but many countries are also instigating their own border security fixations (thereby proliferating "external" games). Barriers are today separating neighbors not just in the West but far beyond, including in the cases of West Bengal/Bangladesh, Saudi Arabia/Yemen, South Africa/Zimbabwe, and Turkey/Iran.[19] While there were some fifteen walls at nation-state borders at the end of the Cold War, the total had risen to more than seventy barely three decades later.[20] Unlike older border fortifications, the new ones are not built to keep state enemies away (or to keep citizens in, as in the case of the Berlin Wall): they are aimed at keeping people out.

Calls for "security" and "border protection" justify not just the building of walls but also a wider architecture of control, separation, and surveillance at national borders and well beyond them. Drones have been repurposed from the war on terror for border surveillance in the United States and the Mediterranean; complex offshore detention and sea patrolling agreements have been rolled out from Australia to the Atlantic; advanced radar equipment and satellite surveillance have proven a boon for Europe's defense industry; and in the increasing number of border security "expos," security firms have flogged ever more intrusive technologies—heartbeat scanners, oxygen detectors, ground sensors, online surveillance—in a market that in one estimate is soon worth more than $65 billion.[21] As for the official side of this stupendous growth, a small indication comes from the

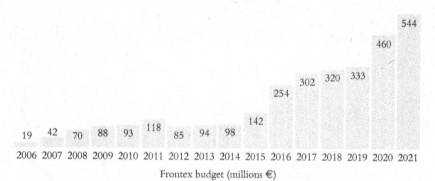

Figure 8 The rising budget of the EU's Frontex. Source: Frontex data.

EU border and coast guard agency, Frontex, which has gone from a budget of 19 million euros in 2006 to more than 750 million euros by 2022, a year in which it was facing mounting scandal over support for illegal Greek "pushbacks" at sea (compare Figure 8).[22]

The United States, as so often, has led the way in this trend while actively heating the global border security market—with the budget of the US Border Patrol increasing almost tenfold in the past three decades, from $363 million in 1993 to nearly $4.9 billion by 2021 (compare Figure 9).[23] While the budget is still small relative to military expenditure, we should note that its remarkable growth rate is strongly related to the wider security marketplace, with great scope for synergies, "dual-use" technology, seed funding, and more across civilian (policing) and military sectors.[24] At the heart of this complex sits the vast Department for Homeland Security bureaucracy, bringing together our various wars and fights in the wake of 9/11.

Besides the escalating border security investments, politicians have put huge amounts of time, money, and effort into the complicated business of getting tough on migration—and being seen to get tough. Yet this has massively backfired on a practical level. Let us look at this briefly with the help of Douglas Massey, a leading migration scholar. Since the 1980s, he and his colleagues have found, the vast expenditure on border security has gone hand in hand with a large *growth* of undocumented migration within the United States. The principal

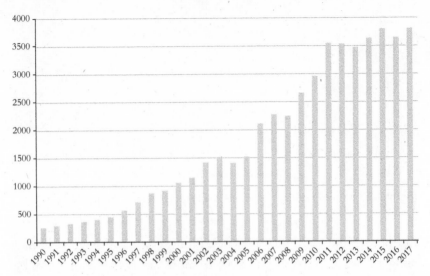

Figure 9 The rising budget of the US Border Patrol (from Keen and Andersson 2018, based on CBP data).

reason is remarkably simple (and mirrored to some extent by North African migration patterns in southern Europe): as it became much harder to circulate back "home" for seasonal migrants owing to harsh controls and barriers, people stayed.[25] So why, if border controls were backfiring so spectacularly, were successive administrations so committed to them?

Academics have long detected a gap between rhetoric and reality in migration policy. This "policy gap" has been especially notable when it comes to "fighting" migration, with significant *political* gains from a strong stance on borders quite independent of enforcement outcomes.[26] Some years ago in the United States, the political scientist Peter Andreas described this as a "border game" with various layers: from the spectacle —and distraction—of border enforcement on the political level to the institutional funding game through to the cat-and-mouse game at the border itself.[27] Racism came to play a prominent role here, reflecting a longer history of racial exclusion in admissions, as shown by studies of media and political representations of Latino migrants in particular.[28] One prominent case of this fear-based discourse came in 1985 from President Reagan as he rather brazenly linked the ongoing Cold War to our wars and fights: undocumented migration, he said, was "a threat to national security," with "terrorists and subversives . . . just two days' driving time" from the Texas border and Communist agents ready "to feed on the anger and frustration of recent Central and South American immigrants." Drawing on this and other examples, Massey summarizes how, over the decades that followed, increasing political "fixation" came together with migration cascades (in our terminology). As he puts it, a racialized "Latino threat narrative was manufactured and sustained by an expanding set of self-interested actors who benefitted from the perpetuation of an immigration crisis, which drove an unprecedented militarization of the border that radically transformed a long-standing migration system from a circularity to settlement."[29] Crucially, this new migration pattern also had clear winners within the wider economy, as an undocumented and deportable labor force was even more exploitable than its legal predecessors.[30]

As in the United States, northern European politicians saw it as expedient to drum up fears over uncontrolled migration, especially after the 1970s economic crisis and its attendant closure of legal pathways for workers from former colonies and neighboring countries. In the 1990s, with the inauguration of the EU Schengen area of free movement and the foundation of an "external border," southern European countries followed suit, cutting legal pathways for North Africans. It was in this context that the migration "crisis" first gestated in the Mediterranean, with small numbers of Moroccans, Tunisians, and Albanians entering Spain and Italy along new irregular routes. As a response, EU member-state governments started to collaborate around external border security and precious little else in the migration and asylum domain (despite plans to the contrary).[31] As in the United States, the rounds of border crises that arose off the back of this border security investment did not make politicians change course; rather, each new dramatic situation was seen as a justification for even more border security. The vicious cycle, as if by magic, turned into a "virtuous" one.

As the crises grew in Europe to unprecedented proportions, with a record of over one million arrivals by land and sea in 2015, politicians and technocrats of different political colors unified around the migratory "fix." While Hungary's Viktor Orbán and Italy's interior minister Matteo Salvini were among those talking actively of a "war" in the Mediterranean (and doing their level best to put it into practice), the European Commission's "liberal" establishment made "protecting the European way of life" through border security and other measures a key plank of its agenda (however much it tried to backpedal on the rhetoric after a backlash).[32] Even in the United Kingdom, far away from the Mediterranean "migration crisis," the Brexit campaign of 2016 staked much political capital on fears over uncontrolled onward migration toward the Channel. "We're from Europe, let us in!" read one tabloid headline to a picture of (non-European) asylum seekers crammed into a truck, illustrating the wider political push at the time.[33]

A large part of the incentive to keep escalating the fight, both in the United States and Europe, concerned the gains to be had from fixating on and fighting "illegal migration" as well as the very limited costs of doing so. Especially in the United States, border closures have brought *economic* gains in rendering the cross-border labor force increasingly exploitable. Meanwhile, the *political* gains are double. On the one hand, a tough nationalist message attracts many voters; on the other, it provides a distraction from problems governments cannot or do not want to solve, including deep inequality and economic insecurity. Irregular migration by land and sea was a boon for this kind of politics in Europe. Yet the numbers have in general been relatively small, 2015 excluded. Most irregular migration in Europe occurs when people overstay their visas, as the European Commission itself acknowledges, while regular immigration dwarfs land and sea arrivals.[34]

In short, what was going on in the parallel political "fights" against migration that we have observed across the North Atlantic was *systemic.* Governments and interior ministries had seen fit, for their own political and institutional reasons, to "securitize" migration with increasing verve in the 1990s; that is, they had increasingly treated human movement (of certain kinds) as a security problem to be solved with force, rather than, say, as a labor market and protection problem. Instead of looking at the complex drivers of migration (including persistent *demand* for workers), all that politicians had to do, in this mode, was to be seen to address the arrivals. By the 2010s, this securitization had become systemic. In the European case, those baby steps in Nouadhibou's port in 2005–6 had transformed into the tramping of boots from Niger to Sudan, and from Turkey to the Poland-Belarus border, where President Alexander Lukashenko—despite his regime's "working arrangement" with the Frontex border agency—was now replicating Gaddafi's brinkmanship by channeling refugees to a frontier no-man's-land where Polish guards fought them back. More and more states and institutions were feeding from the "self-licking ice-cream cone" of the endless fight against migration, in a clear parallel to the war on terror.

The Cascade Grows: Migrant Tactics and Political Instability

In the migration story so far, we might conclude that we simply face the familiar merry-go-round of vested interests, of scheming stall-holders and gullible customers who buy and sell security "solutions." If only it was that simple! With our wreckonomist's glasses on, we get a clearer picture of how wrong-headed "wars" and "fights" may keep escalating not *just* because of nefarious intentions but also through the cascading dynamics within the system itself.

Let us take the example of migrant strategies. Like state officials and wily political leaders, migrants have their own "agency." Rarely has this been clearer than in the fight against migration. "Show me a ten-foot fence and I'll show you an eleven-foot ladder," the saying goes. Ruben has lost count of the times border guards have reminisced about the latest innovative—and dangerous—entry attempts in response to border-building. In the migrant graveyard of Arizona's desert, the US Border Patrol are familiar with "carpet shoes," used by migrants to avoid leaving traces on the desert ground, as well as the use of tunnels, sentinels, and all sorts of ingenious ways of escaping *la migra* (the patrols).[35] In Spain, over the Strait of Gibraltar, migrants have taken to using small inflatable rafts, labeled "toys" by sea rescue services—not just to keep down costs but also to try to avoid detection by Spain's coastal radar systems. In Ceuta and Melilla, the fortified Spanish enclaves, Civil Guards have shown impossible-looking pictures of men hidden inside car seats and van dashboards, eventually detected by heartbeat scanners, leading to other migrant innovations, and so forth. Migrants themselves talked about the right weather to set out across coasts and fences—clouds, even rain, helped distract the sniffer dogs at Ceuta's barriers—as well as the right clothing for climbing the six-meter fences. When Spanish guards added an anticlimbing mesh at Melilla, migrants responded by using hooks to fasten onto the barrier. When Morocco built another fence outside the Spanish fence, old techniques of mass entry via land and sea borders came back in vogue. Tellingly, the term used by Civil Guards to refer to mass attempts to climb the fences was *avalancha*—an acknowledgment, on at least some subconscious level, of the systemic cascade that ensued upon the interaction among policing and migrant tactics.[36]

If migrants' tactics changed with each new border measure, so did their routes. Indeed, we noted above how the closure of legal pathways led migrants to innovate irregular alternatives. This was the case in southern Europe in the 1990s, and had been the case already in the 1960s in the United States, with the end of the agricultural *bracero* program.[37] As border guards cracked down on irregular routes, new ones predictably appeared, in a version of the war on terror's "whack-a-mole." This is how the Canary Islands had been presented with its "crisis" of 2006: as a late-arriving gift sent by the Spanish-Moroccan security operators, who had succeeded in pushing the problem toward the southwest. A few years later, in the central and eastern Mediterranean, the "gift" of migration was being sent around like a game of pass-the-parcel (or, more accurately, beggar-thy-neighbor).[38] Reinforcements by Libya and Italy, and the withdrawal of sea rescues as a "deterrence" measure, displaced routes toward Greece. There, in turn, the fencing of the Turkish land border displaced routes toward the Aegean Sea, which like its Canaries counterpart ten years earlier had opened new opportunities for new groups of migrants. At the same time, and just as in 2005, it was clear to many migrants and refugees that the door was about to close—European politicians said as much. So it was now or never. The migration crisis was becoming a self-fulfilling prophecy both through the incentives of stoking it for "implementers" such as Turkey as well as through migrant and refugee countertactics. Many years later, the cycles of displacements continue, with the latest desperate launch pads including, for a moment, Belarus and Lebanon. Meanwhile, the United Kingdom increasingly started seeing the same patterns and processes that had played out in Spain in the mid-2000s, with routes dispersing and changing in the English Channel amid crackdowns on clandestine entries via trucks in Calais.[39] The panic over rising arrivals was becoming a self-fulfilling prophecy there, too. This ever-shifting nature of routes and tactics in response to border enforcement was leading to a horrific human tally: since 2014, at least twenty-six thousand people are estimated to have died or disappeared around the Mediterranean alone.[40]

The series of largely self-induced migration crises was fueling a swiftly growing illicit market of human smuggling. European leaders have been keen to frame their border security efforts as a "war on smugglers," especially since 2015, when smugglers (frequently mislabeled "mafias" or "traffickers") were conveniently assigned the blame for a set of horrific shipwrecks near the Italian and Maltese coasts.[41] Of course, we shouldn't paint smugglers in a rosy light; theirs is usually a cut-throat business. Yet it is a business that has grown larger and more violent—in short, *cascaded*—on the back of border enforcement not just in Europe but worldwide.

Let us return briefly to Mexico. Here, small-scale "coyote" operations of earlier years have been cornered by larger-scale smuggling enterprises. As anthropologist Wendy Vogt put it in 2013, amid rising enforcement "the markets for humans, drugs, and weapons become intertwined and create new avenues for profit and violence," with the drug cartels—especially Los Zetas at her time of writing—dominating the routes and fueling profitable cycles of violence and predation (often in collusion with the authorities). One of Vogt's interlocutors, a Central American migrant, said that:

> Before on the journey, there were robbers and everyone knew that they would steal whatever you had on you but then they would leave you in peace. But now, with these groups that are kidnapping, well it's a whole other level, now they are organized together with the police and they carry weapons, heavy artillery. The same police that denounce them are the ones who protect them.[42]

In North Africa and the Sahel, the similarly "artisanal" smuggling facilitation of earlier years (often run by migrants themselves) has increasingly given way to organized criminal gangs. In Libya, many such smugglers have held migrants and refugees hostage and even tortured them until their families pay release fees.[43] The taller the barriers, the more captive your market, as "customers" have nowhere left to turn except into the hands of professional criminal organizations.

We can put this in economic terms, as Customs and Border Protection officials in the United States are keen to do themselves. In presentations, econometricians working in CBP have asserted (like their European counterparts) that the aim of enforcement is to destroy the smugglers' "business model." This involves increasing the cost of smuggling (and thus of migration) to the point where revenue takes a hit, in theory leading to attrition in the smuggling market. Yet what this does is favor smuggling economies of scale as both the barriers to entry and profitability rise.[44] In other words, the "cascade" of criminalized smuggling and more dangerous routes is not unpredictable. A systemic view, if officials had wished to consider it, would tell them that the fight against migration and the war on smugglers would produce more of precisely that which they said they wanted to curtail: more dangerous migration scenarios and stronger criminal smuggling operations.

This is where failure and success become more complicated. On one reading, policy was consistently failing either to rein in migration or to weaken the smugglers. Yet at the same time, multiple benefits arose within this apparently failing system. Some of these fell into the hands of smugglers, others into the border control community (with these two groups linked by frequent collusion, as we have noted). More dangerous routes also lent themselves to heightened political rhetoric about the callous human smugglers while also being seen as a highly useful deterrent. In other words, costs and gains were cascading in tandem.

This dynamic—which echoed the cascades of chapter 4's Franken-war—generated serious knock-on effects in the societies where the fight was staged. In Libya, this was seen at an extreme level following the fall of Gaddafi. As one report noted in 2017, "[T]he coastguard, detention centres, and key branches of the fragile Libyan state's security apparatus are largely run by militias, some deeply involved in the illicit economy," with these militias "creating a protection market around human smuggling before eventually taking over the business directly."[45] The political and economic games around European (especially Italian) relationships with the militias are complex and extraordinarily murky. However, it was becoming clear around this time that external involvement and "encouragement" were strengthening the power of the militias, who (like many border guards) could play the dual role of poacher and gamekeeper along Libya's coasts. The strengthening of militias and the ensuing turf battles among them were contributing to prolonged Libyan instability.[46]

Or consider Sudan. With growing urgency since 2015, not least through the so-called Khartoum process for collaboration on irregular migration in the Horn of Africa, the EU has prioritized partnership with a regime that is actually *responsible* for large-scale displacement, in both the past and the present (we should note that the EU has also collaborated with a number of other strongmen in the region).[47] In the aftermath of Europe's border crisis, the militia known as the Rapid Support Forces (RSF)—which incorporated former *genocidaires* from the Janjaweed in Darfur—kept producing news items for the Sudanese press on all the migrant smugglers' vehicles they had confiscated. It was clear they were putting themselves in pole position for being the EU's helpers on the route from the Horn of Africa. This had official backing. In a 2017 report for the NGO Enough, Suliman Baldo noted, "In 2014, the RSF was deployed as Sudan's primary border force, as part of Sudan's effort to demonstrate to the European Union that it could help to contain irregular flows of migrants from and through Sudan to Europe."[48] By 2016, and coinciding with the EU dialogue, Khartoum had redeployed RSF forces to the Libyan and Egyptian borders in Northern State. Officially integrated into Sudan's army, RSF fighters were intercepting migrants and smugglers trying to cross the desert toward Europe.[49] While frequently inflating the numbers to trumpet their success, this patrolling involved significant degrees of "double gaming" as well as widespread abuse of migrants; as one research report states, besides "taxing" migrant vehicles, "the RSF have increasingly become smugglers themselves." At the same time, the RSF continued to attack civilians in Darfur on a significant scale.[50] As the RSF leader, Mohamed Hamdan (known as "Hemedti" and himself a notorious former smuggler), put it, "Once we dealt with the rebellion in South Kordofan and Blue Nile and Darfur, we immediately turned to the great Sahara desert, especially after the directives from the president of the republic to combat illegal migration."[51] Alarmingly, RSF commanders seemed to think that counterinsurgency and migration control could be pursued simultaneously: in September 2016, an RSF commander said his forces had "combed and cleansed the north-western borders of the remnants of rebel movements and of human traffickers and smugglers."[52]

European officials kept denying that funding went straight to the RSF, but this was rather beside the point. Sudan's security and law enforcement sectors are notoriously fluid and secretive, and Khartoum was clearly deploying the RSF as part of its attempt to exploit the EU's fixation on migration by establishing cooperation over border control.[53] A wider systemic risk analysis, if officials had pursued it, would have identified the risk with "border security at any cost," which after 2015 became an EU-wide priority.

In short, the momentum behind fighting migration was leading—as in the war on terror—to an "internal cascade" of subsidiary games, many of them extraordinarily violent and extralegal. Besides these amply documented human consequences, the political consequences of the skewed focus on border security have also been significant. As Alex de Waal has argued, external security collaboration in counter-terror has been important for regional leaders' successful dominance of what he calls the "political marketplace" of the Horn of Africa, and border security was now generating further room for maneuver.[54] Sudan's authorities were benefiting from the new leverage offered by the Khartoum process while its repressive security apparatus was being equipped and strengthened, with little oversight over spending or the risks involved to either migrants or citizens.[55] Benefiting from the new international priority given by the EU to fighting migration, the RSF had also been able to paint themselves in a new light while attempting Gaddafi-style blackmail of Europe—going as far as asking the EU for a "ransom" to continue their efforts "on behalf of Europe."[56] This is not to say that other, internal factors in Sudan are irrelevant in explaining the turbulent politics of the country or indeed the rise of RSF and Hemedti, who has lately been embroiled in a deadly fight for power in Sudan. In particular, the government's policy of waging "counterinsurgency on the cheap" has left a legacy of disgruntled militias whose loyalty depends on expensive and unsustainable payments in the "political marketplace."[57] Yet by turning a blind eye to the history of destructive militia politics in Sudan, European externalization risked doing immense damage in terms of offering repressive state and para-state actors a combination of funds, fig leaves, and fantastic amounts of leverage.

This was by no means a phenomenon limited to Sudan; quite consistently, besides the *economic* stakes in "externalized" border security, there were very substantial *political* payoffs (and consequences). Libya's Gaddafi, as we saw, extracted huge concessions for his role in fighting a migratory "threat" which he himself vastly inflated and mobilized, as did the militias that followed in his wake. In impoverished Mali and Niger, various political leaders have sent clear signals that unless they receive the required political support and economic capital, a migratory crisis will ensue (and we already saw signs of this in the previous chapter).[58] In Morocco and Turkey, authoritarian regimes hold a trump card in wider political negotiations with the EU and regularly turn on and off the migratory tap. In all these cases, authoritarian leaders, interior ministries, and rights-abusing security forces have been the big winners in the fight against migration in terms of power, recognition, and income—with fraught consequences not just for migrants and citizens in these countries, but in the end also for regional stability.[59] Moral hazard, in short, has cascaded uncontrollably.

Staging the Crisis

The European architects of border security know or should have known—to use a lawyerly phrase—that their actions and incentive schemes for fighting migration would lead to reactions among state "partners" as well as among migrants, smugglers, and armed groups with potential skin in the game. This dynamic is a recurring feature of the various "wars" we are concerned with in *Wreckonomics,* as we started to see in the previous chapter, with regimes in Syria and Sri Lanka stoking fears over terrorism to bolster their position. However, in a point we will come back to in chapter 7, there was a twist: as long as the fight could be *presented* as a success in the short term, the problems could keep escalating without threatening the intervention itself. Numerous key actors were involved in a kind of double game in which winks, wrecking, and subverting the rules were all part of the deal, while failure was being fairly systematically refashioned into success.

Coming back to our fairground stalls, there's a simple conclusion to draw from this: we have *all* been played. From a principal-agent perspective, it seems like *both* the instigating government *and* the "partners" behave, perversely, as reckless "agents," with the role of "principal" here taken up by voters (and even their parliamentary representatives). It's tempting to call this a "double-agent problem." Instigating governments have routinely been able to develop their games without concern for the consequences and with little serious public or parliamentary scrutiny, while in turn the "partners" have frequently been able to double-game the emerging systems of migration control. We asked at the start if instigators are like the "suckers" of the funfair or carnival. However, as voters are sold one pointless and expensive fight after another, the suckers, in the end, are *us*.

So far, so bad. But this is also where the usefulness of a neat divide between "principal" and "agent," customer and fairground vendor, starts breaking down. The reason, in short, is that like many economic theories it is not sufficiently *systemic*. As good wreckonomists, one of the first things we have to ask of any intervention is that old question: *Cui bono?* Who benefits? We've seen already that there are many profitable games being played concurrently. One of these, which tends to go unnoticed, is that the principal may be happy for the agent to subvert the intervention in various ways, as long as the system itself is strengthened and prolonged. Indeed, the agent's "deviation" may itself be critical to that objective. The *complexity* of these games and of the interaction among them is a major part of what sustains the border security system, offering remarkable flexibility and resilience under changing political conditions. We do not need to get into the extent to which this is *intentional* to note that the fixation on a migration "threat" has allowed a system for fighting it to develop, grow, and persist over time. In externalization, we have seen that while instigating

governments have set the rules of the game, double gaming and manipulation by the implementers have proliferated. While this has come
with costs for the instigators and underhand gains for the "partners,"
from a systems view *it can still prove beneficial to the instigator in consolidating (or "systemizing") the fight against migration*—in short, setting
the "game" for others to follow, and in this way lending it significant
resilience. Instead of the two discrete and opposing parties that we
find in the principal-agent problem, we here face something more
systemic: a sinister form, perhaps, of three-dimensional chess.

Something similar, incidentally, was happening in relations with
humanitarian actors who also came to be brought into the "fight"
as auxiliaries to the state, particularly in rescue, reception/detention,
and deportation measures. As with security partners, there have been
frictions and resistances aplenty with aid groups, particularly so with
the criminalization of rescuers in recent years in the Mediterranean.
Yet it is notable how, at various stages of the escalating "fight," not
only were aid groups such as the Red Cross helpful in occasionally
lending a "humanitarian" frame to border security, but their partial
co-optation by the "fight" also quietened their critique—as did the
aid money spent on local associations, including those of deportees
in origin countries, as Ruben saw in Senegal and Mali.[60] In chapter 7
we discuss the role of such ancillary actors a little more. For now, let
us return to the political "big beasts" in Europe and to the geopolitical
gaming of migration and displacement.

In 2021, crisis broke out yet again at the EU's external borders.
The site, this time, was the Belarus-Polish borders where migrants
and refugees were congregating following some more or less adept
maneuvering by the Belarusian regime. By this time, EU leaders and
the European Commission had cottoned on to what they called the
"instrumentalization" of migration—that is, the gaming we have
discussed here.[61] Their argument, probably quite correct, was that
Belarusian president Lukashenko was seeking to destabilize the Union
through uncontrollable migration flows. Yet instead of accounting for
its own systemic role in the blatant gaming at the borders, the EU

used this incident to propose what in effect amounted to pushbacks in cases were migration was being "instrumentalized." While these plans were still in the works at the time of writing, the thinking behind it was already severely undermining the rights of people in need of safety and protection at the Belarus-Poland border while risking further escalation.[62]

A symbiosis has emerged between the instrumentalization of migration across both sides of the EU external border, with cruelty and crude state interests frequently masquerading as policy. On the central Mediterranean route, the instrumentalization of migration by Gaddafi and his multifarious successors has been useful not just to them but also to Italian politicians who have used these threats at face value to ramp up antimigration rhetoric, to rally the voter base, and to put blame on the EU—and human smugglers—for the debacle. Part of this has involved conveniently *staging* "happenings" that strengthen their position. For instance, Prime Minister Berlusconi held people in overcrowded conditions on the small island of Lampedusa in front of the world's cameras, the better to spark a reaction—and the reaction he wanted, and got, was more popular demand for border security.[63] This kind of crisis politics has been accompanied by a growing tendency to shift blame onto rescue initiatives on the open sea, with repeated shipwrecks and deaths as a result.[64] In Spain, meanwhile, the former Conservative government cleverly used the crises at the borders of Ceuta and Melilla to broadcast a message of crisis and invasion while putting the blame on the EU (and, sometimes, on aid and activist groups). For a final example from across the Atlantic, while Mexico has often been much less willing to stoke the problem in the way Europe's neighbors have done, this has in no way dented the political appetite in the United States for manipulating border crises and finding new groups to blame. We need perhaps little reminder of how President Donald Trump turned migrant caravans into large-scale political crises, deploying the military to the southern border.

This is a high-stakes game, to be sure, that is anything but stable, especially in the European context, with its bewildering range of state actors. At any moment, one of the "partners" may pitch their demands too high and undermine the position of the instigators, as we have seen from Mauritania to Turkey. This potential for escalation on all sides has been crucial in recent years, with the full machinery of the EU mobilized into the "fight" while immensely raising the stakes for the partners—helping to explain the incentives for Belarus as well as the geopolitical play over Syrian refugees in 2015.

A similar logic of escalation, as we have seen, applies to the war on terror, yet we now have further tools to understand the underlying perverse incentives of wreckonomics. First, we have found that the fixation on migration generates huge risks in terms of the principal-agent problem: strengthening the capacity for abuse, impunity, and double gaming among the partner-state "agents." Second, we have found that the instigator is similarly manipulative in its role as *agent* to the democratic "principal": the voter and taxpayer (as well as institutional structures of scrutiny). Third, while these double games bring huge instability to interventions, we have also found that their proliferation brings *systemic* benefits to the instigator not so much in setting the "rules of the game" as in defining the gameboard. In other words, enabling double games is itself a (systems) game. Fourth, all this entails *escalation,* and especially so as the system responds to cascading migrant and smuggler action. Finally, this escalation presents further risks: it can remain politically, economically, and systemically useful *as long as someone else can bear the costs.* We will look at this last point in more detail as we now turn to the war on drugs—seeing how the ability to offload the costs of intervention onto someone else's backyard helps turn disastrous war and security systems into a remarkably stubborn addiction.

6

Warriors on Drugs

How States Got Hooked on Narcotics and Crime

We have seen how the post–Cold War years became the stage for damaging wars and fights against transnational threats, to the point where the war on terror and the fight against migration came to self-perpetuate and spread. In both cases, had policymakers been willing to reflect and to learn from the past, they may have realized they were about to repeat some very destructive patterns from what in many ways is the mother of all (pseudo-)wars: the "war on drugs." This war has been running, in some shape or form, for about a century. How did it acquire this staying power? Here, our systems-sleuthing takes us from the fairground stalls to the gambling hall, which provides an apt metaphor—and quite a few clues—that will help us to understand this particular war.

How do you leave Las Vegas with a small fortune? The answer is deceptively simple: you arrive with a large one. Now, given that the casino always wins in the long run and given that countless lives have been ruined by addiction and bankruptcy and family breakdown, the rational approach to gambling is, first, never to go near it and, second, if you do find yourself at the gaming tables, to make a sharp exit.

In Vegas, though, they make leaving very difficult. It starts, rather obviously, with the size and visibility of the brightly illuminated cathedrals, each of them more than capable of bringing out our "inner moth," as David found on one of his rare (honest!) visits. Some hotel-casinos lure you in with escalators: there's no need to climb the stairs (though, significantly, it's not so easy to find the exits). Dress code is minimal, so no exclusions there. Once inside, there are neither windows nor clocks to remind you of the passing of time; day and night are indistinguishable, and so are the activities. Hotel-casinos have even been known to pump extra oxygen into their vast gaming halls to keep the patrons awake at all hours. Meanwhile, if anyone wins on the fruit machines, the metal trays will advertise the win with a cacophony of success, while the window on the fruit machines (as elsewhere) cleverly shows you not just the winning (or losing) line but all the "near misses." You are always *so close,* either spatially or in terms of the symbols in front of you, to some kind of win.[1]

No doubt, at some level, the gambler is not even *expecting* to win. If one-armed bandits are fleecing us, the clue would seem to be in the name. Even the size of the hotel-casinos themselves is a pretty gigantic clue that someone is winning at our expense. But for most gamblers, such clues are either ignored or irrelevant. Timelessly, Vegas visitors drift through a highly manipulative environment that has been systematically constructed to maximize its profitability. Let's not think this is limited to the rarefied world of the casino town, however. The signage of large betting companies is a depressingly familiar feature of any down-at-heel British high street, while in convenience stores across the United States, a glitzy wall of state-run lottery tickets lures in the locals with promises of "Blazing Hot Cash" as they wait to pay for their breakfast milk or for the permitted drugs of tobacco and alcohol.[2]

But what can Vegas and gambling more widely tell us about the drug wars? First of all, it shows how addiction—to a substance, to roulette, to lottery tickets—is not simply an individual flaw but depends on a system to sustain it. And that system is shot through with power, inequality, and no small amount of institutional and political maneuvering. The casino analogy may also help us to see *the addictive quality of the war on drugs itself* (and of our other wars, too). Politicians and enforcers, like McNamara's body counters in Vietnam, fixate on their object the way the gambler stares fixedly at the cherries of the one-armed bandit—and the more they stare, the more it seems like they are finally about to win: just one more push (or pull), one more blow against the rebels, one more drug bust. When the win comes, it feels good and is loudly advertised. In short, the incentives of the environment in which the drug warriors operate keep pushing them toward compulsive behavior.

It's notable that governments (including the state government of Nevada) have sometimes become addicted to gambling itself, whether in the form of false-hope lottery tickets or flashy casinos. Indeed, gambling has frequently proven an easy—and spuriously "cost-free"—way to raise revenue.[3] In the "drug wars," this tendency is strengthened. Drugs (and gambling) are notorious for bringing a combination of short-term gain (or pleasure) and long-term pain (whether of individual health, relationships, or financial ruin). Of course, it is this combination that makes drugs so addictive: not only do they provide a powerful high, but the process of immiseration that they induce tends itself to feed the pursuit of a drug-fueled escape. But as we look at the drug enforcement system, we may rather soon be led to ask: Who is addicted here?

There is plenty of evidence that those waging a war on drugs are *themselves* addicted to this process. They receive a number of important short-term benefits or "hits," from political and financial payoffs to the thrill of "winning" (or *almost* winning). At the same time, they tend to be able to export the costs of this endeavor. And when these costs mount up, that itself is routinely taken as necessitating an intensification of the original activity—whether as distraction from misery or because the problem being "addressed" has worsened.

To investigate this further, we start by visiting one of the supposed "margins" of the wider war—the Philippines—before traveling to its historical heart.

Between Cloud Nine and the Killing Fields

In 2016, just as experts and activists were beginning to hope that the global war on drugs was drawing its last breath, it rose again from the dead. No little thanks for this feat of revival were due to the president of the Philippines. Rodrigo Duterte cut a curious figure for a drug warrior: in ailing health, he was himself hooked on the potent drug fentanyl, which made him feel as though he were on "cloud nine"— yet that did nothing to stop his brutal quashing of other drug users.[4] "If you know of any addicts, go ahead and kill them yourself," he said in his inaugural speech, and soon he was taking his own advice: between his assumption of office at the end of June 2016 and January 2017, police and vigilantes killed more than seven thousand people, according to Amnesty International. (The figures remain unconfirmed and contested.) Predictably, most of the victims lived in urban poverty, and Amnesty labeled the campaign "effectively a war on poor people."[5] After barely a few months in office, Duterte ramped up the rhetoric, saying that he would be ready to slaughter the country's "three million drug addicts" while drawing shocking comparisons with the Holocaust: "At least if Germany had Hitler, the Philippines would have [me]."[6]

Besides the kill lists and shoot-to-kill orders, financial incentives for police set up a system for murder that benefited the forces as much as the politician in charge. Police were secretly paid between 8,000 and 15,000 pesos (£130 to £240) per "head," according to Amnesty sources, while also stealing victims' possessions and benefiting from a racket with funeral homes, which "reward[ed] the police for every dead body." Human Rights Watch found that evidence was systematically falsified to label many of the police killings as "self-defense."[7] None of this criticism stopped the police or the president. While Duterte's "war" drew widespread condemnation, it also won praise, including from President Trump, who congratulated his Filipino counterpart in April 2017 on doing "an unbelievable job on the drug problem."[8] Meanwhile, the deaths kept mounting, and Duterte's addiction to the war—like his own addiction to drugs—showed no sign of abating.

That the drug war was brought back from the dead with such verve and violence should not, sadly, be surprising. While it's important to understand the addictive qualities of drugs, the addictive qualities of the *war* on drugs have been less frequently addressed. Both sets of addictions do not just happen; they are systematically encouraged and incentivized, just like our Vegas gambling economy. Economic incentives play a role—police rewards and rackets—as do political and institutional ones. To get our heads around this process, let us travel back in time to where it all began: in the United States of about a century ago.

Anslinger's Gambit

With the distance afforded by decades, it is not hard to see how the drug war became so addictive. At its inception stands the *fixation* on drugs as a huge overriding threat to society. We have already seen how this fixation (or, more specifically, securitization) allows for simplifying a problem, magnifying it out of proportion, and stirring a moral emergency. A further dimension of the "war fix" also rears its head here: demonization. The early drug warriors conjured up a threat that not only built on racist tropes but also served to delegitimize radical politics. And their commander was a single-minded and cynical man by the name of Harry Anslinger.

In 1929, Anslinger joined the US Treasury's Bureau of Prohibition, before becoming the founding commissioner of the Federal Bureau of Narcotics the following year. For all his fighting spirit, he would himself—like Duterte—eventually become hooked on drugs (morphine, in Anslinger's case) while helping to supply the notorious anti-Communist "witch-hunter" Joe McCarthy with his own narcotics of choice. Anslinger's addiction to fighting wars on intoxicating substances drew sustenance from his revulsion against the supposed degeneration of his time. And his first target was booze. In *Chasing the Scream,* this is how journalist Johann Hari conveys Anslinger's approach to the offshore alcohol business that had grown up in places like the Bahamas during Prohibition:

> "Just give me a high-powered rifle. I'll stop the bastards," one of Harry's colleagues said, and in this spirit, Harry announced to his bosses that there was a way to make prohibition work: Use maximum force. Send the navy to hunt down smugglers along the coasts of America. . . . Massively increase prison sentences for alcohol dealers until they were all locked up. Wage war on booze until it was just a memory.[9]

Alas, this was a war that booze would win, with rackets and profiteering proliferating off prohibition.[10] But failure did not deter Anslinger. Now at the heart of the new Bureau of Narcotics, he was launching another war that was to prove much more "successful," at least in terms of its sheer endurance: the war on drugs. Anslinger was clear on the institutional incentives for ramping up the drug prohibitions of the 1910s into an outright "war." As Hari writes, "A war on narcotics alone—cocaine and heroin, outlawed in 1914—wasn't enough. They were used only by a tiny minority, and you couldn't keep an entire department alive on such small crumbs. He needed more." And "more" meant marijuana—and with it came the conjuration of specific racial and political demons that are still with us today.

Anslinger proceeded to "fix" the information environment for this war, ignoring the vast majority of experts who saw drug and especially marijuana use as best treated through the public health system.[11] Anslinger actively searched out the few voices who could back up his hardline approach. He cherry-picked cases that revealed the dangers of weed. And he racialized the issue of drug use with help from the media.[12] As Hari writes, Anslinger "believed the two most-feared groups in the United States—Mexican immigrants and African Americans—were taking [marijuana] much more than white people, and he presented the House Committee on Appropriations with a nightmarish vision of where this could lead." Anslinger warned that it could lead to "coloured students . . . partying with female [white] students" and impregnating them, to insanity, crime, and "delirious rage" from what he called the *loco weed* of the Latinos. Anslinger even recruited the monster we invoked in chapter 4: "The drug turns man into a wild beast. . . . [I]f the hideous monster Frankenstein came face to face with the monster Marijuana, he would drop dead of fright."[13]

The campaign worked. At times, Hari's compelling journalistic investigation seems to suggest that a moral panic was born in the service of one man's ambition and paranoia. Yet the drug war was not simply irrational, a fight against demons of the mind. Despite the emphasis on Anslinger, Hari's account also makes it clear that serious political and institutional rationales were at play. Institutionally, the Federal Bureau of Narcotics was turning into *a system in search of a problem*; now it had found one in weed and turned it into a monster, a beast, an enemy. Instead of learning from the failed experiment of alcohol prohibition, the authorities were now generating a self-sustaining system with huge capacity for wrecking people and even whole societies.

The logic underpinning the war on drugs went something like this: the threat preexists our actions in the world and acts upon us from the *outside,* and it can be stopped and neutralized in interventions that crack down on the *supply* of it. This "supply-centric" view of the drug problem conveniently ignored the "Las Vegas" environments in which people become addicted to substances in the first place. It consciously downplayed a wider understanding of the market and the *causes* of the trade and of drug-related suffering. Why do people smuggle drugs across the border? Why are people selling them on street corners? How do people get hooked? Few officials seemed to care for an answer. For all the very serious differences in our wars' respective fixations, a similar blinkered logic was applied in Vietnam (the body count of the enemy), the war on terror (the "kill lists"), and the fight against illegal migration (arrival figures, smugglers intercepted)—a logic that privileged visible symptoms while downplaying underlying causes. Reverting momentarily to our systemic lens, we

Figure 10 The dance of enforcement during US Prohibition, 1920–33. Credit:
Winsor McKay.

can say that the *war system actively and consistently strengthened itself by
ignoring any holistic systems analysis of the "threat" itself.*

Even this, as we shall see, is not the full picture of the perverse
logics at work: for the war on drugs *preceded* the emergence of drug
gangs, the criminal smuggling across the border, and the widespread
drug abuse of recent decades. In fact, it largely created them.

It was known already in Anslinger's time that if one shuts off legal
routes to drugs or drinks—routes that existed for opiates and cocaine
prior to the 1914 Harrison Act in the United States—then criminal
providers will step in to fulfill the demand (see Figure 10). Yet even
though the great drug warrior himself acknowledged this problem in
the case of alcohol, he ramped up the crackdowns on legal drug sup-
pliers. Clinics that persisted in providing addicts with safe doses into
the interwar years faced crackdowns, which in many cases involved
drug enforcement working in cahoots with the mafia. Meanwhile,
the policing of the real "drug lords" was frequently reduced to a
"puppet show" thanks to the deep pockets of the entrepreneurs of
the new illicit market, who in Hari's words had quickly realized that

"the prohibition of drugs and booze was the biggest lottery win for gangsters in history."[14]

If all kinds of drug "games" were already being staged in the 1920s in this way, it would take a few decades for the full political gaming to come into its own. In 1971, President Richard Nixon declared his "war on drugs" as a riposte, in part, to President Lyndon B. Johnson's "war on poverty." Johnson's "war"—despite its name (which should make any wreckonomist suspicious) and its many critics—did eventually lead to some public gains.[15] The emerging drug war, by contrast, was to be defined by high public loss and rampant self-interest. Protestations from Nixon's economic adviser, Milton Friedman, were in vain: a fervent free-marketeer, Friedman had warned of the ethics of using state force to halt people taking drugs.[16] Yet the wider political environment was propitious for "war." On the one hand, the legacy of heavy drug enforcement since Anslinger's days had already set the relevant institutional games. On the other hand, the permissive counterculture was ripe for targeting in an early variant of the "culture war," especially given protests over Vietnam. After a hiatus during the Jimmy Carter administration, the crack epidemic of the 1980s allowed President Reagan to escalate the war.[17] Antidrug funding further rocketed, as did the "prison-industrial complex," along with swiftly ballooning rates of incarceration (see Figure 11). Specifically, the number of people behind bars for nonviolent drug law offenses rose from 50,000 in 1980 to more than 400,000 by 1997.[18]

Meanwhile, programs for the prevention of drug addiction, treatment, and relevant education were severely scaled back, as were social programs. In her landmark study of the burgeoning US prison system, *The New Jim Crow*, legal scholar and rights advocate Michelle Alexander noted that Reagan's large cuts to state expenditure on welfare went hand in hand with increases in expenditure for law enforcement agencies in the context of a relaunched "war on crime," including especially the drug wars.[19] She wrote, "When it came to the bellicose branches of government . . .—what Reagan called the 'legitimate functions'—he countenanced bureaucratic bloat at every turn.

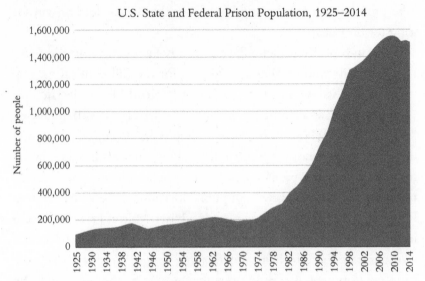

Figure 11 US state and federal prison population, 1925–2019 (overall figure excluding jails). Data source: https://www.sentencingproject.org/research/.

The crime war became his domestic equivalent of the cold war."[20] Thanks to Reagan and Nixon, Anslinger's initial interwar project was coming to fruition: a runaway enforcement apparatus was guaranteed a long institutional life and ever-growing resources on the back of mounting crime and health emergencies. This was something Anslinger's detractors working in public health (before he shut them down) could have predicted. Studies have noted that overdosing may severely increase with prohibition and harsh enforcement, while others have suggested that violent crime rates often track the criminalization of drugs (or of alcohol during US Prohibition).[21] The abuse, crime, and violence were part of the war's *cascade*: once you prohibit and wage war on a product, criminals will step in to take over the market—with violent and all too predictable consequences.

Rising criminality was not only a problem but also an opportunity, especially once the category of criminal was extended to end users. Indeed, the targeting of *particular* "drug criminals"—from marijuana users in Anslinger's early days to crack users in the Reagan years—was part of a wider project of intimidation with distinctly racist and class dimensions. Anslinger's conjuration was working its nefarious magic. Under Reagan's drug wars, crack users were treated far more harshly than richer cocaine users, who were disproportionately white. By the early 1990s nearly 90 percent of crack prosecutions targeted Black Americans.[22] Before this phase, significantly, Nixon had originally launched the domestic war on drugs in the context of widespread social unrest and antiwar protests. He was also responding to reports that US soldiers in Vietnam had been widely using heroin and marijuana (the latter often for calming down after fighting, a pattern that David also found in Sierra Leone, incidentally).[23] Nixon's "war on drugs," announced just after the publication of a congressional report on soldiers' drug use, illustrated how our wars feed into one another with disturbing frequency. It sent out an intimidating message not only to the Black population but also to antiwar protesters.[24] John Ehrlichman, a former White House counsel, echoed Anslinger's old tropes in 1994 when he recalled that Nixon "had two enemies: the antiwar left and black people":

> We knew we couldn't make it illegal to be either against the [Vietnam] war or black, but by getting the public to associate the hippies and marijuana with African Americans and heroin, and then criminalizing both heavily, we could disrupt those communities. We could arrest their leaders, raid their homes, break up their meetings, vilify them night after night on the evening news. Did we know we were lying about the drugs? Of course we did.[25]

Nixon was well aware of the electoral benefits from getting tough in the wars on crime and drugs. As Christian Parenti notes in his *Lockdown America*, surveillance increased sharply, and Nixon's Organized Crime Control Bill was used to summon protesters before secret "special grand juries" for interrogation.[26]

The political and institutional games around the drug threat have staged a remarkable symbiosis, including in more recent years. Consider the case of Arizona, where Sheriff Joe Arpaio's "tent cities" and chain gangs for convicted drug users (and irregular migrants) became a spectacular scene of sadistic enforcement spanning many years. When the courts caught up and voters finally had enough (with some significant help from antiracist protesters), President Trump saw fit to pardon "America's toughest sheriff."[27] Yet Arpaio was not a mere outlier: he was in many ways an exemplary member of the system of enforcement set up by Anslinger's bureau and later militarized by Nixon and Reagan. Torture and rape in detention, brutal isolation in desert camps: these were among the forms of violence with impunity that proliferated under the escalating war on drugs, as rights advocates have cataloged.[28]

Since Anslinger's time, fixating on the drug threat had worked its sinister magic in various ways. It had created a rationale for a huge "supply-centric" enforcement apparatus, which in turn fed the problem and so created justifications for further enforcement, all of which helped in demonizing particular parts of the population for political reasons.

In other words, both institutionally—for the Bureau of Narcotics, its various local partners, and its international equivalents—and politically, the gains from the "war fix" were very significant. But let us now turn back to more subtle institutional games played in the shadow of high politics.

Selective Enforcement

In the 1980s, amid the increase in police counternarcotics operations as part of President Reagan's revived drug war, one major focus was the interstate highway I-95, known to be a major conduit for drugs coming from the south into New York City, Washington, DC, and a number of other towns and cities along the route. So the heightened operations were understandable. But something peculiar was afoot.

Rather than targeting the drugs that were coming into these cities from the south, police were intercepting vehicles coming in from the *north*. The police confiscated large amounts of cash from these southbound vehicles—and all the while the northbound drugs continued to arrive and to circulate. Between 1989 and 1992, the sheriff in Volusia County, Florida, seized more than $8 million from motorists on that same highway, with a focus on southbound travelers. Few of these seizures led to criminal prosecutions.

Patrick Murphy, formerly the police commissioner of New York City, explained this selective enforcement to Congress. He said police had "a financial incentive to impose roadblocks on the southbound lanes of I-95, which carry the cash to make drug-buys, rather than the northbound lanes, which carry the drugs. After all, seized cash will end up forfeited to the police department, while seized drugs can only be destroyed."[29] In fact, local police forces were increasingly funding themselves from such asset seizures, something that proved especially attractive amid budget cuts. According to an investigation in the *Harvard Law Review*, some budgets were being cut *in response to* police departments' raising their own revenue through asset seizure, "in turn spurring police to raise even more money in these ways."[30] According to a 1993 report commissioned by the US Department of Justice, "Asset seizures play an important role in the operation of [multijurisdictional drug] task forces. One 'big bust' can provide a task force with the resources to become financially independent. Once financially independent, a task force can choose to operate without Federal or state assistance."[31] This had very serious repercussions on policing within a democratic system. At the extreme, the drug policy advocate William Boyd suggested, "Self-financed police need not justify their activities through any regular budgetary process."[32]

Meanwhile, even as the drugs continued to make their way up from the south and US prisons began to fill up at a rapid rate, major drug traders—or "kingpins"—tended to escape long prison sentences. This was in large part the result of their ability to engage in plea-bargaining, trading valuable assets, from yachts to houses, for drastic reductions in prison sentences.[33] The overwhelming majority of those sent to prison were those who were simply buying drugs or selling very small quantities. The surge in drug convictions, especially among Black Americans and Hispanics, helped to swell the numbers held in prisons and jails from around 300,000 when Reagan became president in 1980 to more than 2 million by the year 2000.[34] By 2015, the United States housed about one-quarter of the global imprisoned population, and every year from 1993 to 2009 saw more people being imprisoned for drug crimes than for violent crimes. Black Americans make up a disproportionate part of those arrested for drug crimes. Even if the past years have seen a decline in absolute prisoner numbers, rolling back the full consequences of the system built by the architects of the wars on drugs and crime will take enormous effort— if indeed political will for such an effort can be found.[35]

A wide range of actors, from policymakers to private prison companies and private investors, were in effect cashing in on an unwinnable "war" on a commodity. For them, this failing policy was a more or less continuous success. Meanwhile, people and institutions further down the chain—drug users and dealers, US social services dealing with the consequences of the narcotics trade, countries in Latin America destabilized by the burgeoning drug trade—were the losers.

By 1993, after more than a decade of an intense war on drugs, the price of an average milligram of heroin in New York was one-third of the 1979 price—and it had ten times the purity. The RAND Drug Policy Research Center reported in 2005 that "[t]he overall trend in cocaine and heroin retail prices during most of the past two decades has been downward (after adjusting for potency)" in the United States.[36] Even when drug prices have risen, consumers have often resorted to dangerous means of consumption under the auspices of strengthened criminal networks.[37]

In a careful study published in 1998 in the *University of Chicago Law Review*, Eric Blumenson and Eva Nilsen wrote:

> [The] Drug War has been an extraordinary failure.... Drug dependence in the inner city and among teenagers has increased substantially. And the drug problem continues to produce massive amounts of crime, $20

billion in annual medical costs, one-third of all new HIV infections, prisons filled with drug-related offenders, and the attendant decimation of inner-city communities.[38]

They then asked a highly pertinent question:

Given these facts, and a general consensus that the Drug War has been a failure, one might wonder why essentially the same strategies persist year after year, untouched by the wisdom of twenty-five years of experience. And why do so few public and law enforcement officials speak out against this policy?[39]

It's the kind of question that can illuminate not only the "war on drugs" but also the occurrence and persistence of all our other wars and fights. Blumenson and Nilsen continued, "The answer is that the Drug War has achieved a self-perpetuating life of its own, because however irrational it may be as public policy, it is fully rational as a political and bureaucratic strategy,"[40] a statement that could equally be applied to the disastrous "war on terror" and the floundering "fight against illegal migration." Perpetuating the war on drugs has become hugely addictive—yet it's only by understanding the rational and cynical mechanisms that allow for this addiction to flourish that we stand any chance of stopping it.

Fleece Me in St. Louis: Visiting the War on Crime

Ferguson, Missouri, part of the St. Louis metropolitan area, became notorious in August 2014, when residents took to the streets to protest the killing of Michael Brown, an unarmed Black teenager, by a white police officer. In response to the protests, the police pointed military weapons at peaceful protestors, injecting the optics and apparatus of war into the standoff. Naturally and rightly, a range of observers put the killing and the protests in the context of institutional racism within US law enforcement as well as within the charged racial context set by drug and crime warriors from Anslinger to Nixon.[41]

Yet tension between Ferguson residents and the police is also difficult to understand without comprehending the peculiarly perverse
incentives that have grown up around the justice system in the city,
and indeed more widely across the United States. From prison companies that write "occupancy guarantees" into their contracts to police forces that fund themselves through asset seizure and on to private
debt-collection companies that strip assets from poorer people and
drive them into jail, a remarkably powerful set of interests has grown
up in the United States around the very phenomenon—crime—that
they claim to be combating.[42] Many of these law enforcement activities, broadly understood, have ended up feeding the deprivation that
fuels crime, while richer criminals have been able to gain exemption
from punishment. We may say, in fact, that crime and punishment have
been coexisting in a strange kind of symbiosis, while crime fighters
of various kinds have systematically benefited from (and sometimes
colluded in) precisely what they claim to be suppressing. Naturally,
this has deepened underlying grievances, often structured along racial lines, with grave political ramifications. To see this in more detail,
let us stay with Ferguson and look at a remarkably disturbing case of
"Fleece Me in St. Louis."

For Tom Barrett, the fleecing started in April 2012 with his theft
of a single can of beer. When Barrett appeared in court charged with
stealing the can from a convenience store, he was offered a court-
appointed attorney for a fee of $80. Declining this expensive offer,
he pleaded "no contest" to a shoplifting charge and was promptly
fined $200. Barrett also had to rent an alcohol-monitoring bracelet
for more than $400 a month, payable to a private company, Sentinel
Offender Services. Barrett's only source of income (including to pay
this huge bracelet fee) was selling his blood plasma. Yet this double
economic predicament soon led to a catch-22. He was skipping meals
in order to pay Sentinel, and as a result his protein levels fell to the
point where he was ineligible for giving plasma. As Barrett's debt
grew to over $1,000, Sentinel got a warrant for his arrest. He was un-
able to pay and was jailed.

This is not an isolated case. In 2013, Ferguson's population of around 21,000 had been issued with an astonishing 32,975 arrest warrants for nonviolent offenses—an average of more than one and a half arrest warrants *for each person*.[43] Many people were hiding in their homes and even missing work out of fear of being arrested. At the same time, the per capita income in Ferguson was only just over $20,000, with nearly a quarter of residents below the poverty line.[44] Court fines and fees, meanwhile, were bringing in $2.4 million in revenue in 2013—Ferguson's second-largest source of income. Documenting these figures, the *Harvard Law Review* noted, "Widespread hostility toward Ferguson's municipal court is the tinder that helped set the town on fire after Michael Brown was killed."[45]

In Barrett's case, the system of extraction had quickly extended not just to his meager financial resources but also to his *biological* resources.[46] Meanwhile, a progressively tighter web of debt was being woven around him, drawing in more actors. In the 1980s, Missouri had become one of the first US states to let private companies buy the probation systems of local governments, so that debts owed by individuals as a result of criminal proceedings were sold to private companies, which then added fees and interest. At the time of the Ferguson protests in 2014, anyone imprisoned for fees they owed (and awaiting the next court session) would be charged between $30 and $60 a night.

We start to see here how law enforcement and private companies have colluded in extracting rent from ordinary citizens to the point of becoming addicted to it. The reason for this addiction is not hard to see: amid pressure on police to "fund themselves" and incentives for business to use raw human material as their resource in deprived communities, and with few legal safeguards or political obstacles, there is really little stopping this extensive "gaming" of criminal justice. But to understand what fundamentally sustains it, we must move from our second "wreckanism," gaming, to the third, the *externalization* of costs. It was ordinary people, and the wider public good of the community, that shouldered the burden of this extractive operation; indeed, they were the blatant source of extraction. With a lack of negative institutional consequences for their behavior, police and private companies "fighting" crime and drugs were lurching further into the addictive spiral with no apparent end in sight.

We have brought in more subtle, and recent, trends from the "war on crime" here to show how the drug wars do not operate in isolation; rather, the logic of the "war" and in particular its underlying economic incentives permeate much wider sectors of law enforcement. This is an aspect that has often been missed out in calls to "defund the police." Defunding, as we have seen, had in many cases served as a direct incentive for police forces to extract rent from local populations. Without addressing such underlying mechanisms and perverse incentives, reform will not get far. Our systemic and wreckonomic lens is relevant in another way too: to the extent that one reduces or even "prohibits" state security, other actors—vigilantes, militias, criminal gangs, and security companies—will likely plug the gap and be *more* dangerous. That is certainly a lesson from highly unequal countries with minimal state provision, including the fragile states of the kind we considered in chapter 4.

But let us turn back to drugs. If the calculated brutality and the police profiteering at least had managed to address the downsides of drug use, a cynical case could have been made for keeping the United States (and other countries following a similar path) on a war footing. However, state suppression was rather aggravating these downsides. We have mentioned research suggesting that criminality has frequently risen with waves of prohibition and enforcement. We have also noted how antidrugs policy in effect spawned the drug gangs. The criminal market did not just peacefully replace the previous legal drug provision; the gangs and syndicates (including the mafia) started *escalating* their use of violence in order to establish their turfs in the absence of any workable legal framework, leading to a spiral of increasing sadism that has reached its apogee in neighboring Mexico, as we will soon see. We have also heard how the rate of overdosing severely increases with punitive responses, given the lack of safe injection sites and the presence of adulterated drugs on the black market. Part of this dynamic comes down to the "Iron Law of Prohibition": once a substance is outlawed, the criminals purveying it have an incentive to make their product as potent (and thus dangerous) as possible, given the costs and difficulties of transport and sale. A potent drug will fetch a high price while renewing demand through addiction. During alcohol prohibition, whisky substituted for beer; during drug prohibition, heroin, cocaine, and later crack substituted for over-the-counter tinctures; and skunk substituted for marijuana. Today, powerful and deadly fentanyl seems an apogee of this process, as public health experts have found.[47]

Another facet of the drug market that exacerbates the situation is the phenomenon of onward sales. As drug users are themselves likely to be involved in selling drugs to finance their habit, business tends to grow under prohibition along with the number of users and addicts. In other words, our *cascade of costs* has been in full operation in the drug wars, with each round of enforcement further consolidating and proliferating the violence, health risks, and user base of the drug market.

Within a liberal democracy such as the United States, there is at least some hope of accountability when things keep going terribly wrong in policing, as the antiracist protests of 2020 showed. While these did not quite put the finger on the business model of wreckonomics or fully address concerns with violent crime in deprived neighborhoods, they represented a powerful fight-back. As we now turn to the international dimension of the war on drugs, such checks and balances are often extremely fragile—while the potential for *externalizing costs* grows hugely.

Mexico, Colombia, and the Mirage of a "Drug-Free World"

As we have noted, the war on drugs has a blinkered focus that, with some important variation, besets all our wars: it relentlessly aims to crack down on the *supply* of the perceived threat rather than addressing the wider context of demand and "root causes." Field operatives, in their more lucid moments, know that this spells trouble. Border patrol agents speak frequently of their line of work as a "game of tag and catch," while counterterror officials talk of their game of whack-a-mole. These are not just sarcastic remarks but point to the futility, as even many operatives see it, of cracking down on the "supply side" of the problem that is ostensibly being "combated." The war on drugs is in many ways the originator of this floundering model. Numerous studies have noted that the "war" focuses on cracking down on the supply of narcotics rather than targeting persistent *demand* in destination states.[48] The key metrics of Western governments targeting drugs concern levels of drug production, arrests of drug lords, and restrictions on particular routes. While demand persists, drugs—and people—will find a way. In what is sometimes referred to as a "balloon effect," crackdowns in one place tend to push trade elsewhere. And so the game continues.

These repeated "failures" have not deterred the funders, however. Spending on drug control has increased massively—reaching an estimated $50 billion a year from state and federal budgets in the United States alone by the 2010s, and global spending estimated at about twice that amount.[49] And it is that global dimension that we must now consider.

The United Nations has proclaimed the aim of a "drug-free world"—based, critics quite correctly say, on the illusion that the human urge for mind-altering substances can simply be canceled out "through prohibition, enforced by repression."[50] Yet this mission did not come about by chance; rather, the *global* war on drugs was largely the US drug warriors' gift to the world. UN drug conventions were effectively "authored by Anslinger," in Hari's words, with the drug warrior's bureau (and the US government) strong-arming less powerful states into playing their part on the battlefield. This was the case, not least, with Mexico and Central America, where attempts from the early twentieth century to pursue a public health approach were stamped out with the help of US enforcement.[51] By the 1980s, the balloon effect was turning the region into a "corridor" to the US market amid US crackdowns on routes for Colombian cocaine via the Caribbean. The region has since that time starkly illustrated the externalization or unequal distribution of costs, while also revealing how deeply the drug war was being "gamed."[52] In fact, authorities in origin and transit countries for drugs have, like Ferguson's crime warriors, managed to extract substantial economic and political rent from the drug wars while successfully exporting much of the cost of the "externalized" war to ordinary civilians caught in the line of fire.

So let us consider, first, the huge externalization of costs to the societies stuck on the front line of the war, which we already glimpsed in Duterte's Philippines. One prominent report on ending the drug wars, LSE's Expert Group on Drugs Control, summarizes the global consequences:

> [T]he pursuit of a militarized and enforcement-led global "war on drugs" strategy has produced enormous negative outcomes and collateral damage . . . [including] mass incarceration in the US, highly repressive policies in Asia, vast corruption and political destabilization in Afghanistan and West Africa, immense violence in Latin America, an HIV epidemic in Russia, an acute global shortage of pain medication and the propagation of systematic human rights abuses around the world.[53]

In *Transforming the War on Drugs*, Annette Idler and Juan Carlos Garzón Vergara explain that prohibitionist drug policies have transferred a large portion of the economic and social costs to producer and transit regions. State coercion has tended to focus on "persecuting small-scale growers, people who transport small amounts of substances, low-level offenders, or drug users," while "countries like Afghanistan, Mexico, and Colombia have seen real wars in the name of the fight against drugs, which have caused hundreds of thousands of victims."[54]

Let us consider Mexico, which has for a long time been at the front line of "externalization." Since President Felipe Calderón decided to launch his version of the drug war upon assuming office in 2006, deploying more than six thousand soldiers to the state of Michoacán, the human costs have been adding up, to the point where Mexico has higher death rates than many countries undergoing civil war. More than 360,000 homicides have been registered since the start of the war, a staggering figure; more than 79,000 people have been disappeared, "primarily at the hands of criminal organizations such as the cartels, though government forces also play a role," in the words of the Council on Foreign Relations; and human rights abuses, including against rights organizations, activists, and journalists, have become routine.[55] Crucially, much of the violence is committed with guns imported from the United States, whose guns industry has long systematically exported some of the human costs of its trade while insourcing the benefits. Experts estimate there to be about *half a million weapons* entering Mexico illegally from the United States each year, large numbers of them "military-style weapons that end up in the hands of drug cartels and other violent criminals."[56]

Abuses have not just been committed by the cartels, whose power has grown immensely on the back of the drug war, but by state actors. As the Human Rights Watch board of directors—including a former foreign minister of Mexico—stated already in a 2009 *Washington Post* letter to the editor, "By abusing civilians, Mexican soldiers have contributed to the climate of lawlessness and violence in which drug cartels have thrived. These abuses also deter the public cooperation essential to curbing trafficking."[57]

Besides the strengthening of cartels and the undermining of public support, a third perverse effect of the globalizing drug war has been the constant relocation of routes and the subsequent relocation of violence. Crackdowns tend to be associated with rising violence in the new sites of transit, as suggested by the rising homicide rate in Mexico following the large-scale interdiction in Colombia beginning in 2007 (see Figure 12).[58] To take one specific example, recent research posits that the horrific and much-publicized murders of women around Ciudad Juárez can largely be explained by reference to the drug-related balloon effect.[59]

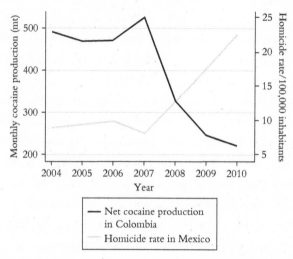

Figure 12 Net cocaine supply from Colombia and homicide rate in Mexico. Source: Mejía and Restrepo (2014).

While the costs of the war are immense, they are rarely accounted for in full. In Colombia, which has finally moved toward a reckoning with its brutalization during the war on drugs, the catalog of violence and suffering is decades long. We cannot do justice here to that long history; suffice it to note that the much-touted US-funded Plan Colombia for combating the drug trade has been actively counterproductive. The supply-side measures of forceful interdiction, crop eradication, and spraying fed our familiar balloon effect, with growers using ever more ingenious methods while transporters found new routes, as we saw with Mexico. The militarized crackdowns ramped up drug prices (as supply was constrained while demand was left unaddressed), leading drug traffickers to increase production to capitalize on the seller's market. Yet what stands out in Colombia, as in Mexico, is the export of the costs to ordinary civilians. One 2020 review summarizes the evidence thus: "Since its inception in 2000, Plan Colombia has displaced more than four million people, with Afro-Colombian and indigenous people being disproportionately impacted. This staggering number places Colombia only behind Syria in terms of the number of internally displaced people." Meanwhile, the Colombian military killed almost six thousand civilians in the decade from 2000 to 2010; six million people have filed restitution claims for harms inflicted due to the Plan; and US military aid has been found to lead to an increase in paramilitary attacks.[60] And this is before we consider the severe political consequences of the drug profits themselves, which have helped to fuel both government-linked paramilitaries and guerrillas.

Having looked briefly at the staggeringly "successful" fixing of the fallout of the war on drugs through externalization, let us move on to the games through which benefits are realized. In the global war on drugs, the benefits of at least *appearing* to collaborate have often proven substantial for partner states, institutions, and individual police. Colombia is one prominent case; Mexico, predictably, is another. In his analysis of "narcocorruption," Peter Andreas explains that already by the late 1980s, *fixation* (in our terminology) was kicking in as successive presidents declared drugs a top national security threat with a keen eye on improving US–Mexico relations. This set the scene for large investments in collaboration with the US "principal." As Andreas writes, "Mexico tripled its federal anti-drug budget between 1987 and 1989, and tripled it again in the 1990s," while one-third of the military's budget was spent on drug control. Counternarcotics also started to dominate the criminal justice system at a time of deep cuts in government spending overall.[61] The potential for "gaming" this environment of existential threats and external "support" was profound. Since this time, arrests, seizures, crop eradications, and so forth have all been part and parcel of showing the "principal" that one is collaborating, echoing the politics of the "body count" metric of Vietnam. Meanwhile, the authorities have found themselves sitting on a prize asset: the service of nonenforcement, which can be purchased by drug smugglers. And the more intense the enforcement, the higher the stakes become in this market, to the point where selective enforcement starts to play a very direct role in the nature and shape of drug-related violence and profiteering. The game, Andreas and other scholars noted at the time, was becoming multilayered as police forces staged turf wars of their own over the (notional) control of lucrative drug corridors while drug traffickers had to negotiate the nature of the bargain so that each player gained something from the unseemly game—from free passage for the trafficker to praise and promotions for police, all the way up to the PR and good statistics required by the US drug enforcers.[62]

Let us look at more recent times to see how this multilayered gaming has persisted, and worsened, since scholars wrote excoriating 1990s texts with telling titles such as *Studies in the Failure of US Narcotics Policy, The Economics of Organized Crime,* and *The Price of Denial.*[63] US aid to Mexico has continued to encourage a clampdown on drugs, conspicuously ignoring findings on the high price of business as usual. Between fiscal years 2008 and 2017, for instance, Congress appropriated nearly $2.8 billion for Mexico under the Mérida Initiative for combating drug trafficking and organized crime, mirroring Plan Colombia.[64] Such programs have kept creating perverse incentives to promote the persistence of the problem while spectacularly failing to learn from earlier "failures." These programs also rarely acknowledge the long-standing symbiotic relationships between senior military officers, law enforcement, and the drug cartels. By late 2011, such was the corruption in the Mexican police that the entire police force of Veracruz, a major drug conduit, was dissolved.[65] In the northern Mexican state of Chihuahua—infamous for the Ciudad Juárez murders—the Zeta cartel had law enforcement so firmly in its pocket that it was at one point allegedly "running" the state altogether.[66] In Colombia, a pre- and post-9/11 war on terror further combined damagingly with a war on drugs, propping up abuses by counterinsurgency actors while at the same time minimizing the attention paid to grievances that helped inform rebellion.[67]

In "partner" states, the repressive apparatus of the state has depended on positioning itself as an ally of the United States in one or more supply centered security interventions. Here, gaming the war on drugs—at arm's length from a "principal" seemingly oblivious to the perverse consequences—has fed illicit gains and a spiral of escalation and violence. It has also helped consolidate an oppressive security

apparatus, especially in countries with fewer democratic safeguards
and in contexts where various of our wars and fights interact. One
such case is Guatemala, our coda to this sorry saga of an externalized
drug war.

Guatemala reminds us of war's frequent inability to end as long as
the underlying incentives remain and a new threat or enemy can easily
be fixated upon. The country had gone through a vicious and long-
lasting civil war, fueled by Cold War anti-Communism and involving
the perpetration of a genocide against the indigenous Mayan population. Yet the end of the Cold War slowly opened up new opportunities for peace, and when the civil war was finally brought to a close
in 1996, there was an obvious opportunity for reform—a chance to
address the country's notoriously unequal landownership and to re-
allocate to development all the energy and money that had been spent
on fighting the war.

But that is not what happened, as David found during his visit in 2002.
Instead, with the help of US largesse and political pressure, a "war on
crime" and a "war on drugs" came center-stage like two bolting horses
of the apocalypse. Issues like low taxation, poor social services, and extreme land inequality remained largely untackled, while high military
spending was maintained amid a much-trumpeted threat of crime
and drugs. During David's research, several key informants stressed
that shadowy structures linked to the old counterinsurgency were
now involved not only in the new imperative to combat crime and
drugs but also in some of the criminal enterprises that they claimed to
be combating. At the country's northern border, meanwhile, Ruben
found on a separate visit some two years later how extracting bribes
or *mordidas* from migrants had also become a growing racket for police who were turning a blind eye to the gangs.[68] All of this was classic
"double gaming" of a kind we have already documented in all our
wars and fights. In Guatemala, powerful groups were also using violence to intimidate political opposition as well as the criminal groups
that they publicly highlighted. Edgar Gutierrez, head of civil intelligence, said that clandestine intelligence organizations were being used

to fight organized crime, and "this same apparatus and method have been used to intimidate the human rights organizations." A fixation on the threat of crime was now helping to sustain flows of external aid (especially from the United States) as well as continued impunity for official and semi-official attacks on "subversives."[69] A careful study of Guatemala City, based on research in the 2010s, showed how the national army had continued to recover from its vulnerable situation at the end of the Guatemalan civil war by projecting itself as one of the less corrupt institutions involved in combating crime and drugs. Meanwhile, a range of politicians had benefited from being seen as "tough on crime."[70] Yet in reality high-profile (and ostensibly "successful") crackdowns on crime had tended to shunt the problem into other parts of Guatemala City and beyond. In other words, the problem and the security "solution" were both maintained, locked in our familiarly destructive—and lucrative—symbiosis.

Addiction through Externalization

We have emphasized that the "war on drugs"—like our other high-profile wars and fights—has been failing even on its own terms. Those who defend the war on drugs, of course, are not completely without argument or evidence. They can bring in the counterfactual that drug consumption in destination states might have been even higher if there had been no attempt to limit supply.[71] On their part, reformists argue that consumption itself is not the problem but rather drug *abuse* and the social and health consequences that follow from it. On this more meaningful metric, the security approach to combating a potentially harmful set of substances is spectacularly failing.[72] Reformers point to the partial legalization and public health approaches being rolled out, despite national and international (US-led) resistance, in Portugal, Switzerland, and Uruguay. All of these have their problems, and the idea that there is a simple nonbelligerent "fix" to drugs should in our view be avoided (a contention also borne out by the decidedly mixed attempts in different

US states to liberalize drug use). However, in countries taking a public health and harm reduction–led approach to drug abuse, evidence tends to point to less dangerous drug use, less crime on the streets, and a marked improvement in the well-being of addicts.[73]

Yet however evidence-based the public gains from a harm reduction approach, this does not necessarily undermine the appeal of the war—or indeed the political *addiction* to it. Since Anslinger's time, the political gains from enforcement have been enormous, especially as regards targeting and stigmatizing minority groups while diverting attention from the underlying social and economic problems feeding addiction. We have also seen how the *institutionally* beneficial "games" being played by the enforcers have bred impunity and rent-seeking, especially where the war on drugs has combined with the associated fights against migration, crime, and terror. We have put particular emphasis on a third and often hidden element of "success" via the *externalization* or export of costs, risks, and consequences. In particular, large-scale costs and risks from the "war on drugs" have been displaced onto poorer citizens as well as onto communities in producer and transit countries—and this in turn has enabled the addiction to war to continue as the instigators and enforcers have rarely been made to face the consequences.

In poorer partner countries, this dilemma of where the chips fall has been acute, as courageous campaigns by citizens and advocates have highlighted for years—setting the pace for a global alliance against the war on drugs. States collaborating in drug control have suffered from a growing drug problem among their own citizens as well as catastrophic levels of criminality and violence. Yet elites and enforcing institutions in these "collaborating" countries are typically afforded sufficient benefits in terms of resources and impunity-for-repression that they tend to exhibit at least some degree of cooperation. That cooperation is usually conditional and always a matter of negotiation—a negotiation in which actually removing the problem would radically undermine the bargaining power of many key actors at the local and national level.

The greatest risks and costs accrue not to core security actors within the system, in other words, but rather to groups that have little or no say in the system. Ordinary Mexicans have suffered severe violence in the course of the global war on drugs, while public authority there has been significantly undermined; a somewhat similar case was observed in Ferguson in the context of the wider war on crime. This mirrors the uneven distribution of costs in our other wars and fights. In the "war on terror," the regions and countries targeted (or launching their own version of the war) have borne the brunt of casualties besides widespread displacement, as seen from Afghanistan to the Sahel. In the fight against migration, a similar exporting of the costs has long been under way, leaving some of those very same countries as buffer zones and dumping grounds. This highlights a crucial aspect of our war systems: the way they *interact* and are often located in the very same space, where their brutal logics of cost distribution combine to devastating effect. Such costs can be seen as "negative externalities," in the sense familiar from environmental economics: they are not of central concern to the security players perpetuating the "game," and they are rarely accounted for when the gray suits finally show up (if ever they do) to take stock of the value of the war investment. Accounting for these costs is key to counteracting the war systems, as reformers and activists have realized, and especially so in the increasingly successful fightback against the war on drugs. We will return to this more hopeful point in the final chapters of the book. But first we must consider how the mounting costs (and skewed benefits) of our wars and fights are consistently hidden from view: through the "knowledge fix" that we have already alluded to in all our cases. It is time to exit the casino and visit the hall of mirrors, where nothing is ever what it seems.

7

The Hall of Mirrors

The Distortion of Disastrous
Interventions

In previous chapters, we have shown how in wars and fights against amorphous threats, "failure" has become its own perverse form of success. Vested interests, from politicians to law enforcement and corporations, have routinely turned the threat that is ostensibly being combated into an endlessly renewable resource, a gift that keeps on giving. Interactions between interveners and targets have tended to escalate the problem while feeding the intervention in a complex systemic cascade. In the process, core interest groups have typically exported the costs of their disastrous interventions to others.

That, in a nutshell, has been our argument. But even acknowledging the perverse distribution of costs and benefits arising from failing policies, we should still be a little puzzled. Why is the failure itself not more threatening to policymakers? Why are they not held to account? How exactly is success extracted so deftly and so often from the jaws of endemic failure?

To answer these questions, we need to get deeper into our fifth and final "wreckanism." This is the *knowledge fix*—the distortions that let the fixers and wreckers get away with it. We will examine distortion in four steps. First, we consider the environment in which it has flourished and festered. Second, we look at three specific ways in which it has been achieved in our wars and fights. Third, we draw on our initial Afghanistan example to add political complexity to the picture. Fourth, we critically (if briefly) examine the frequent complicity of the media, aid groups, and academia in the process of distortion and distraction.

Since one prominent feature of our war and security systems is their tendency to simplify and fixate, let us start by acknowledging complexity and nuance. Engaging with power structures is not always futile. Some officials inevitably listen; things do change. Yet our wars and fights often seem particularly impervious to such change. Like those crime-series detectives trying to persuade their superiors about a new and risky line of investigation, we have often found ourselves hitting our heads against the wall of official intransigence. Instead of bruising our skulls in this way, we must start by at least trying to understand how the world looks to policymakers and civil servants. What is success to *them?*

Let us offer one anecdote. In 2019, Ruben was on his way to a Brussels think tank to present a critical report we had just co-written for the NGO Saferworld, a report that showed how Europe's "fight against illegal migration" was leading to instability and abuse in partner states.[1] It all started rather inauspiciously. Ruben showed the well-honed travel skills that had taken him from Bamako to Bandung by losing his luggage between Oxford and London. Arriving in Brussels, he hastily borrowed an ill-fitting suit from someone at Saferworld. With bare ankles and tucked-in belly, he made his entrée into the boardroom of the think tank, where assorted EU officials, diplomats, and other higher-ups had congregated to debate the report.

It turned out the potentates-in-waiting were less concerned about the ill-fitting suit than the ill-fitting argument. Ruben outlined the report's main findings, highlighting that the EU had funded, trained, and pushed partner-state forces to crack down on migration in often the most brutal manner, with such incentives predictably escalating the "border crises" over time. Even setting aside the dire human consequences, it seemed obvious that policymakers should care about the mounting financial and political costs, including the growing threat to stability and good diplomatic relations in Europe's neighborhood. Some of the more humanitarian and development-oriented officials in the room seemed to nod along, and one NGO worker even suggested the report's title—*Partners in Crime?*—could lose its question mark. Yet soon the skeptics got the upper hand. A border security architect from the European Commission said everyone knew about the consequences already, adding that there was no political appetite for a different approach. Besides, his colleagues added, the system was *working*. One diplomat suggested that sending gunships to the Mediterranean might add to the current success, while the chair of the meeting emphasized that migration was "not *our* problem": Europe was doing as well as it could in handling *other* people's problems. In politics we are not virgins, he said. We can't be pure. We need to "crack a few eggs to make an omelet," he added, while emphasizing that there was no appetite among European politicians and electorates for any other approach.

As an ethnographer, Ruben found it important to understand what success and failure meant to those gathered in the room. Nevertheless, if this was a case where academics were being regarded as "unrealistic," here it was surely the official "reality" that was, in some rather fundamental way, being twisted out of shape. The kind of official thinking manifest in Brussels was dissected many years ago by Hannah Arendt in her critique of the politics of the "lesser evil." In her essay "The Eggs Speak Up," she stressed that lesser evils can easily pave the way to greater ones, especially where official blinkers did not countenance robust challenge. Relatedly, she took issue with the idea that "you can't make an omelet without breaking eggs."[2] Yet in the case of strengthening and outsourcing border controls, it did not seem to matter how much the "eggs" spoke up—or the eggheads! With or without protest, officials kept getting away with cruel and destructive policies. How was this possible? How could politicians, bureaucrats, and security actors so routinely snatch success from the jaws of failure? And why do voters so often fall for this ruse?

Back to the Funfair

In many ways, the knowledge environment of our wars and fights resembles that old funfair or carnival attraction, the hall of mirrors, in which large-scale distortion is all around. Such distortion is to be expected amid the well-known "fog of war." Indeed, one of the problems with combating or waging war on something is that the political stakes for success become so high that it may not be possible to admit failure. But the problem goes beyond war-fighting. If we listen to systems iconoclasts such as our old friend John Gall (chapter 2), they might tell us that distortions to the knowledge environment are common in any bureaucratic system. In *Systemantics,* Gall notes that it's almost impossible to find proper criteria for evaluating a system of intervention—especially when the system and its actors effectively advocate against such evaluations. Bringing these observations together, we can say that distortion is magnified when bureaucracy and the "war fix" come together. In this context, how precisely is a distorted image of success produced from the raw material of failure?

We can start by noting, along with Gall, different layers of "success" in our war and security systems. In the fight against migration, we should consider first the *stated purpose* of border security: to "combat" irregular migration, to stop it, or at least to limit it as far as possible. Another stated purpose is often the "humanitarian" one of limiting suffering and exploitation. Seen in the right light with the right set of mirrors, all kinds of "success" can be observed, recorded, and rewarded despite terrible death counts and perpetual crises. "Wins" in the stated goal of acting in a humanitarian manner may be registered every time a boat full of people is "rescued" only to be pushed back into Libya, for instance. More fundamentally, hard border security can be presented as "successful" provided that "success" is defined in narrow, short-term, and self-interested ways. Land and sea arrivals into Europe have fallen dramatically since 2015, thanks to precedent-setting and dirty agreements with Turkey and Libya, among others. If you pour enough money into a particular aspect of the fight over a particular timescale, and if you ignore the "balloon effects" and the sound of eggs cracking, it will produce "results." These may hold up until the next crisis hits. And given that the underlying problem remains un-resolved or indeed exacerbated by the intervention, the next crisis *will* come.

Behind the stated aims, there is usually a set of *unstated* aims that are key to understanding what drives our interventions. While it's not easy to know the "real" aims, wreckonomics helps us peek under the hood. We find, for example, that "looking tough"—and reaping the antici-pated political benefits from doing so—is often a rather fundamental feature. More broadly, we tend to find an attempt to outsource the risks and costs that the system keeps generating alongside a simultan-eous "insourcing" or monopolizing of the gains. Now it may be that outsourcing costs gives some kind of boost to the stated purpose (for example, the stated aim of controlling migration). Turning Libya into what a UN report called a "hellhole" of mass detention and abuse was one such "success"; inside the EU itself, converting Greece into a vast buffer zone was another.[3] But such projects tend to be *undeclared*, not least because of the inhumanity—and often the intentional creation of suffering and of problems-for-others—that they involve.

The Brussels meeting and our migration chapter suggest that the key unstated aim of border security is to produce a strong political "win" based on short-term optics rather than longer-term consequences, and that an integral part of this project is hiding (and exporting) those consequences. This maneuver has also strongly characterized the war on terror and the war on drugs. In all three cases, moreover, the wars and fights have frequently served as a *diversion* from other problems that politicians cannot, or do not sufficiently want to, address. On this count, fighting migration has been at least intermittently "successful" in the EU: a "tough" stance has meant fewer headlines about the pol-itical failure to deal with the migration crisis. The EU's institutions have at times seemed robust in the face of crises, and their recurring "solutions" have presented excellent opportunities for a wide range of national politicians (especially those on the right) to advertise their hardline credentials and divert popular attention from other pressing social issues.

Here, as so often, we need to distinguish between shorter-term and longer-term gains. Political gains are often temporary, with a constant risk of being hoisted by one's own petard. We see this with the rise of far-right forces in Europe today, riding the coattails of the "lesser evil" and looking to turn it into a greater one. If the game is about "getting tough," the far right will always play it better. This does not take away from the shorter-term gains of looking tough and resolute in the political market, but it does add a fundamental risk of being outflanked or punished for deviating from a hardline path. In the United States, voices on the right attacked the young Biden administration for opening the door to further migration across the US-Mexico border through its more "humane" approach relative to Trump's—and Biden was soon taking this on board as he started enforcing tougher border policies that mirrored those of his predecessor.[4] In this way, some degree of political "success" may be assured, however temporarily.

Many migration and borders scholars have increasingly come round to agreeing with Peter Andreas that "'successful' border management depends on successful image management" rather than on levels of actual deterrence.[5] "Success," in this model, cascades through the system from those political gains down to institutional gains, which similarly depend upon good optics and metrics. The same can be said about our other wars and fights, which all have a circular quality. Again, "self-licking ice-cream cones" keep justifying themselves, however damaging or pointless they may be.

Gall draws our attention to a kind of subcategory within what we have called the unstated aims. He says the system wants to live: it is often very good at rising, time and again, from the dead.[6] Image and knowledge management—our hall of mirrors—clearly form a key part of this. However, to understand why taxpayer-funded wars and fights are so successful at "getting away with it" and surviving, we need an expressly *political* systems analysis rather than an abstract

systems theory that risks anthropomorphizing "the system." Part of
what we need to understand here—and it's something we discuss
in more detail in our section below, "The Road to Turf-dom"—is
interbureaucratic competition. This was already significant during the
Cold War, as we saw in our discussion of Vietnam. Yet it is notable
how, since the dying days of the Cold War, public bodies have increasingly been treated as businesses through "new public management."
The market logic permeating state administrations has fed the proliferating security marketplace we identified in chapter 4, while offering
institutions an incentive to market their "success" in an increasingly
competitive funding environment. Within this emerging political
ecology, self-promotion has become an increasingly central priority,
good optics and metrics have increasingly trumped outcomes, and
taxpayer-funded war and security systems have found ingenious ways
to outwit calls for proper accountability. For now, though, we should
turn to some of the more specific "mirrors" through which the reality
of disaster may get distorted into an image of shining success, with or
without the help of such institutional incentives.

Three Mirrors

The first mirror is **the manipulation of the timeline of success**.
In 2010, Ruben experienced a blatant example of this amid Europe's
on-off "migration crisis." He was meeting the Spanish central government delegate in Tenerife, an island that had seen large migrant
arrivals a few years earlier. Seated on an undersized chair in front of
the delegate's massive wooden desk, Ruben thought the encounter
had the distinct air of a naughty schoolboy called in for a talk with
the headmaster (perhaps another case of "Honey, I shrunk the academic!"). In this case, the headmaster's message was a cheerful one.
He was keen to show that the Socialists' fight against irregular migration was successfully pushing back the supposed human tide from
West Africa—and that it was doing so in a humane and transparent

fashion. To this end, he produced a printout of a graph showing how migrant arrivals by wooden fishing boats into the Canary Islands had dwindled from more than thirty thousand in 2006 to just a few thousand four years later. Spain's Conservative opposition liked to criticize the government for failing to halt irregular migration, the delegate said—but look, we've done what they *never* accomplished! There was a hitch, however. His timeline had been chosen to start at the record year for irregular maritime migration into Spain, which had happened under the Socialists' watch; so it rather conveniently left out the sharp *rise* that had preceded it.

Somewhat similarly, if more subtly, politicians have in recent years been able to present a picture of "success" in fighting migration at Europe's borders by taking the record, one-off year of 2015 as their reference point (as happened in that Brussels meeting). This quite conveniently ignores the longer trend, which is of much smaller yet quite consistent numbers of arrivals and interceptions since the early 2000s (see Figure 13).

Across all our wars and fights, politicians and policymakers have been able to disguise and distort the reality of longer-term failure (in terms of expressed goals) with the image of short-term success. As we noted, the nebulous, nonterritorial nature of the threats they target has enabled new levels of make-believe, with the war on terror offering

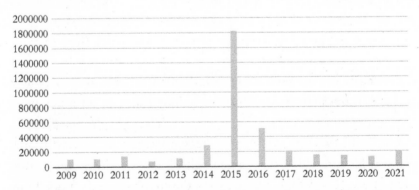

Figure 13 EU irregular entries between border crossing points. Note: Frontex double-counts where individuals cross multiple times. Source: Frontex data.

the biggest distorting mirror of all. When George W. Bush prematurely declared the Iraq invasion "mission accomplished" on board his aircraft carrier in May 2003, few suspected that this was to be but one in a long string of "successes": defeating al Qaeda in Iraq, defeating ISIS, killing bin Laden, taking out terrorists with drone attacks, and so on. A mostly "failing" long war can be broken into a set of smaller wars, each of which can in this way be conveniently framed as successful within its own narrow frame of reference. We cannot reasonably leave out of the picture the disastrous concatenation of small wars that has been actively helped into existence by the intervention itself, as we will see if we stare into our next distorting mirror.

This mirror is **the failure to account for the counterproductive effects of intervention itself**—or, worse, to turn these effects into a sign of success. Let's return to the Spanish borders of 2005, the year before the Socialist government delegate's calculations of success began. The autumn of that year was to prove pivotal in Europe's escalating fight against migration as one of Europe's earlier "border crises" played out at the perimeter of the Spanish enclaves of Ceuta and Melilla. You may recall that the crisis itself had a lot to do with the already announced plan to reinforce the fences; that is, border security was creating an *anticipatory effect*. Further, it generated a displacement or *balloon effect,* with the crisis in the Canaries of 2006 owing much to the crackdowns around the enclaves and the Strait of Gibraltar.[7] Yet instead of acknowledging and accounting for this cycle of crisis and reinforcement, politicians and border agencies saw the 2005 scramble across the fences as *justifying* the very planned reinforcement that had contributed to triggering it. It was a similar story with the 2006 crisis, which was framed as *sui generis* and "not *our* problem," to echo the Brussels diplomat. This crisis in the Canary Islands became an excuse to experiment in the externalization of border security, pushing routes further into the Sahara desert. Around the Mediterranean, we have noted how a similar pattern has developed, with little public reckoning of the cascading consequences of more border security.

The same is true of the way in which border security "collaboration" has fed predatory security actors in undemocratic or barely democratic states. Instead of acknowledging the costs and risks, these collaborations have frequently been chalked up as a "win" not just for "security" but even for "development" (since better border management is seen as a key developmental objective, with development aid actively being channeled to cooperating states' security apparatuses).[8] In short, the practical, political, and human consequences of border security—the diversion of routes and the attendant loss of life, as well as the wider impact on public safety, stability, and rights—have quite consistently been "externalized" in the public accounting, insofar as there has been one. No holistic costs-and-benefits analysis of the EU and member states' vast investments in border security has, to our knowledge, been carried out by officials.

Despite the penchant for cost-benefit analysis in management and accounting circles, proper and comprehensive assessments of costs and benefits—whether in-house or more publicly—tend to be gravely lacking in each of our wars and fights. Consider how stories of "success" have similarly been constructed out of carefully chosen metrics in the war on drugs. One incisive analysis of these official metrics finds that "[m]ost conventional indicators are process-oriented, in that they track the extent of drug crops sprayed, producers put out of business, and arrests and incarceration of traffickers and consumers. They do not, however, demonstrate whether drug supply or demand is increasing or declining." Meanwhile, and as we have seen, counternarcotics initiatives have often been "associated with the most egregious forms of violence, including tens of thousands of intentional homicides and disappearances per year." In this context, it is striking how favored metrics give a sense of "how tough we are being, but do not tell us how successful we are"—that is, how successful in achieving a positive human outcome.[9]

The war on terror has actively spawned the enemy it was purportedly designed to defeat, yet this has not deterred politicians from chalking up win after win. "Liberating Iraq" and "defeating ISIS" were framed as two compartmentalized "successes," yet the two were intimately interlinked; the brutal occupation, the detention and torture sites, and the "de-Ba'athification" of Iraq all substantially *contributed* to the rise of ISIS from the ashes of Saddam Hussein's regime. As one policy analysis put it, corroborating wider findings, "had the United States not invaded Iraq, it is doubtful that ISIS would even exist."[10] We must add to this the way in which the terrorist threat proliferated, creating new "moles" to "whack," *and* the way in which the whacking kept generating more popular anger, resentment, and resistance that fed into violent insurgency. Wider UN findings on counterterror suggest government repression is a major recruiter to insurgencies.[11] Such findings suggest that chinks in the mirror do exist. Yet again, rather than triggering a rethink, the emerging threats simply led to further opportunities for declaring new wars, and new successes, within the overarching war. Disastrous failure was being magicked into a string of successes.

That brings us to our third mirror: **the failure to include in the tally the wider "negative externalities" of intervention on third parties.** This point is crucial for anyone keen on finding a way out of our various wars and fights. We have already seen in the war on drugs how the costs have been transferred downward and outward, to deprived communities within instigating states and to poorer partner countries. The same pattern applies to our other interventions. Notwithstanding the numerous terror attacks in the West, one calculation suggests that only 3 percent of deaths caused by a growing number of global terrorist attacks occurred in Western countries in the period 2000–2014, with the bulk of terror attacks concentrated in a handful of mainly Muslim countries where the war on terror or its piggybacking smaller wars have been staged (see Figure 5 in chapter 4).[12] In counterterror operations, further, the use of drones and "vertical" forms of power minimizes the risk to Western combatants, as does the focus on "hard security" for the reduced numbers of personnel deployed on the ground, which transfers risks to inadequately protected national workers and unprotected ordinary civilians.[13] By contrast, countries that collaborate in the war on terror have often found themselves on the front line of violence and even retaliation. The "risk-transfer" mode of warfare in counterterror, as in the Cold War proxy wars before it, outsources huge risks to populations in poorer and frequently formerly colonized countries, reproducing and indeed reinventing an old and disturbing pattern.[14] Yet it is remarkably rare for politicians, the media, or prominent security think tanks to take proper account of these outsourced risks and costs; if these are recognized at all, they are frequently framed as "collateral damage."

Our other wars, as we have seen, similarly generate huge costs, which are largely borne by those who are relatively powerless and have no stake in the intervention. The war on crime has severely hit the livelihoods and civil liberties of poorer people and minorities; the war on drugs similarly so. Both the drug wars and the fight against migration have led to large amounts of human suffering and needless deaths. In the drug wars, deaths and suffering range from the lethal violence in transit countries and crime-hit neighborhoods to accidental (and preventable) overdosing, the latter tally reaching beyond 100,000 in the United States alone in 2021.[15] On migration, the UN has recorded some fifty thousand deaths on migrant journeys since 2014 worldwide, in what is likely to be severe undercounting.[16] However, the death, suffering, and many other adverse consequences are "off the books," at least in most official reckonings. Insofar as the costs are successfully externalized, the fight is succeeding, however many disasters and double-game scenarios it happens to generate. Coming back to our stated and unstated aims, this may in fact be the greatest "achievement" of our various wars: not just a double but a *triple game* that ensures a win every time.

The tendency to generate self-justifying metrics in ways that exclude the true costs of an intervention, corroborated by a wealth of studies,[17] has a lot to do with the quashing of dissent enabled by the "war fix." It also has a lot to do with bureaucratic "target culture." You may remember the frequent obsession with metrics for winning: body counts, kill lists ticked off, smugglers detained, drug lords arrested, migrants halted or deported, and so on. "You can't manage what you can't measure" is a familiar refrain—yet this focus on metrics has been used politically to distort the picture. Besides the human fatalities, a whole host of unmeasured impacts routinely goes unaccounted for, while what cannot be counted routinely "doesn't count." Let us break some of these unmeasured impacts down in terms of *public goods*, as opposed to the *private rents* the system provides.

First, we must account for costs to fundamental rights. The fight against migration has undermined the right to safe haven and non-refoulement for those escaping violence and persecution. In a wide range of countries, we find refugees and displaced people contained in terrible conditions, in ways that frequently make a mockery of the Geneva Convention.[18] More widely, the "fight" has also undermined freedom to move, often along lines of class and race. In North Africa (as well as within Europe itself) a suspicion of illegality has frequently led to documented migrants and citizens being stopped and detained. In Niger, a signatory to free movement accords with fellow West African states, migrants from the region (and Nigeriens too) have been effectively prevented from traveling within parts of the country owing to European-supported crackdowns and draconian laws.[19] In the war on terror, we know that rights to due process have been trampled amid arbitrary and prolonged detention, torture, and extrajudicial killings.

Second, freedom of expression has been undermined. A "war" framing has silenced dissenting voices in all our case studies, and especially so in the war on terror. If this is the case in richer instigating countries, it is all the more so in poorer countries with weaker democratic institutions.

Third, and very much related to this, there are costs to trust in authorities and democracy. Policing by consent has been fundamentally undermined by all our wars, from the arbitrary and extractive enforcement seen in the wars on crime and drugs to migration crackdowns in destination and "partner" states alike—and on to draconian antiterrorist measures. The provisioning and bolstering of partner state security forces has shifted the balance of institutional power within fragile and weak polities, often further undermining public trust in the legitimacy of government, as seen for instance in Niger and Afghanistan.[20] In richer countries, the "emergency" measures used by border forces and law enforcement more widely have given rise to concern about the arbitrary exercise of power. When rights and even international law are set aside, this is a threat not just to the populations that are being "targeted" but also to those who are helping them as well as to wider populations whose well-being *also* depends on respect for rights and law.[21]

Finally (though we could go on), our wars have generated significant costs in terms of international solidarity and collaboration. The way the war on terror severely cracked down on humanitarian assistance in the name of cutting terrorist funding has contributed to famines and severe shortages in Somalia, Yemen, Syria, and elsewhere.[22] Meanwhile, a fixation on security threats has come to reshape relations between richer donor states and their poorer counterparts, as we saw in the brinksmanship and bargaining of the fight against migration as well as in the export of war on terror rhetoric in countries such as Sri Lanka.

In sum, our three "mirrors" pinpoint three aspects to the fixing of the knowledge environment: *the manipulation of timelines, of blowbacks, and of costs to the instigator's advantage.* While we can't assume that these distortions or manipulations are always conscious and "strategic," it is striking how they nevertheless tend to produce the same systemic patterns over and over again. The "mirrors" habitually mask the failure to achieve expressed goals, and they simultaneously obscure the unexpressed goals—and internal functions—of our various wars and fights. More particularly, the mirrors mask the cost-distribution logic of these wars and fights; they turn accountability for the wars into something akin to an oil company's balance sheet, from which all "negative externalities"—mass pollution of the public domain and the public good—have been excised from the accounts. This, in turn, offers an opportunity to bring the costs into the open. We can learn here from the process by which many big polluters have finally had to reckon with more of the costs of their profit-making activities, a point to which we return in chapter 9.

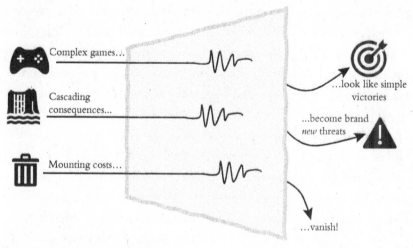

Figure 14 The distorting mirror.

The idea of a hall of mirrors is a neat way to show how distortion occurs within the wars (see Figure 14). But perhaps it is a bit *too* neat. The mirror is cracked and foggy; not everyone agrees on what they see there. Among those who depart from official "wisdom" are academics, activists, reporters, civil society groups, and survivors—but also many of those tasked with carrying out the wars and fights. Yet while we have often found implementers to be the among the sharpest critics, we also find that their internal critique can usually be masked or muffled through the political, institutional, and career incentives of war. Let us look at these political games one final time, now with the "knowledge fix" uppermost in our minds, by revisiting Afghanistan and a belated public reckoning with the war on terror.

Afghanistan and "the Best Picture Possible"

In 2019, the story of the "Afghanistan Papers" broke in the *Washington Post,* showing with stark clarity—well ahead of the Taliban takeover and US withdrawal of 2021—how the occupiers had stacked the information cards in their own favor. "Every data point was altered to present the best picture possible," said Bob Crawley, an army colonel who served as a counterinsurgency adviser.[23] Summarizing their interviews and the evidence, the *Post*'s reporters wrote that "officials issued rosy pronouncements they knew to be false and hid unmistakable evidence the war had become unwinnable. Several of those interviewed described explicit efforts by the U.S. government to deliberately mislead the public and a culture of willful ignorance, where bad news and critiques were unwelcome."[24]

This willful (or functional) ignorance was replicated elsewhere in the war on terror, including in the Baghdad Green Zone, whose loose relationship to reality was revealed in the tellingly titled *Imperial Life in the Emerald City* by the Post's Rajiv Chandrasekaran.[25] In Afghanistan as well as in Iraq, we see how the incentives were systematically stacked against a full accounting of the costs—and how the resulting hall of mirrors was gradually transforming into its own make-believe reality.

Part of this had to do with political secrecy and expediency in war, which was by no means limited to security and military actors. David has had his own experience of these dynamics, and one of these experiences takes the form of a "shaggy dog" story. The 2010–16 Cameron government had recently come to power and the UK Department for International Development (DfID) expressed interest in a paper from David that would sum up what we knew about the difficulties of "winning hearts and minds" in Afghanistan in the context of a corrupt government and an ongoing conflict. But soon there was an about-face, and David was being told that the topic was too politically sensitive. "Okay, how about a paper on the Vietnam War?" David suggested. His contact was enthusiastic, and they agreed that this was an interesting and politely indirect way of raising some key "hearts and minds" problems in relation to a war that had, after all, unfolded some forty years earlier. But then word came from higher up in the department: this would also be too sensitive in the "current climate." Resisting the urge to suggest a paper on the Hundred Years War, David gave up. (We did say it was a shaggy dog story.)

Besides the politics of war, it is also important to understand how the bureaucratic environment helped maintain some form of silence or *omertà*, at least for some time.[26] We will get to this "political ecology" side of the story further in our next section. Suffice to note for now how in Afghanistan, besides incentives for having the right metrics and optics, government departments and agencies also faced the risk of losing out in the funding and relevance game. In the context of the global financial crisis, DfID (and related development organizations, such as USAID in the United States) had been facing budget cuts. (Today, DfID has been incorporated into the Foreign Office.) Given the war on terror and given the precarity of development ministries themselves, the argument *that development promotes security* became an especially attractive one—and in the context of Afghanistan, this meant arguing that development aid can win hearts and minds. In this funding environment, NGOs, too, have been tempted to sell their interventions as promoting security.[27]

The distortions in the knowledge environment of the Afghan occupation were fueled by secrecy, sensitivity, and official inaction in the face of potentially unwelcome evidence. Yet, going further, such distortion also occurred as a result of *direct action,* which has very often served as a form of propaganda in war and security operations. Part of this has been "action as distraction." Just two weeks after 9/11, Secretary of Defense Donald Rumsfeld was already suggesting a grand diversionary maneuver to a meeting of the US National Security Council: "Look, as part of the war on terrorism, should we be getting something going in another area, other than Afghanistan, so that success or failure and progress isn't measured just by Afghanistan?"[28] In many ways, this is classic wreckonomics: you start one fire to take attention away from another. Two years later, the Iraq invasion followed. Yet amid the subsequent quagmire, officials and politicians again attempted to extract an image of success from endemic failure. One former UK Foreign Office worker told David that there was pressure to ensure things were seen to be working in Afghanistan so as to provide a distraction from things going so badly *in Iraq.*

Within this mindset, even bad news could be wrestled into good through some clever diversionary tactics paired with a good fog machine. A senior US National Security Council official said there was constant pressure to show that the 2009-11 troop surge in Afghanistan was working, despite evidence to the contrary, adding, "It was their explanations. For example, attacks are getting worse? 'That's because there are more targets for [the Taliban] to fire at, so more attacks are a false indicator of instability.' Then, three months later, attacks are still getting worse? 'It's because the Taliban are getting desperate, so it's actually an indicator that we're winning.'"[29] Back in 2001, Deputy Defense Secretary Paul Wolfowitz said the bad news that the Taliban were getting reinforcements was also good news since it would *create more targets.*[30]

We must again add a very large dose of *political* systems analysis to how we assess the distortion of the knowledge environment. As the saying goes, the fish rots from the head.[31] But the capacity for distortion, deception, and self-deception did not stay at the political level. As we have seen very briefly in Afghanistan, it also reproduced on institutional level, given the many bureaucratic incentives to "play into" the war fix.

Notably, these incentives fed down to the *individual* level. If we consider, briefly, the incentives for those deployed militarily in Afghanistan, we find that career success was quite compatible with endemic failure—which, moreover, created incentives to present the war in the rosiest light possible. US diplomats tended to say that they themselves were doing a good job, and so did army brigade and battalion commanders. The retired army general Michael Flynn, a key figure in military intelligence in Afghanistan and later Trump's controversial national security adviser, said of the latter:

> So they all went in for whatever their rotation was, nine months or six months and were given that mission, accepted that mission and executed that mission ... Then they all said, when they left, they accomplished the mission. Every single commander. Not one commander is going to leave Afghanistan ... and say, "You know what, we didn't accomplish our mission." ... So the next guy that shows up finds it

[their area] screwed up ... and then they come back and go, "Man this is really bad."[32]

The British were no better. As Simon Akam wrote perceptively in the *London Review of Books* in a 2019 stock-taking of the British military, "Few would argue that the Iraq (2003–9 for the British) and Afghanistan (2001–14) campaigns didn't go badly . . . [yet] almost everyone in uniform who ran these wars, even those who directly supervised failure, was subsequently promoted and decorated." It would be hard to find a clearer distillation of wreckonomics than this. Individual as well as institutional incentives of the kind already familiar to us played their part, as the army was determined "to fend off cuts by demonstrating its prowess and constitutionally disinclined to admit that things might not be going well." The result was yet more make-believe, leading to Akam's scathing review of a book by a lieutenant colonel on "why British army leadership works":

> [T]here is no sense that these were conflicts that cost trillions of dollars and thousands of lives, that sought to remake foreign states and didn't succeed. Eight years after the withdrawal from Helmand, it is still uncomfortable to think about Iraq and Afghanistan, therefore they didn't happen, therefore British army leadership works.[33]

You might say that hindsight is always 20/20 and we did not know that Kabul would eventually fall so precipitously to the Taliban. It's true that there is an element of unpredictability in every historical event. David originally trained as a historian, and he likes to say that it is hard enough to find out what has already happened, never mind predicting what will happen next. But when he wrote in his 2012 book *Useful Enemies* that the war in Afghanistan "has been a counterproductive failure," he also spelled out the essentially unwinnable character of a war-cum-reconstruction that was fueling anger at corruption even as it claimed to "win hearts and minds."[34] The point is not that this was especially insightful or foresighted but rather the reverse: anyone who knew something about the war in Afghanistan knew that it was going pretty badly. But that was not a problem in the hall of mirrors.

The situation in Afghanistan was, in many ways, an odd mix—a kind of fearful optimism that one might more readily associate with Soviet Communism, a world where official statistics almost always pointed in the right direction and if you were the bearer of bad news, beware. The official accounting of the war on terror, like the accounting of the Vietnam War before it, was looking like a tractor production report. One reason for this, we have suggested, has to do with the politics of war. Another has to do with the politics of bureaucracy: target culture, career advancement, and interagency competition all presented huge possibilities for manipulation. A further factor feeding into the distorted nature of the accounting concerns the growing number of participants in our various wars and fights. This expansion has allowed for dispersing responsibility and reframing objectives on a massive scale, fogging the mirrors still further. Let us look at this through a slight digression into the wider pattern beyond our war and security systems.

The Road to Turf-dom

We have raised the possibility that what we call "wreckonomics" extends well beyond our wars and fights. Indeed, one observant reader thought our argument recalled Friedrich Hayek's in *The Road to Serfdom,* that midcentury call to arms against Communism and the evils of central planning.[35] The reader put the parallel eloquently:

> Because of the inescapable tendency of centralizing systems of administration to simplify the world around them, to overestimate what they can know and change and to fail to recognize alternative realities, they instead nurture an ecosystem of special interests that becomes nigh-impossible to reverse (or even reform), in the process quashing dissent even when this leads to manifestly poorer and poorer outcomes that exact a higher and higher toll on society.

Of course, some bureaucracies have made a huge positive difference, and one might think, for example, of the United Kingdom's

National Health Service. But while we are no fans of Hayek in general, there is something in his critique of bureaucracy. Some of the worst examples of the kind of self-deluding and self-reinforcing cycle we have identified are to be found in totalitarian systems where the "fix" brooks no dissent and the political "steer" on cascading consequences and games is particularly acute—Mao's Great Leap Forward with its government-made famine being one terrifying example.[36] Yet we would also like to give Hayek's critique an important twist, with all the caveats that should go with the brevity of our argument here. It is this: that the very market-based logics advocated by Hayek and others (especially his fellow Chicago economist, Friedman) have *intensified* some of the dangers that surround bureaucracies. Ironically, these dangers escalated after the end of the Cold War, which was supposed to be the death knell of sclerotic state bureaucracies. The market-oriented logics of new public management (NPM), developed in the 1980s and increasingly popular in the 1990s, have constrained public accountability while creating a competitive environment within the bureaucratic worlds of richer democracies. The NPM combination of "audit culture and fetish for short term quantitative indicators" has spread across sectors as diverse as warfighting and university life—greatly contributing, in the view of war scholar Tarak Barkawi, to a mass production line of "self-licking ice-cream cones" of the kind we saw in our Cold War chapter.[37]

In his study of the deployment of NPM within academia—a field we will get to in a moment—Chris Lorenz, a history professor in the Netherlands, notes that "NPM managerialism ironically shows extremely interesting similarities to the type of managerialism found in former Communist states," not least in its focus on tightly regulated metrics.[38] More generally, the rise of NPM encouraged public service providers to compete with one another, leading to a fierce scramble for resources. This in turn encouraged a growing focus on image-making and a gaming of the wider political system. Amid growing competition over power, status, and money, different state institutions were increasingly determined to put a favorable gloss on their own performance, reinforcing the pattern that Morton Halperin had already observed in the 1970s.[39] This was not so much the road to serfdom, in short, as the road to turf-dom.

It was in the meeting of Reaganomics and wreckonomics that our wars and fights escalated. This was also the moment, we should recall, when the Cold War was unwinding and a newly competitive market-place for "security" opened up, adding further political impetus to fixating on and gaming various threats. In this environment, holding the biggest threat was the winning card in intra-agency competition, especially when accompanied by a confident promise to reduce it and by an impressive set of metrics. However, the competitive funding environment was not only affecting the behavior of core security actors in our wars and fights; it also affected a range of ancillary actors, from aid organizations to academia and media outlets. In this highly competitive environment with its penchant for quick image fixes, our war and security systems found a propitious chance to extend their longevity and reach.

We note here the stupendous expansion of aid (which was partly a *redirection*) that accompanied the rebranding of the war on terror as a suitably far-reaching and long-lasting humanitarian mission: res-cuing Afghan women from Taliban oppression; liberating Iraqis from Saddam Hussein's tyrannical rule; and treating humanitarian groups, infamously, as a "force multiplier" in the theater of operations. As we saw above, aid funders and groups were often happy to participate in this "game," competing in the humanitarian marketplace.[40] Let us now return to the fight against migration one more time to see how a range of actors were similarly being dragged into core security actors' framing of the problem.

By 2013, some two years before the migration crisis grew to unpre-cedented proportions, European officials were facing a dilemma. How to deal with the dramatic shipwrecks—and deaths in the thousands— in the Mediterranean? The short answer was: through deflecting the blame. European leaders were soon reframing the recurrent mass drownings as a "humanitarian" problem caused by unscrupulous human smugglers. This redirected shame, and blame, onto those who were cornering the market for migrant crossings that had emerged and expanded as a direct result of Europe's "fight against irregular migration." The maneuver even reframed increased border security as a kind of *humanitarian mission* that rescued people from evil smugglers.[41]

Any genuinely "humanitarian" aspects to this move receded when the Italian Navy's Mare Nostrum sea rescue mission was ended in late 2014. Yet the humanitarian emergency frame did persist into the 2015 crisis. Besides blame-shifting, it drew in a larger and larger range of actors, ensuring that many potential critics were congregating "inside" the border security system rather than raining on the parade from the outside.[42] European leaders were greatly aided in this systemic expansion of the mission by the huge range of ancillary actors being drawn, by default or design, into border security's field of gravity. Humanitarian organizations such as the Red Cross were among them, wittingly or unwittingly helping to ensure the humanitarian branding while working closely with state authorities in rescues, reception, and even detention and deportation, as we saw briefly in chapter 5. In some ways, this mirrored a long-standing tendency in which self-consciously "humanitarian" operations have sometimes fed into and legitimized violence while trumpeting their own virtue. A relatively early example was the 1988 Sudan famine in which concentrating aid on the edge of the famine zone helped to depopulate an area coveted for its oil. Coming back to Europe's "migration crisis" of 2015, the International Organization for Migration (IOM) provided a misleadingly neutral gloss on an intensely political situation through its "humanitarian" data-gathering efforts and its "voluntary" removal campaigns in North Africa. Through such initiatives, funded via its close links with powerful donor states, the IOM was growing into a key player and eventually a UN-affiliated agency on the back of recurrent "migration crises" that it was itself increasingly helping to frame.[43] As a recent careful study has argued, both IOM and UNHCR are tapping into a "refugee rentier" market where claiming parts of the "mixed migration" population in North Africa as "theirs" comes with political, economic and institutional benefits.[44] A wide range of NGOs fed into this process, as Ruben saw firsthand in the rollout of Spanish development programming in West Africa after the 2006 "boat crisis." Boondoggles included "risk awareness-raising" campaigns for potential irregular migrants and much else besides.[45] Add to this the externalization of controls into countries such as Libya, whose officials and militias-turned-guards were paid and trained (including in human rights!) to push back migrants,[46] and the list of security *and* ancillary actors with a "slice of the cake" is long indeed.

In short, and coming back to a theme from chapter 5, key political and security actors have been able to reinforce, legitimize, and "systemize" destructive operations by bringing more and more ancillary actors into their *framing of the problem*—in this case, framing irregular migration across land and sea as an emergency and framing the border as the site to address it. We should not exaggerate the steer on this process, which frequently cascaded uncontrollably in ways that were uncomfortable for instigating governments. We should also not exaggerate the unity of purpose; conflicts and tensions run through this very messy wider system of intervention, as seen again in the struggles between volunteer aid groups, authorities, and nationalists around the Mediterranean in recent years. However, it is notable how donor-instigators have in key moments generated "buy-in" among potentially critical sectors. At its worst, this was a kind of engineered complicity. It is also notable how this bewildering variety of actors has served to *diffuse responsibility* away from the instigators of the system such as state and EU authorities. Usefully, *blame* could also be diffused, including eventually to humanitarian rescue workers who were being framed in Greek and Italian courts as complicit in human smuggling.[47]

Among the ancillary actors in our war and security systems, we find "knowledge workers"—academics and journalists. Let us say a brief word about each sector. Like our colleagues in aid, academics are caught up in "audit culture" and "value for money" criteria that owe much of their strength to NPM and to various bouts of cutbacks.

For universities chasing research income as well as good metrics on "excellence" and "impact," jumping on political bandwagons may sometimes look very attractive—especially as governments (themselves under pressure to have a strong "impact" of their own) have increasingly been inclined to give a political steer to the funding process. Since "crisis" was yet again announced at EU borders in 2015, new migration research centers have sprung up across the continent; lucrative "urgency grants" have been announced by research funding bodies, attracting more academics into the crisis fold; and innumerable panel events have brought policymakers and academics together in attempts to work out new solutions. In the United Kingdom, academics have been told that "impact" on policy—and, strictly, it didn't have to be *good* impact!—would be rewarded if it could be demonstrated. Of course, practical steps to change the dire border situation are crucial. Yet when academics are playing this highly structured system, we are also at risk of being played. Like NGO workers, we are sometimes co-opted into the official frame and the official accounting rather shifting our gaze to see the highly political nature of the emergency-generating system in which we are operating.[48] When it comes to the causes, consequences, and functions of this broader system, many of the key incentives direct attention to consequences and a rather token account of causes, while deeper causes—and proliferating functions—routinely go missing.

Of course, a good amount of critical work has emerged from academic quarters, just as a great deal of good work in dire circumstances has been done by NGOs and UN practitioners. But we must always be aware of where our gaze is directed and how our findings may be co-opted. In academia, market logics and crude metrics have bolstered some very perverse incentives. In this context, rather than tuning out and retreating into what some critics would see as a "purer" kind of research,[49] we need to examine the political system in which we ourselves are operating. In the case of our various wars and fights, this involves actively investigating the framing of situations *as an emergency*—and we need critically to examine *what kind of emergency* they are said to constitute.[50]

This takes us to the media, which has of course played a funda-mental role in all our wars and fights in setting the crisis or emergency frame. Media outlets have done so alongside—and sometimes at log-gerheads with—political and security actors. Rather than looking seriously at the causes and functions of underlying problems (and at the functions of floundering interventions), a great deal of coverage focuses on visible symptoms and on the optics of a "tough" interven-tion. A longer book could easily spend a whole chapter on the role of the news media, and we have ourselves recently studied the emo-tive aspects of emergencies including the media's role in them, with a focus on fear (Ruben) and shame (David).[51] Having both trained in earlier incarnations as journalists, at the same university to boot, and having worked in different news organizations in London, we are very much aware of the constraints of mainstream journalism. One of those constraints (or perils) is the political steer given by proprietors. Another is the changing news environment. "If it bleeds, it leads" is the old adage, which we may well pair with a second one: "If it scares, the reader cares." Newspaper proprietors with political agendas, and editors trying to corner a fast-changing market, have strong incen-tives to ramp up whichever crisis politicians have fixated upon—and not infrequently the fixation emanates in the first place from media outlets themselves. Often the "coverage" takes the form of talking heads or loud commentary (sometimes parroting officials' anonymous briefings) rather than expensive on-the-ground reporting.[52]

We are also aware that journalists, especially of the freelance or investigative variety, have helped to shine a bright and critical light on the various disastrous wars that we have discussed in this book. But the increasingly competitive and temporally compressed media market is greatly incentivizing the emergency framing. Indeed, the escalating cycle between the huge media attention to dramatic border crossings and dramatic political responses has not been lost on migra-tion scholars examining the "border spectacle" (or image-oriented

"game"). It has also not escaped the attention of politicians, who seek
to give this dramatization a suitable steer, as we saw in our earlier discussion of brinksmanship at the borders. Nor has it been lost on target
groups. This is especially notable in the war on terror, with terrorists
finding in the twenty-four-hour news cycle a propitious environment
for staging and escalating the impact of their violent "propaganda of
the deed."[53]

What we face here is a complex set of systemic incentives toward
fixation upon (or the "securitization" of) a particular problem, reaching from parliaments to newsrooms, NGO offices, and even academic
institutes. We do not wish to simplify this process, which has a long
history and involves a large range of conflicts among these security
and "ancillary" actors—including conflicts over different framings of a
given problem. Yet we also find that the nature of the post–Cold War
marketplace of security *and* of bureaucracy has contributed to generating this buy-in. Our wars and fights have come to include a bewildering range of organizations that have for quite rational institutional
reasons seen benefits from somehow addressing the relevant "emergency." In this environment, ancillary actors have contributed to the
resilience of these security systems. This has happened in three ways.
First, they have frequently helped strengthen the emergency framing;
second, they have frequently helped to frame or diffuse the *objectives*;
and third, they have crucially helped diffuse *responsibility* for these operations' disastrous consequences. All this points to an important feature of wreckonomics: the more actors, and the more games, the better
the opportunities not just to diffuse and externalize the costs but also
to diffuse and distort the knowledge environment around them.

History, Accountability, and Policy-Based Evidence-Making

In this chapter, we have added important pieces to our crime-scene
puzzle. We have seen how the "knowledge fix" is a crucial part of

what makes our war and security systems so durable and even self-propelling. Relevant here is the nature of the "war fix" and its quashing of dissent. But we have also suggested that this "fix" is greatly helped by market-driven changes in public administration, in the media landscape, and in the aid sector in recent decades—as well as by the opening of a "security marketplace" at the end of the Cold War. Here, then, is part of the reason why we call failure the new—or at least "newish"—success.

We have noted Gall's arresting view that "the system wants to live." Yet so do all those who make it up—and any political systems analyst ignores this at their peril. Institutions and individuals within our disaster-prone systems do not just want to live, but often to live well, whether as decorated officers, reelected politicians, high-ranking UN officials, promoted professors, or well-funded and powerful organizations. You might point out that these political, institutional, and individual incentives are going to be very difficult to change—and you would be right. But let's start by at least recognizing how incentives have been consistently skewed, and how the "political ecology" of the post–Cold War years has actively contributed to this. We also need to recognize the huge costs of a single-minded focus on very particular objectives. Let's then examine the complex networks of self-interest that grow up around such single-minded interventions. And let's recognize the deceptions and self-deceptions that are deployed to give the impression that laser-focused interventions—at the extreme, an actual war—are working when they are not.

We have seen how the "knowledge fix" depends on a very significant degree of political steer. Yet it is frequently insufficient to shame or denounce those "at the top." Rather, we must look at "co-creation" across many different levels. The hall of mirrors—indeed our whole infernal fairground—is sustained by interests and mechanisms large and small. Some of these interests are of the kind that we routinely see congregating around existential threats and wars. Others have more to do with the workings of bureaucracies. Their penchant for fixed ideas and promise to "deliver" on them can easily be co-opted politically, as we saw in Afghanistan. The result, all too often, is what some insiders have called "policy-based evidence-making," or fitting the facts around a policy that has already been "fixed" for other reasons. The Iraq invasion is a case in point, with MI6 chief Sir Richard Dearlove telling a meeting at Downing Street in 2012 that in the United States, "the intelligence and facts were being fixed around the policy."[54]

Like politicians, those working within ministries and within a wide range of other bureaucratic organizations are likely to develop a sophisticated sense of what kinds of information are inconvenient, unwelcome, and even downright dangerous. Alongside the questions habitually emphasized (How can we make ourselves useful? How do we respond to this threat? How can we grow or at least retain our staff and funding?) there are likely to be many questions that are neglected. The latter are often *historical* questions: How did this problem come into being? How did we, as an institution, get to this point? And perhaps most neglected of all: What have we been doing that *contributes* to this problem?

Here, a blatant refusal to *learn* and a kind of functional or strategic ignorance can easily come into play.[55] In late 2022, to take one symptomatic case, the Conservative UK home secretary announced that England was facing a migrant "invasion" across the Channel and that the migration system was "broken"—that is, the very same system that the Conservative government had presided over for the previous twelve years.[56] Similarly, EU politicians have repeatedly clamored for a secure border, as if this had not already been attempted for decades. In such contexts, and alongside all the declared wars that we've been highlighting in this book, we may detect an undeclared "war" on history. Routinely, the discussion remains trapped in a kind of perpetual present which "fixes" the terms of debate. Whether it's financial reporting, aid situation updates, TV news, briefings for ministers, or academic policy papers, the knowledge environment is often geared toward short attention spans, crisis response, and the chosen political frame. This is a tendency, we suggest, that has worsened in a "market" context where each institution (in the media, public administration, universities, NGOs, and more) is inclined to play its own games by fixating on narrow problems and metrics, preparing the path for demonstrating "success" by narrowing its focus. Again, we do not wish to underestimate the complexities and *struggles* over how emergencies are defined, or how solutions are decided upon, or over the kind of knowledge that should "count." Yet all too often, as we cast an eye back to the hall of mirrors, what we see reflected back is an image of the system's shining success.

If the hall of mirrors serves as a useful metaphor for the distorted "optics" that surround our failing interventions, we should notice something else. Funfair mirrors take ordinary people and turn them into the grotesque. By contrast, the *knowledge fix* that surrounds our various wars and fights—as well as many other interventions that are mobilized around an existential "threat"—is taking something grotesque and making it look somehow normal and acceptable. That is central to the business (and in many ways it *is* a business) of extracting success from the jaws of failure. It also keeps us locked into policies that are constantly generating suffering on a massive scale.

The vanity of the powerful is a familiar theme from fairy tales, from *The Emperor's New Clothes* to *Snow White*. "Mirror, mirror on the wall, who's the fairest of them all?" the Queen asked of the mirror, and the answer came back: "Thou, O Queen, art the fairest in the land." What we need is some "speaking back," as when the mirror tells the Queen quite truthfully that she is no longer the fairest in the land. When it comes to our various "wars" and "fights"—and when it comes to failing-but-succeeding systems more generally—solutions, logically, begin with freeing ourselves from these various distortions and inquiring more closely into the nature of the phenomena that we are investigating and ostensibly trying to remedy. This also means investigating the interventions themselves—not least the incentives that are operating within them. That is the beginning of restoring accountability, and we have emphasized that there is no accountability without history, including a careful examination of how our interventions came to be.

8

Wreckonomics Goes Viral?

The Costs of Laissez-Faire and Lockdown

At the start of this book, we asked you to join us in becoming "systems detectives" on a wide-ranging "crime scene investigation." We have since visited several terrible crime scenes, from wars on terror and drugs to the fight against migration. On the way, we have seen how war and security systems tend to leave a trail of fraud and destruction. More often than not, your two author-detectives have been almost eerily in agreement with each other on the nature of the relevant "crimes" and on the interests and perverse incentives that underpin them. Whether or not you like the theme-tune of our Oxford noir, we've been singing in harmony.

But perhaps we are close to that point in many a detective story where the inspectors are starting to bicker. The reason is a disaster—and in some people's eyes a crime scene too—that has caused more than a few arguments in workplaces and households around the world: the COVID-19 pandemic and the responses to it. Could it be that a note of discord is spilling into the quiet and historic streets of Oxford, with Inspector Morse beginning to snipe at Sergeant Lewis and vice versa?

Let's call it a creative tension. In the first section (in which David leads the investigation), we look at the case against the laissez-faire approach to COVID-19 that was sometimes favored within prominent democracies, including the United Kingdom and the United

States. In the second section (with Ruben as inspector), we bring out some of the dangers in the heavy policing of the pandemic.[1] In our third section—perhaps a grumbling reconciliation in one of Oxford's grubbier pubs—we emphasize some important common themes across these two critiques.

Why talk disease? Ignoring such a major crisis would be odd, we think, in a book about crisis intervention. Further, the pandemic sparked our curiosity as nonexperts on public health: we felt COVID-19 responses might help us to see the extent to which "wreckonomic" patterns apply beyond war and security systems. Certainly, we must acknowledge important differences from our other wars and fights. While the history of waging "war on disease" is a long one, it is clear that pandemic politics still differs quite significantly from military and security interventions in the strict sense.[2] A key difference is that the target of the "war" is a virus.[3] This means that the dynamics of games and cascades will diverge from our other cases: the virus will react to human intervention, but it won't react the way human target groups would. It will not become annoyed at those intervening against it, for example, but instead will display great "patience" in waiting for its next opportunity. Another key observation is that, unlike our other systems, COVID-19 interventions have largely *ended* in most parts of the world.

Given these differences, it is quite remarkable how COVID-19 policy still shows very significant overlaps with our wreckonomics of war and security. It is more remarkable still that the two extreme-case versions we will consider—simplified as "laissez-faire" and "lockdown"—*both* exhibit these overlaps, albeit in sometimes distinct ways. A rather fundamental point that unites our analysis in this chapter is that each mode involved creating a system that distributed costs in very particular, very uneven, and very politicized ways. A second point that runs through our analysis is that alongside this skewed distribution of costs was a (shifting) knowledge environment that served to legitimize this distribution. A third unifying point is that a single-minded fixation—often involving the language of war—tended damagingly to constrain debate and to legitimize the imposition and toleration of hidden costs.

With this throat-clearing complete (hopefully it's not a bug), let us begin our systems investigation.

Viral Nationalism? A (W)reckless Combination

We both remember standing in seminar rooms at the end of February 2020, fielding questions from our students: Would exams go ahead? Would there still be lectures? At this point, lockdown was not in our mind. The UK government, led by Boris Johnson, was resisting the kind of hard closure seen in Wuhan, China, where the pandemic had begun. Yet the epidemiological dashboard was blinking red. Soon the country would be in the throes of erratic policy shifts and radical experimentation in pandemic management. In practice, policy moved from "taking it on the chin" (in Johnson's words of spring 2020) to lockdown, with a good deal of subsequent yoyo-ing between the two. Something similar was also happening in the United States, though political pressures to "keep the economy going" were stronger there. We start our critique with the first phase of "laissez-faire" responses in these two prominent democracies, with particular focus on our UK home. We find that unscrupulous politicians there were often adept at *manipulating* disaster to their advantage. Nationalist framings, including invocations of war and sacrifice, contributed to this potential for manipulation. Such manipulation was, initially, also helping to paper over growing public costs amid a "let it rip" tendency that was proving to be a large gamble in the no-vaccine context of 2020.

How far did the laissez-faire experiment fit with the *fixation* element in our framework? At first glance, not well at all: instead of fixating on a threat, here was an attempt to ignore it. Indeed, politicians were pushing back against the kind of radical "fix" that many epidemiologists and citizens were calling for. Yet there *was* a distinct fixation at work: a fixation on the economy. When it came to our other W.R.E.C.K. mechanisms, from rigging the response to exporting costs and knowledge-fixing the results, the laissez-faire approach tended to exhibit them rather strongly; it also invited a notable cascade in terms of escalating viral infection. Instead of "wreckonomics," laissez-faire offered—with apologies to Stephen Dubner and Steven Levitt—the kind of "Freckonomics" we were so studiously avoiding in chapter 2 (with the F for fixation).[4] Yet as we will see shortly, the temptation to war-game this approach was to prove irresistible especially once costs rose.

Many official pronouncements around this time had a chilling aspect. On the one hand, the narrative had elements of "natural complexity" thinking to it: from this perspective, there was little point in trying to interfere with and regulate a virus that would "naturally" spread through the population. Moreover, this natural spread could be presented as virtuous resilience-building. In the United Kingdom, Graham Medley, one of the government's expert advisers, said on March 13, 2020, "We are going to have to generate what we call herd immunity. . . . And the only way of developing that, in the absence of a vaccine, is for the majority of the population to become infected."[5] The thinking, conveyed in newspapers around the time, was that the government was "concerned that if not enough people catch the virus now, it will re-emerge in the winter, when the NHS (National Health Service) is already overstretched."[6] The point being made— though politicians would later go on to dispute this—was that the government actually *wanted* infections (and this at a time when vaccination was not available and treatments were poorly developed). In any event, the already fragile public healthcare system was soon buckling under the load.

In spring 2020, as the virus took hold, it seemed that some people were more dispensable than others—and not just the "front-line workers" in health and other essential services. *Sunday Times* journalists spoke with special advisers, Downing Street staff, and civil servants, noting how Johnson's then senior aide, Dominic Cummings, had outlined the government's strategy at a private meeting at the end of February. "Those present say it was 'herd immunity, protect the economy and if that means some pensioners die, too bad.'"[7] While this account was disavowed by the prime minister's office,[8] Cummings himself (as part of an increasingly bitter public fallout with Johnson) later said that herd immunity "was literally the official plan in all docs/graphs/meetings until it was ditched."[9] The idea of saving the economy while strengthening the "herd" was enthusiastic-ally embraced by assorted right-wing commentators. One columnist for the conservative *Daily Telegraph* wrote that "from an entirely dis-interested economic perspective, the COVID-19 [pandemic] might even prove mildly beneficial in the long term by disproportionately culling elderly dependents."[10]

The first wave did severely impact those elderly dependents who as a rule couldn't "take it on the chin." By May 2021, at least forty-two thousand care-home residents in England and Wales had died of COVID-19.[11] Until mid-April 2020, those discharged from hos-pitals into care homes were not tested, and by this point a thousand care homes had suffered outbreaks.[12] An Alzheimer's Society survey of more than one hundred care homes discovered that one-third had taken in COVID-positive patients discharged from hospital.[13]

In this context, it was not surprising that old political dividing lines were being reactivated—a point we return to in our third section. "Herd immunity is epidemiological neoliberalism," read one critique from spring 2020.[14] The idea, widely shared at the time, was that the laissez-faire approach hit the poorest and most vulnerable the hardest, while this was being justified with the deceptive gloss of individual choice. At times, the "herd immunity" approach followed the neo-liberal habit of combining laissez-faire with a token concern for "the most vulnerable."[15] Yet, as care-home residents found—and not just in the United Kingdom—there was often a long distance between rhetoric and reality. Laggards in the herd, on this account, were on their own.

And yet, even the most carefree of politicians in Johnson's vein found that survival of the fittest wasn't quite enough by way of a national narrative. It was here, through the back door, that our "war fix" snuck in. Laissez-faire was not just about keeping "the market" open—the nation had to be mobilized in the spirit of wartime sacrifice.[16] The nature and extent of this varied from country to country (in Germany and in lockdown-resistant Sweden, for example, such language was largely absent).[17] In the United Kingdom, there was more than a hint of the Blitz spirit in Johnson's initial "take-it-on-the-chin" approach. A key feature of this framing was the willingness to dispatch particular categories of people to some kind of "front line," notably the "essential workers" who were deemed indispensable to the economy or to health and social services but evidently far from indispensable as individuals.

Language aside, the specific cost distribution was far from a UK-specific phenomenon. In Italy, the first country to be hit heavily in Europe, a fellow systems detective by the name of Professor Colombo referred to the "expendable lives" of those deemed necessary to keep the economy going.[18] In a range of countries, the fate of these groups turned out to be markedly different from the middle-class groups that disproportionately shaped the pandemic response. As we will see, this was the case whether the response was in lockdown or laissez-faire mode; it is notable that the unequal costs were such a frequent rallying point among critics of both.

The "war fix" started to take on more importance as costs (and fears) started to mount. This was not least the case in Trump's United States. In May 2020, the US president told reporters, "The people of our country are warriors. I'm not saying anything is perfect, and will some people be affected? Yes. Will some people be affected badly? Yes. But we have to get our country open and we have to get it open soon."[19] The war framing, skeptical observers thought, allowed Trump "to call for the collective sacrifice of laborers without taking the measures necessary to ensure their safety."[20] Back in the United Kingdom, critical voices in *The Lancet* worried that a war meant "sacrifices have to be made." A key question, then, was: *Whose* sacrifices? One notable feature of the UK response in the early stages of the pandemic was that variations of "herd immunity" were in effect being advocated by people who were in a much more privileged position than those who bore most of the risks. In other words, framing the laissez-faire approach to COVID-19 within a nationalist narrative of (wartime) sacrifice served to distort its vastly uneven cost distribution.

Dissent was another problem. In April 2020, *The Lancet* suggested that war metaphors "encourage the view that criticizing government strategy is somehow unpatriotic."[21] Also at this time, as COVID-19 deaths were mounting, Trump swatted away critique of his adminis-tration by attacking the journalists asking challenging questions. "You should be praising the people who have done a good job," he told one reporter. "It's dangerous, it's going to a battlefield."[22] In effect, Trump was invoking the old chestnut that criticizing a war equates to criti-cizing the soldiers who are fighting it.

In the United Kingdom, with medical staff struggling to access even basic protective equipment, doctors and nurses were warned not to raise concerns publicly. One doctor wrote to *The Lancet*, "I never thought I lived in a country where freedom of speech is discour-aged."[23] Meenal Viz, a hospital doctor, wrote:

> We are being silenced. In our own hospitals. By our own managers. A lot of people are afraid for their own safety but they're also afraid of losing their jobs. Some of them have visas tied to their work or families to feed. . . . It's not a "war." . . . This is systematic negligence. I'm not a warrior. And none of us should have to "sacrifice" ourselves to do our jobs.[24]

UK healthcare workers lacked even basic masks, let alone the hazmat suits available to their counterparts in East Asia. Increasingly, "sac-rifice" substituted for protection. In the United Kingdom, ritual-ized "clapping for carers" had official backing. Yet many doctors and nurses expressed their unease with the praise, particularly given that 20 percent of responding healthcare workers in Italy had become in-fected.[25] Another UK doctor wrote, "We are not being treated with

the dignity and care due to frontline workers. Instead, it feels like we
are being treated as cannon fodder."[26]

Adding to the overtones of a "war" when the pandemic hit were
some distinctly nationalistic elements in many official responses,
whether this was in relation to governments hoarding scarce supplies
or trying to boost the strength of the national "herd." Later there was
fierce competition for vaccines. Those favoring herd immunity (in
name or in all but name) effectively set aside any kind of collective
strategy to keep infections at a minimum at a time when no vaccine
was available. A kind of "public health patriotism" was running high.
In fact, this was something that increasingly seemed to unite countries with very different strategies. The relatively low-interventionist
Sweden, critics noted at the time, also experienced a significant narrowing of opinion and rallying around the national solution in the
face of the rest of the world. While this, to some, looked admirable,
it also carried risks—among them, ignoring the scandal brewing in
care homes that eventually came to undermine international interest
in the trust-based Swedish model while leading, as in the United
Kingdom and elsewhere, to an unnecessary loss of lives.[27]

India was another instructive case. After an early national lockdown
(on which more later), Narendra Modi's Hindu nationalist government started speaking of the innate strength of the Indian people as
a reason to open everything up. Besides the fallout of the first lockdown, Modi had clear political reasons for this about-face: regional
elections were under way, with substantial political campaigning by
his party as well as popular religious festivals that were largely seen as
part and parcel of the Hindu nationalist cause. The festivals, especially
the millions-strong *kumbh mela* in the Himalayan foothills, ended up
fueling a cascading rate of infections.[28] In May 2022, the World Health
Organization put India's excess deaths during the pandemic thus far
at a staggering 4.7 million people; Modi's government argued the
figure was ten times lower. This was in keeping with the undercounting of deaths during the phases when COVID-19 ravaged a largely
unvaccinated population, and when infections were being blamed on

minorities—disturbingly feeding into India's existing "communal" politics and crackdowns on Muslim citizens.[29]

In the United States, the tone was equally belligerent, though here the blame was largely directed outside the nation. Trump constructed COVID-19 as an "invisible enemy" or as the "Chinese virus," tying the threat narrative to geopolitics as well as to overtly militaristic frames, calling COVID-19 an "attack" that was "worse than Pearl Harbor" and "worse than the World Trade Center" that "could have been stopped in China."[30] The virus was also used as an excuse to tighten controls at the southern border with Mexico.[31] It was not hard to see how Trump's militaristic framings offered a helpful distraction from—and a scapegoat for—his inept response and the rising death rate.

One part of war's "sacrifices" is frequently the embrace of mass casualties. At the end of February 2020, the UK government's own scientific advisers were predicting 52 million infections, with a 2 to 3 percent death rate, a calculation that gave between 1 and 1.5 million deaths in the scenario labeled an "unmitigated" epidemic.[32] Whatever we make of the modeling (and there was eventually plenty of critique),[33] what was striking was that these calculations by the government's own advisers did not initially prompt a strong response. Lockdowns were imposed only after a March 16, 2020, Imperial College paper predicted an overwhelmed NHS. Again, the numbers were later challenged—yet with the virus surging, this was a long delay.[34] Significantly, records from the early scientific advisory meetings were not published until the end of May.[35]

In India, the United States, and the United Kingdom (as well as in Brazil), governments decided to ignore parts of the scientific advice and push their own versions of what anthropologist Malini Sur has called "viral nationalism."[36] This contributed to a *cascade* of cases at a time when public health systems were ill-prepared and vaccinations scarce or nonexistent. Unlike in the "wars" and "fights" we discussed in earlier chapters, the most nationalist and belligerent rhetoric was pushing in the direction of *nonintervention*.

Some of the anxiety around the early inclination toward nonintervention (and in particular around the lingering "herd immunity" approach) was the sense that plans were being made without significant consultation with the public or parliament. In the United Kingdom, it was as if the need for infections now to protect the NHS later was suddenly being considered necessary by unknown modelers using unknown methodologies. At the extreme, once war rhetoric entered the picture, this suggested a perverse cycle of escalation: insofar as Britons were now in a "war," the virus was being positioned by some leading politicians and influential health officials as *their ally.* The idea of "herd immunity" was potentially a wonderful boon here in magicking failure into success, for it neatly inverted a disaster (mass infection) and framed it as a triumph.[37]

The careless (and, to many, callous) approach of populist Western leaders may have owed something to a sense of exceptionalism. Relatedly, it involved actively ignoring lessons from elsewhere, with governments in East Asia in particular faring much better in their pandemic response on many counts. A February 2020 study in *The Lancet* suggested, "In most scenarios, highly effective contact tracing and case isolation is enough to control a new outbreak of COVID-19 within 3 months."[38] But when it came to the United Kingdom, the government initially did not put much store by contact tracing, which was seen as intrusive, difficult, expensive to organize, and problematic when infection was asymptomatic. Taking a different view, Annelies Wilder-Smith, an epidemiology professor, argued in April 2020, "To anyone who tells me that contact tracing is too expensive or not do-able, I just say, rubbish. We are now basically quarantining 68 million people. That is so much more expensive."[39] One overall possibility—pursued with vigor in South Korea, for instance—was quarantining people with the virus rather than everyone. Serious questions have arisen about surveillance, human rights, and control in the pandemic, which we will get to shortly.[40] However, regardless of one's position on novel tracking capabilities, the fact remains that countries such as the United Kingdom and the United States could have mitigated their deadly "first waves" through a better use of existing public health measures and judicious learning from responses elsewhere.

The erratic and disaster-prone laissez-faire strategy was informed by strong elements of self-interest and bolstered by the language of war. COVID-19 was simultaneously "just another flu" and a major enemy requiring stoic sacrifice. We have found that the distortion of the knowledge environment related very strongly to the uneven cost distribution, or our *externalization* mechanism. There was clearly a strong relationship, too, between distortion and the political gaming of the system in the approach of laissez-faire-leaning leaders. Let us look at this a little more.

In India, Sur has argued that a self-consciously embattled Hindu nationalism "morphed into a viral nationalism that ironically derives strength from every crisis, including the pandemic."[41] In the United States and the United Kingdom, Trump and Johnson were able to obtain significant payoffs from policies that contained elements of recklessness, ruthlessness, and even magical thinking.[42] Before the pandemic, Johnson had said, in his usual off-hand way, that the mayor in the movie *Jaws* was his hero; this was a character, let's remember, who wanted to protect tourism and so kept the beaches open despite a hungry shark just off the coast. In September 2020 (when coronavirus infections in the United Kingdom were rising rapidly), Johnson brought this admiration up again, and "allegedly told aides in Downing Street that he would rather let coronavirus 'rip' than impose a second lockdown because of the economic harm further restrictions would cause."[43] But since systems for controlling the spread of the virus or limiting its severity (or indeed supporting people to stay at home if sick) were generally not being put in place, getting back to normal meant a return to the cycle of rising infections and more lockdowns.

Meanwhile, in the United States, as long as the problem could be denied or minimized and the economy "kept strong," Trump could hope that the economy would give him a second term in the White House. The Trump administration (like counterparts elsewhere) was keen to declare "success" against the virus and to "get back to normal" as soon as possible. And "normal," clearly, meant another term in office. In this context, Trump's knowledge-fixing perhaps reached its nadir when he justified the extreme slowness in rolling out testing in the United States with these words: "When you test, you find something is wrong with people. If we didn't do any testing, we would have very few cases."[44] This is a striking example of a leader trying to construct a "hall of mirrors" and create an image of success out of endemic failure.

In general, the laissez-faire tendency rather strongly displays our mechanisms of rigging, export, cascade, and knowledge fixing. And while this was certainly not a war, war language was very often invoked. The war—or nationalist—framing was at times used to legitimize particular policies and to stifle dissent. This was particularly useful when there was a clear need to obscure the *cascade of costs* in the pandemic. In other words, the laissez-faire tendency corresponded quite well to the pattern of wreckonomics, while showing that the "war fix" is not necessary for the other mechanisms to kick in. Yet there is a very important *difference,* too. While the laissez-faire tendency had a certain resilience, it did not quite pass our wreckonomics "test" in the sense of persisting indefinitely. After a delay, lockdowns and partial lockdowns were imposed, and often these were remarkably far-reaching. In the medium and longer term, the political costs of escalating infection and mortality eventually proved substantial both for Trump (who lost the 2020 election) and for Johnson, who was ousted while being widely condemned for not observing lockdown in Downing Street parties. In Brazil, President Jair Bolsonaro was similarly disadvantaged by his flippant approach to the pandemic (though we note that India's Modi is still very much in power). Quite apart from the political costs, the laissez-faire approach also increasingly gave way—with complex local and temporal variations—to a hard lockdown approach. As an understated Oxford detective might say, this brought its own problems.

A People's War? COVID in the Crosshairs

By the time Johnson and Trump were working (or not working) on the details of their erratic pandemic response, Beijing had moved hard against the virus. Displayed in spectacular fashion through silent streets roamed only by workers in hazmat suits, the Communist leadership was launching a "People's War" against COVID-19. Even if other countries did not go as far for nearly as long, "hard" health security involving extensive population controls was to be rolled out to different extents in country after country in the spring of 2020.

We have seen examples of nationalism, laissez-faire, and gaming combining (w)recklessly in supposedly advanced democracies. While the laissez-faire mode tended to involve a fixation on the economy, the hard push for "health security" involved a different kind of fixation—a fixation on the virus itself. Within this framing, the virus was an overriding existential threat that demanded a kind of war. Meanwhile (and linked to this war framing), those highlighting the hidden costs were often framed as dangerous dissidents.

As the early stages of the pandemic unfolded, many politicians, health officials, and media outlets fixated on a single threat—the virus—stressing that it needed to be combated with every means available. Beginning in March 2020, this single-minded focus was typically maintained through government communications and media reporting. Belatedly the United Kingdom itself also got on board, if intermittently, leading to the erratic on-off approach we have touched upon. Media organizations and public health authorities contributed to the fixation. Decontextualized ticker data on COVID-19 cases and fatalities, with no benchmark to other diseases or case fatality rates, failed to give a comprehensive picture of a complicated health crisis. War rhetoric crept into the lockdown approach, not just in China but also in more liberal countries and quarters. When France's president Emmanuel Macron ordered people to stay at home and for borders to close in March 2020, he said simply, "[W]e are at war." The same sentiment was voiced by the UN secretary-general António Guterres: "Our world faces a common enemy. We are at war with a virus."[45] In the United Kingdom, meanwhile, Health Secretary Matt Hancock declared, "[W]e are at war against an invisible killer."[46]

As in other policy spheres we have examined, governments were under pressure to show that they were taking tough measures and were in control of the situation. Whether governments decided to invoke war and nationalism—and not all did—the clarity of lockdown seemed to be *cascading* through international politics, in a way that in some ways echoes our war and security interventions. It became harder to justify why one was *not* locking down along with everyone else. A good wreckonomist should be wary here: whenever there is a chance to press the "big red button" of emergency, the playing field for political gaming expands substantially (and we will see some examples of this in due course). The emergency politics frequently involved the deployment of fear in order to ensure compliance, as eventually became clearer, for instance, in evidence from behind the scenes of the UK approach.[47]

Whatever the political calculations, the *economic* gaming of the crisis was certainly notable. Revealingly, this was happening in *both* the laissez-faire and lockdown stages of the UK approach (as well as in the United States and elsewhere). No one seemed to be keeping tabs. Private businesses with close links to government figures managed to land multimillion-pound contracts for protective equipment, leading to losses to the public purse tallying in the billions.[48] The credentials of these firms were often very dubious.[49] Contractors of personal protective equipment (PPE) included eminently unprepared businesses, including a Miami jewelry designer (receiving £250 million), a pest control company (£109 million), and a T-shirt manufacturer in Turkey that produced only a fraction of the 400,000 gowns ordered (which were then found to be unusable).[50] In a case brought against the government's high-priority access lane for contracts, the High Court found that it "was in breach of the obligation of equal treatment."[51] In a pattern that is again familiar from our wars, the "emergency" frame meant little due diligence on the cynical or downright illegal gaming of the pandemic response. In the United Kingdom, this included the huge sums spent on businesses and jobs hit by stringent lockdowns; while such payments were often a lifeline, the operation ended up facing a write-off of £4.3 billion in fraud.[52]

Naomi Klein, in a rare early reckoning with the instrumentalization of lockdown within Western democracies, argued that for some companies the disease represented a chance to push through technological and organizational changes that they favored in any case. Here was a chance for extensive innovation in security and surveillance technology for companies already invested in our long-running wars and fights. Among them was the data company Palantir, which had already been controversially involved in US migration enforcement. Amid the rush for "health security," Palantir started seeking business across a wide range of sectors in Europe, according to a special investigation that found evidence of data-sharing on European citizens with very few safeguards.[53] Beyond specialized data and surveillance outfits, major corporations used the crisis to insist on high-tech solutions within the spheres of health, education, distribution, and so on, with "Big Tech" companies emerging as big winners—again frequently with a strong surveillance component.[54] This included initiatives such as telecom giants cellphone-tracking whole populations or developing "bossware" for monitoring the home-workers who were proliferating amid lockdown. One early study of technologies of control deployed during the pandemic found that Big Tech companies "have been able to use the crisis as an opportunity for legitimizing their privacy-invasive economic models while forging new partnerships with health authorities—for instance to optimise the resource allocation of medical supplies, strained by dint of budget cuts."[55] From Western business leaders came positive noise about high-tech investments suggesting that only such a course would prevent global dominance by China.[56] Yet in the United Kingdom, there was precious little sign that the huge investments were yielding this hoped-for competitive advantage: when an efficient vaccination program (run by the NHS) eventually arrived, it contrasted with a calamitous £39 billion track-and-trace program (which was outsourced to private contractors and provided the lowest financial compensation for isolation in any OECD country).[57]

Pharmaceutical companies, of course, were among the innovators, and some played a key role in eventually controlling the pandemic via their life-saving vaccines, developed at record speed. Yet the emergency also allowed such companies (with the partial exception of AstraZeneca) to reap huge profits in "captive markets" of confined citizens while negotiating nonliability clauses and special privileges and protections with governments desperate for vaccines.[58] Notably, Big Pharma companies also firmly resisted (together with powerful Western governments) any attempts at loosening patent law despite concerted campaigns to bring vaccines to poorer parts of the world, contributing strongly to pandemic inequities.

Amid the gains, the *costs* were also adding up in the context of lockdown and health security enforcement. Let us start by looking at these in the context of wealthier democracies such as the United Kingdom. Particularly given the extreme difficulty of isolating older people from the rest of society, stringent measures did help to protect millions of the most vulnerable people, especially when vaccines were unavailable. But the costs hit disproportionately. In a parallel with the laissez-faire approach, hard lockdown shifted costs onto relatively powerless groups, generally along the fault lines of class, ethnicity, nationality, age, gender, disability, legal status, and more. Since the unevenness of this cost distribution was usually not recognized (amid a habitual emphasis on the claim that "we are all in this together"), it proved difficult to counteract or compensate for this unevenness.

The ability to work from home depended, unsurprisingly, on the nature of one's work and domestic circumstances (see Figure 15). Class played a major role here, as did generational gaps. The

Figure 15 Herd immunity. Illustration by David Keen.

(libertarian) think tank the Brownstone Institute put the problem this way:

> The initial lockdowns had a strong class-based component. The working classes were assigned the job of delivering groceries, tending to the sick, driving the trucks filled with goods, keeping the lights on, and keeping the fuel running. The professional class, among whom were the people who pushed lockdowns in the name of disease avoidance/suppression, were assigned the job of staying home in their pajamas and staying safe.[59]

The relatively "successful" lockdown of many privileged groups contrasted with major risks elsewhere. Healthcare professionals shouldered huge burdens, but so did others, in different ways. "Essential workers" had to keep commuting, delivering goods, and providing crucial services. Where schools were part of lockdown, the young faced risks to their social and educational development and mental well-being, as has now been amply documented. For small children, the United Kingdom's schools and early learning inspectorate Ofsted found "delays in learning speech and language; problems with social interaction and confidence, such as not knowing how to take turns and struggling to make friends; and delays in walking and crawling, with more obesity as a result."[60] Commenting on a similar situation in Italy, Enzo Colombo reported, "Young people have been the group least listened to and least considered during the pandemic. They have often been seen only as subjects to be controlled to prevent their behaviors . . . from spreading the infection."[61] This neglect was especially severe among families in cramped or otherwise difficult living conditions, compounding the class dimension of the cost distribution. Among adults, this class dimension—itself tied into race/ethnicity, gender, and other vectors of inequality—was prominent. Further, those suffering from diseases other than COVID-19, who saw consultations and operations greatly postponed as medical workers focused on the novel coronavirus, have faced huge costs to their health.[62] Those who bore the costs included—seemingly paradoxically—the elderly in care homes and other institutional settings, where insufficient testing combined with massive restrictions on social interaction with loved ones and even with carers. These restrictions were intended to protect residents yet brought huge costs, with one cross-country report suggesting that neglect was "one of the biggest killers in care homes" during the pandemic.[63]

Putting aside wider welfare questions, let's consider an area that relates directly to our security systems: the policing of the pandemic and its very significant public costs. Around the world, COVID-19 encouraged many governments to relabel dissent as disloyalty, to step up surveillance of the population, and to claim emergency powers that look set significantly to outlast the emergency itself.[64] In states where democratic checks and balances were already limited, law enforcement agencies were able to "game" the crisis for their own ends, whether this involved consolidating institutional power, trialing new modes of intrusive policing, or simply exerting violence and extracting money with impunity, usually from minority groups and the poor. Extensive police violence against suspected lockdown breakers or others transgressing the new rules was reported from South America to East Asia. Mature democracies have seen severe curtailments of free movement and of the right to protest, which was already under threat in many cases. One review of fifty-two emergency orders from thirty-nine countries found about half of all orders included criminal sanctions related to lockdown violations, frequently with "significant latitude to law enforcement in determining individual punishments."[65] To take a pick of the consequences of this punitive approach, Human Rights Watch found deadly police violence and abuse "under cover of the COVID-19 pandemic measures and an anti-drug campaign" in Sri Lanka, shooting and beating citizens venturing to market "even before the daily start of the curfew" in Kenya, and the use of COVID-19 restrictions as a pretext to impose harsher controls on migrants in Greece. Mediterranean states such as Malta also used restrictions as a reason for closing ports to rescued migrants and refugees.[66] In the United Kingdom, reports eventually surfaced showing that enforcement had disproportionately targeted minorities and poorer sections of society.[67]

In China, the "war" on the virus was bringing control of the population to a staggering level. It was clear that the administration was using the crisis as an opportunity to roll out an enormously repressive set of measures aided by advanced surveillance technology. This was combined with Beijing's existing "grid-style management," with neighbors reporting on one another, as well as with other intensified forms of social surveillance, including by employers.[68] Socioeconomically vulnerable groups were hit the hardest, including the millions of rural workers without urban residency rights under China's strict *hukou* system, who suddenly found themselves without income or support.[69] Rigidity worsened the consequences. In one example, a pregnant woman lost her baby when she was denied hospital entry because her COVID-19 test was four hours too old.[70] Prolonged citizen detentions and lockdowns became more erratic and abrupt as the omicron variant gained the upper hand. More so than in a democracy with its checks and balances, here local authorities were frequently second-guessing the leadership in escalating interventions, while extensive "knowledge fixing" was possible with some help from official, journalistic, and popular quiescence.[71] It is quite clear that the increased surveillance, whatever its effects on this virus, will have served important political functions in deterring dissent more generally. Yet eventually, the cycle would break. By late 2022, reports of lockdown-related tragedies were leading to unprecedented protests from Urumqi to Shanghai.[72] Until this late reckoning with the costs of "zero COVID," it had seemed the leadership was managing to keep the virus in its crosshairs in a manner reminiscent of our various wars and fights. As Beijing was now heading from hard lockdown to laissez-faire, it was nevertheless sustaining its tight control of information—notably over the mounting death toll.[73]

Globally, the most serious costs of lockdown and laissez-faire approaches were seen in poorer countries with weaker welfare infrastructure for absorbing the shock. Consider India, where we have already seen how a drastic reopening fueled a huge COVID-19 death toll. Before this phase, Modi's hard and sudden lockdown had wrought its own damage, forcing internal migrants back to their villages, confining slum-dwellers within their often unhealthy dwellings, and cutting the lifeline of welfare support for many poor citizens. Sur wrote of India's initial hard response:

> With India's unplanned lockdown in response to COVID-19 and the brutal ways mobility has come to be policed through beatings and deaths, leaving the city to return to a village even in neighboring states entails days of walking. The lockdown has affected the lives and livelihoods of migrant laborers, who have been stranded without food, shelter, or transport—and who suddenly became visible on TV screens, walking across the country with heavy bags and children.[74]

Of course, lockdown proponents would argue that *not* locking down would have led to an even more staggering death figure from COVID-19 in many countries. Yet lockdown itself led to huge and underrecognized costs, including large-scale fatalities. UNICEF estimated some 239,000 maternal and child deaths in South Asia due to disruptions in healthcare and welfare services—a staggering number in its own right, notwithstanding the country's enormous toll from COVID-19. In research carried out together with the World Bank and UNESCO, the agency further found that there has been a "nearly insurmountable" loss of schooling in poor countries globally amid COVID-19, with up to 70 percent of ten-year-olds in low- and middle-income countries unable to read or understand a simple text, up from 53% prior to COVID-19.[75] These are but pickings of the huge impacts on people's life chances and on mortality from non-COVID causes in a picture that is only gradually becoming clearer. Yet frequently, as reports emerged of these costs, they were framed in prominent media outlets as simply due to COVID-19 itself, rather than due to the response. We have seen in our various wars and fights that it's been common to focus on the problem or threat while failing to reflect adequately on the costs of the intervention itself. The pandemic "war fix" certainly seems to suggest a similar pattern.

In Africa, the consequences of hard COVID-19 responses were acutely felt. While some states took a more holistic approach, many governments were following the lead of the West in locking down.[76] In contexts where most people depend on making a living in the informal economy, severe restrictions on movement frequently had devastating impacts.[77] Though reliable data has frequently been scarce, various careful studies are starting to emerge that focus on the links between economic and epidemiological patterns in the region. In one such study, building on the work of Thandika Mkandawire on informal economies in Africa, Kate Meagher suggested that lower levels of COVID-19 mortality in West African countries accompanied lower levels of lockdown, reflecting in part the lower risk of infection in outdoor market environments. In South Africa, by contrast, severe lockdown accompanied much higher mortality figures, with lockdown restrictions and even social protection schemes sometimes feeding into overcrowding.[78] In many African countries, ordinary people were often very sceptical of the wisdom of fixating on a virus. For instance, when international aid organizations and the South Sudan government urged citizens to make radical behavioral changes in response to the pandemic, many people protested that they were actually facing *multiple* crises, including conflict, malnutrition, unemployment, and a range of potentially fatal diseases. They stressed the importance of balancing the response to the virus against other crises that often seemed more real and more pressing. Many of those pushing a strict response were seen as trying to protect richer countries rather than promoting local welfare in a holistic way. The perceived bias helped undermine trust in public health in South Sudan, one study found.[79] More widely, vaccinations and protections against other diseases posing large risks to African populations (including malaria and tuberculosis) have been hampered across many countries in the region. The tally of costs, as elsewhere in the "war on the virus," remains shockingly incomplete, and a clearer picture is only gradually emerging.

Fixation Squared: The Virus Goes Viral

We have noted that the two policy poles of "laissez-faire" and "lockdown" shared some similar shortcomings, notably a damaging downplaying of major costs associated with the favored position. Also striking is the very skewed distribution of costs (and benefits) in both cases, with various vulnerable groups bearing the brunt. Whether in laissez-faire or lockdown mode, many of these costs disappeared from official radar screens—with war rhetoric significantly facilitating this process. A broad-based systemic analysis that puts the full costs *on* the radar screen has been all too rare since the pandemic began, notwithstanding a common insistence to be "following the science." This reflects the highly politicized way in which health policy has been conducted and debated. As the pandemic progressed, it became increasingly evident that there was not just a war on the virus on the one hand and viral nationalism on the other, but also a "war of words" that was brewing between "the two sides." This frequently took the form of a "health versus economy" binary, with one camp focusing on "fighting the virus" (and often wary of "business interests"), while the other camp emphasized the need to "soldier on" so as to keep the economy going.

On top of the fixations within each (contrasting) strand of the response, then, there was a kind of metafixation of the debate into two fixed positions. In particular, the fixing of the debate into "your money or your life" dangerously oversimplified matters and led to some very damaging exclusions. In the course of this battle, important health conditions and vulnerabilities were set aside, as were important human rights. The possibility of assisting the economy through effective track-and-trace or support measures also tended to be marginalized. Further, the battle brought damaging political consequences, opening rifts in the heart of already fragile democracies.

The binary reflected, to a large degree, important underlying political tensions and schisms. In many respects, it was thus incorporated into the "culture wars." Many of the issues we have covered in this book, from migration to the policing of drugs and crime, are central arenas in these "wars"—certainly in the US context but also elsewhere. With COVID-19, preexisting battles were in effect finding more fuel through the fixation of the debate around laissez-faire and lockdown poles. On the face of it, this standoff seems to allow for dissent and disagreement. Yet insofar as it *was* a debate, this "war of words" showed the limitations of the common idea that "both sides" need to be heard on any major issue. Just as debates on migration are not helpfully reduced to "put up a wall" versus "open borders," and just as debates on drugs are not helpfully reduced to crackdowns versus legalization with no safety nets, so too the binary debate on COVID-19 tended to constrain thought, debate, and policy options.[80] Within both the "health" and the "economy" framings for pandemic response, there seemed to be relatively little room for a more broadly conceived approach that tried to consider *all important aspects* of public health and public well-being, including a concern for human rights and a practical and workable concern for the most vulnerable.

We saw the intersection of COVID-19 and culture wars when academic criticism of lockdowns started to emerge. The British historian Toby Green had in 2021 been one of the few academic voices criticizing what he called the "covid consensus" while highlighting lockdown's devastating impact in many countries around the world. One can take issue with his arguments. But responses to Green illustrated the danger of dismissing important critiques as the work of "the other side": one article in the *Guardian* accused Green of siding with the right and went so far as to call his work historical revisionism and "a travesty of the facts."[81]

Another example of the escalating COVID-19 battle concerned the "anti-vaxxers." Many doctors were understandably furious as hospitals filled up disproportionately with patients who had refused a vaccination. Yet the accompanying politics was soon becoming infused with shaming and blaming in a way that took it far from traditional public health approaches. In many countries, vaccine hesitancy was said to require mandates, with people losing jobs or their ability to interact with others if they did not agree to injections. In France, President Macron went so far as to say that those refusing to be vaccinated were not actually citizens.[82] Particularly when we remember that Macron had been among the most explicit in declaring war on the virus, his outburst illustrates a danger that runs through all our wars and fights: namely, that a war on *something* tends rather quickly to become a war on *someone*. Of course, it did not come down to an actual war. But in many countries, "responsible" citizens were separated from "irresponsible" ones, whether through speech or through physically excluding the unvaccinated from venues and activities. The term "anti-vaxxer" itself saw substantial inflation over time—encompassing, in many cases, those who were objecting to vaccine *mandates* rather than to the vaccines themselves. There were important class dimensions to such divides, and frequently ethnic and religious ones as well. In an example of class-related tensions, Canadian politicians denounced truckers who were protesting mandates that were hitting their line of work.[83]

The "war on COVID" had a righteous air that could quickly turn to aggression and the pushback could be aggressive too. Indeed, each "side" tended to become more self-righteous as the crisis unfolded. This fundamentally included those who railed against restrictions, some of whom were hardening their stance to extreme extents. Some protesters were actively drawing on antisemitic conspiracy theories, while others—including among the Canadian truckers—went so far as to deploy Confederate and even Nazi imagery.[84] Meanwhile, Trump supporters in the United States actively invoked a war framing as they chanted "Live free or die."[85]

One could delve further into the disturbing politics of the far right in relation to the pandemic. But let us return to the meta-fixation with which we are concerned here. Seen as a *system,* the binary politics of COVID-19 was going into overdrive through mutually reinforced differentiation, deepening divides while impeding genuine and open debate. In this context, expert voices emphasizing a holistic approach to public health (so as to include other diseases and risks to livelihoods and mental health) were sometimes attacked as "COVID deniers," "let-it-rip" advocates, or "COVID minimalists," while finding themselves excluded or "shadow-banned" from social media. Conversely, many of the public health experts advocating for a robust epidemiological approach were targeted by abuse and attacks.[86] One Cambridge University study, while suggesting that there was a waning of support for populist leaders during the pandemic, drew attention to a "disturbing erosion of support for core democratic beliefs and principles."[87] The way in which the pandemic debate became "fixed" and rather restricted seems to resonate with that conclusion.

By the later stages of the pandemic, it was becoming clear that the fixation of the debate around the rigid binary of prioritizing health or prioritizing the economy had contributed greatly to the invisibilization of the wider, less easily quantifiable costs of lockdown responses in particular. In the United Kingdom, where the binary was

particularly prominent, media reports voicing critique of the lockdowns often focused on impacts on businesses rather than focusing
on the wider social and psychological costs of lockdown. The space
for expressing alternative or dissenting opinions, while not closed, was
being seriously curtailed.

Public Health and "War"

Can we learn lessons from COVID-19 in relation to wreckonomics
more widely? One limiting factor is that pandemic intervention was
in some important ways a different beast from our other wars and
fights. A major difference was the magnitude of the underlying threat.
The 15 million excess deaths (all-cause mortality) cataloged by the
World Health Organization during the pandemic makes a terrible
tally.[88] A second major difference was that the interventions, as noted,
did not involve a human adversary in the strict sense, which meant
they were subject to quite different cascading dynamics. Relatedly,
there is no vaccine against high-risk migration or drug-taking (despite
some attempts by government campaigns to gloss their work in such
terms).[89] The nonhuman "enemy" and the advent of vaccines help to
explain another difference that we mentioned at the outset: the fact
that COVID-19 interventions failed our "longevity test." While they
"self-perpetuated" at certain points, such as in China's zero-COVID
phase, and while aspects of the response are likely to remain for years
to come, COVID-19 interventions did eventually melt away.

That said, there are also similarities with our various wars and fights
against terror, migration, crime, or drugs. In particular, the "war on
COVID" drew on a "martial script" for dealing with disease that persists despite having repeatedly been found wanting, as Alex de Waal
reminds us in his important book on "two hundred years of war on
disease and its alternatives."[90] As in our other wars and fights, we often
saw remarkable political consensus develop around the "war fix," with
left and right frequently united in commitment to lockdown. As in

those cases, what tended to disappear from view were the huge costs that hard lockdown and similar measures entailed—and not just in monetary terms. In poorer and less democratic countries, costs were still more pronounced. When the laissez-faire mode saw war conceptualized as demanding a strong "herd" and sacrifices from "front-line" workers, this also encouraged and legitimized an extremely uneven distribution of costs (and of gains). In both laissez-faire and lockdown modes, moreover, we saw the "fixing" of the knowledge environment to suit the given policy, a phenomenon evident most starkly in China's about-face but also in countries such as the United Kingdom.

So where does this leave us in terms of evaluating COVID-19 responses—or in reconsidering our other interventions? The difficulty with the critiques of both lockdown and laissez-faire stems, in part, from the problem with counterfactuals. This is also the case, to a large extent, with our other wars and fights. With COVID-19, certainly, the stakes were extraordinarily high. Wherever we land individually in our assessment, there were genuine dilemmas and trade-offs for politicians and public health officials when faced with a large and fast-evolving threat. In some ways, our criticism of both major modes—a plague on both your houses?—may look too easy. But the case of COVID-19 illustrates rather well that wreckonomics does not necessarily tell us which political approach to take on a given problem. Rather, our framework points to the grave dangers that stem from suppressing debate on the true costs of any given intervention, and it calls correspondingly for the fullest possible assessment of the costs and benefits of each approach in the round. Whether the intervention is "worth it" will remain up to politicians—and, fundamentally, to their electorates.

In this context, our framework can help us to understand two approaches that were in many ways diametrically opposed. Within both poles of the pandemic response, there was a strong element of *fixation*: fixation on the economy for fans of "let it rip" and fixation on health (or rather *a particular aspect* of health) for proponents of hard lockdown. Importantly, both sets of fixations evolved in the context of public health systems that were not properly equipped to deal with the virus (including an inability, particularly in the early stages of the pandemic, to find out exactly who had it). That underlying weakness could feed into a kind of "herd immunity" fatalism; it could also feed into the quite drastic conclusion that everyone had to be kept at home.

COVID-19 shows, too, how fixations are not set in stone. Influenced by changes in the distribution of cost and benefits—and by changes in the way these are discussed and perceived—interventions can change quite swiftly (a point that Foucault also emphasized).[91] Sometimes this change illustrates how failure cannot *always* be harnessed to success, as we saw when Trump was defeated in November 2020 in large part because of his incompetent handling of COVID-19. But even when things change, there may still be windfalls from failure, as when Shanghai's hardline leader was promoted to Chinese premier in 2022 despite overseeing damaging and botched lockdowns in the megacity.[92]

We have seen that the language of war was often invoked in the pandemic response. A key point is that in both "laissez-faire" and "lockdown" modes, a war framing seemed to serve a function in legitimizing high costs that would otherwise have been unacceptable. Yet we found that the laissez-faire mode was also a kind of anti-intervention, a strong denial of threat that separates it rather sharply from our other interventions. War rhetoric was more overt in hard-lockdown mode—most obviously in the idea that we were now collectively "at war" with the virus itself. We have already seen (for example, in the discussion of interventions in the drug trade and in border control) that the language of war may be imported into situations that are not wars or not exactly wars, and we've noted that this move may add an extra layer of legitimacy and energy to the intervention—not least by making dissent more difficult.

Legitimizing a particular policy choice in the face of a crisis, and legitimizing a very particular distribution of costs that comes with that choice, does not always depend on invoking a "war"; there are other ways of doing this. One of these, familiar from the field of humanitarian aid, is to portray needs in such a way that they match the favored response—for example, through talking about those humanitarian-disaster victims who are "needy and reachable."[93] Another is to present the situation as a case of "letting nature run its course," as we saw with laissez-faire. Yet another strategy is to dismiss or stigmatize those who are being made to bear the greatest costs or those who speak up on their behalf. With COVID-19, there were references to those deemed "unhealthy" or "about to die anyway" (in "let it rip" mode) or to "just kids," "hedonistic teenagers," "super-spreaders," and "conspiracy theorists" (in lockdown mode).

There are both positive and negative takeaways to be had from the pandemic in relation to wreckonomics, war, and wider societal challenges. Above all, perhaps, the COVID-19 crisis—as crises tend to do—brutally revealed the underlying cracks in social and public health systems, leading to calls for a genuinely different politics of renewing and even reinventing the public good. It also eventually opened up spaces for acknowledging the trade-offs involved in handling a virulent new disease. Again, and to return to the framing of the COVID "wars," setting up the debate as "saving lives" versus "saving the economy" left out the vast realms that lie between epidemiology and economics, including the social and wider health costs of getting fixated on either of these two simplified poles. A more determined effort to put resources into public health over a long period would have removed or at least reduced the incentives for such radical approaches. For instance, the United Kingdom had the second-fewest hospital beds per capita in Europe, while the proportion of intensive care units before the crisis was also among the lowest.[94] If robust health systems had been in place and if there had been confidence in the ability of the NHS to cope with a "winter surge," then the early attractions of "herd immunity" would also have been less. Italy's Lombardy—whose soaring death toll made it resemble a "conflict zone" with war-style triaging of care—had helped trigger lockdowns across Europe, with warning bells ringing especially loudly as the region's healthcare was supposed to be excellent. Yet reckonings with the fallout have suggested that a highly fragmented and privatized healthcare system "contributed to making Italy more vulnerable and unprepared to tackle the COVID-19 pandemic."[95]

Behind the vulnerability of healthcare systems was the lack of resilient welfare systems. The United States was a stark case. As Ed Yong noted in *The Atlantic*, "The decades-long process of shredding the nation's social safety net forced millions of essential workers in low-paying jobs to risk their life for their livelihood."[96] Lack of paid sick leave was another huge problem in the dwindling welfare nets of the United States and the United Kingdom alike.[97] One behavioral scientist working on the UK Scientific Advisory Group on Emergencies drew comparisons to how individuals were being blamed for collective failures on the climate, with the "government blaming the public for breaking lockdown or not self-isolating when infected, when the real problem was the lack of government support to allow them to do so."[98] Revealingly, the British public was repeatedly asked to stay at home to "protect the NHS." Yet one would naturally assume (and a public health approach would urge) that a national health service will *protect the population*—and be supported over a long period so that it is able to do so.

★★★

We are left with one simple and one complex conclusion. The simple one is that framing public health as a "war" of sorts is not a very good idea, whether it's in the context of laissez-faire, lockdown, or the locking of horns between the two. The fixation of the terms of debate and its attendant definition of enemies—from the virus itself to migrants, foreigners, students, or critics of those who are waging a heroic "war"—was distracting from the urgent need to improve public health systems, economic safety nets, and social protection. Also distracting from this task were nationalist invocations of stoic British traditions, American liberty, or Indian strength. In Italy, Enzo Colombo noted that "the language of war rather than the language of care" was becoming predominant, with the virus quickly emerging as "an enemy to be defeated." Cautioning against the erosion of public trust in a climate of increasing surveillance, he continued, "Rather than informing citizens, making them aware of the risks and responsible for their actions, the discourse on the COVID-19 threat and the war against the virus has often resulted in a paternalistic and police state attitude."[99] The rhetoric of fear and emergency, Colombo and others remarked, was eroding trust and faith in the individual citizen.[100] Managing a fast-moving pandemic was not easy, but whether we were being told some version of "Nature will take its course" or "Don't be naughty," the message was oddly and rather consistently disempowering; at times, it verged on infantilization.[101]

Our "simple" conclusion has perhaps become a little more complex than we thought. But we still have our more "complex" conclusion to relate. What we find here is that both responses were fundamentally *antisystemic*. There was a failure to understand that "in a system one cannot do just one thing," as Robert Jervis reminds us.[102] Each course of action (or inaction) was setting off a cascade, which should have been, if not predicted in any degree of detail, at the very least acknowledged and mitigated by acting more fully on various vectors at the same time. Of course, states with sufficient resources and welfare nets did put in place protections such as the United Kingdom's furlough scheme of off-work pay, alleviating a great deal of hardship. Yet the fixation on objectives, together with the "fixation squared" of the polarized debate, made it very hard to discuss, let alone account for, the trade-offs in a genuinely systemic manner, whether in the United Kingdom or elsewhere.

Signs of change are sprouting amid the wreckage. As countries came out of COVID-19 restrictions, there were encouraging signs that debate and dissent were eventually being reinvigorated. It was also clear that a public reckoning was actively contributing to "systemic reflection" on aspects of the response, including school closures and the need to address the underlying inequalities and crumbling public infrastructures that had contributed to the pandemic's huge and unequal impacts. More generally, COVID-19 is also important for us in showing how even the most "fixed" of debates can eventually come unfixed, to great public benefit. The gradual widening of the public debate allowed many people to recognize the problems that ensue when our "wreckanisms" have been pushed too far—that is, when the fixation on simple renditions of complex problems starts to show obvious cracks. An early example came when the fixation on the economy and laissez-faire looked set to generate huge mortality along with collapsing health services. As awareness of these (mostly impending) costs grew, it led to strong pushback. Throughout the pandemic, the "fight" against the threat of COVID-19 generated major gaming opportunities for vested interests, and these eventually began to come to light. Meanwhile, the *costs* of the interventions were increasingly visible. In this, there is one final and rather crucial difference with our other wars: while the export of costs on to the poor, vulnerable, and powerless groups is a shared feature of them all, in COVID-19 the magnitude of costs accumulated was such that it could no longer easily be "knowledge-fixed." A lot of this had to do with the fact that, unlike in our other wars, *externalizing* costs "extra-territorially" was largely impossible. Amid this dawning awareness of costs, there was the beginning of an awareness, too, that crackdowns on dissent were damagingly silencing the exchange of views among scientists and citizens.

Even if all the lessons of COVID-19 cannot be incorporated into our war and security systems, there are still rays of hope here. Insofar as wreckonomics is a runaway system, it also has some built-in brakes. As citizens, it's in our power to use these brakes. How to start *deploying* the brakes more effectively in our wars and fights is what we will look at next.

9

How to End the War on Everything (In Four Complex Steps)

The many "wars" and "fights" that we have discussed in this book have generally been characterized by damaging and counterproductive policies. Self-reinforcing war and security systems have been fueling the problems that they feed off—a key mechanism by which failure becomes a peculiar kind of "success." Yet this is not all. As political systems analysts, we may also see such systems as particular *ecologies* that get progressively more complex over time. As they have grown in scope and as the number of games played within them has increased, these various systems have exhibited remarkable adaptability. The Cold War machinery adapted over time to the global war on terror and now, amid the resurgence of geopolitical conflict, is in the process of adapting yet again. The war on terror itself has mutated over time, with elements proliferating across borders from Narendra Modi's India to rising crackdowns against "ecoterrorists" in many countries and even to US Democrats' rhetoric around "domestic terrorism." Border security, counterterror, and drug wars have all interacted with and reinforced one another. Frequently, actors "at the top" of a given system of intervention have switched—for example, the Russians step into the breach vacated by the French in Mali—while the system itself has persisted in some shape or form. In this process, our war and security systems have developed increasing diversity and complexity, as we have seen in the manifold collaborations with aid groups, companies, academia, and other ancillary sectors. All of this has rendered our systems resilient.

While this makes them extremely hard to dismantle, we have offered some tools for understanding why they have proven so persistent and resilient. In terms of our five "wreckanisms," we have found that the **war fix** essentially transforms a complex, systemic issue or problem into an oversimplified threat that is then met with an oversimplified solution. Within such a framing, wider considerations—notably, the causes and the complex nature of the problem, and the problematic and often counterproductive nature of the intervention—tend to get sidelined. In highlighting the **rigging** or fixing of the game, we suggest that the aim of defeating the enemy or eliminating the relevant threat cohabits with other games that often interfere with the ostensibly overriding objective of "winning." In a form of the "double game," covert winners have frequently undermined their own loudly expressed cooperation for self-interested ends. In **exporting**, the costs of floundering interventions have tended to be perversely distributed in ways that minimize negative impacts on the "winners," again helping to explain why our various destructive "wars" and "fights" persist despite the damage they inflict. In a process of **cascading**, reactions from targets (migrants, smugglers, insurgents, or a wider population) have tended to escalate and complicate the underlying problem or "threat," while the failing responses have tended to proliferate on the back of this failure. Moreover, these various failing "wars" and "fights" have cascaded into complex overlapping crises by fueling one another. Finally, we have suggested that the **knowledge fix** has involved distorting the knowledge environment around the relevant threat and the proposed or implemented "solution." Indeed, this environment has been shaped in ways that have tended to inflate the threat and to obscure the failure to address it, while responsibility for this failure has been outsourced and spaces for dissent constrained.

Now we've discerned a rather dangerous systemic pattern. But as Marx would have told us, interpreting the world is one thing; the point is to change it.

In many popular academic books, there is a tendency to present a diagnosis and follow this with a list of recommendations that the world is somehow supposed to embrace. We are reluctant to follow in these optimistic footsteps. Indeed, the idea that there is one "fix" for a given problem is precisely what we are criticizing! It's nevertheless important to think about remedies. We need to do the opposite of the instigators of our wars and fights and make sure that *learning* is at the heart of the response and the fightback against destructive wars and fights. Part of what drew us to our comparative political systems analysis in the first place was the hope that by thinking across a variety of crises and interventions, we could learn some fundamental lessons about how to start dismantling the wreckage. Here we propose four broad "wreckommendations."

First, *foment dissent and dialogue.* "Fixation" on a threat has tended to quash dissent and has made it exceedingly hard for instigators to change course. As we saw with our COVID-19 account and in elements of our other wars, opening space for dissent and dialogue is a fundamental first step toward mitigating or reversing problematic interventions.

Second, *require proper cost and benefit analyses.* We have seen how the "hall of mirrors" has tended to twist and distort public and political understanding of the real costs and consequences of our wars and fights. Instead of such distortions, we need proper diagnoses of the functions of failing interventions. This involves producing a genuine *systemic* analysis of costs and benefits as well as of how these are distributed.

Third, *build coalitions against complicity.* Broad and reformist coalitions can be built—and indeed *are* being built—around a shared recognition of these (often hidden) costs and benefits. Building such coalitions involves analyzing and to some extent reverse-engineering the process that has drawn so many actors into our wars and security systems. It also involves active listening and finding friends in unexpected places.

Fourth, *unfix the problem*. Our war and security systems are all characterized by a very simplistic understanding of the threat they are ostensibly addressing. Here we need more focus on causes and less on symptoms. This "unfixing" of the problem must happen in parallel with proper accounting for how the "solution" is framing and frequently feeding the problem.

These steps are all tied up with our mechanism of the knowledge fix. Perhaps this is a natural bias for academics, but we do believe that positive change is possible only if there is a far-reaching improvement to the knowledge environment. An "unfixing" of this environment is moreover relatively feasible, if not exactly easy. It can in turn significantly contribute to an unfixing of the gains and costs—and of the problem itself. In this way, our analytical tools for understanding destructive systems may also become wrenches in the works, contributing to more humane and rational policies and interventions.

Foment Dissent and Dialogue: Opening Up the Information Environment

It is common to hear, when critics raise their voice against the abuse of migrants or drug users, that any right-thinking individual who believes in "defending our borders and way of life" could not countenance a different approach to the current (abuse-generating) one. Worryingly, a similar pattern was present during COVID-19, as we saw in the previous chapter—with supporters of rival approaches painting themselves as the real defenders of fundamental societal values, while opponents were assigned to a "deplorable" moral position. We have seen how one key quality of our various "wars" and "fights" is that they typically involve a sense of existential threat and a (related) sense of self-righteousness. Winning becomes imperative for survival, and the cause is portrayed as a just one. Yet these very qualities have routinely invited a kind of systematic failure. Fixation and its associated righteousness tend strongly to discourage self-reflection and a change of course. Furthermore, they tend damagingly to facilitate the suppression of disagreement.

A key problem here is that two of our "wreckanisms" are in effect joined at the hip, with the war fix fueling the knowledge fix and vice versa. Once we have a blinkered and simplistic view of the problem, it may become easy to convince an audience that it's the nail that matches one's hammer. This tends to make war seem not only inevitable but also the only option that any rational and right-thinking person would countenance. In this context, dissent may be painted not only as disloyal but as divisive and even (at the extreme) as "treasonous." We find that abusive war and security systems have tended to be reinforced when the category of the enemy is expanded so as to include critics of these abusive systems.[1] Truth may not only be the first casualty of war but also of interventions that are *not* in any ordinary sense a "war" while nevertheless being presented as part of a struggle for survival. Yet if failing or flawed interventions are to be corrected, they need to be critiqued. It is crucial that dissent from the officially approved path is not discouraged or actively punished. Indeed, we cannot envisage any change without such spaces of dissent. Crackdowns on "dangerous" views have tended to lead to the kind of pattern we have seen in our wars and fights, in that they haven't quashed these views but rather pushed them to other sites in a version of the balloon effect. If alternative views can be encouraged and debated rather than suppressed, we can move toward a less brittle information or knowledge environment. And as this informational "ecology" grows more complex and resilient, new solutions can begin to emerge.

Dissent is all well and fine, you may say, but what if no one is listening? This is where the importance of **dialogue** becomes very clear. In a polarized environment, dissent can quite easily spill over into intolerance—and stigmatizing those who hold unpopular views can often reinforce divisions, with disagreement escalating into denunciation. In these circumstances, conflict may be ignited rather than resolved. Polarization has been promoted by social media, where algorithms encourage opponents to lock horns and escalate their shaming rhetoric to admiring followers.[2] Polarization in the political systems of many countries, notably in the United States, has added further kindling. So have our wars. The with-us-or-against-us rhetoric became a fundamental feature of the Afghan and Iraq invasions; in the fight against migration, opponents of hard security at the borders have often been framed as advocates for mass migration across "open borders"; in the war on drugs, opponents were portrayed as hippies and stoners and decadents. Sometimes opponents of these wars have countenanced no opposition to their own struggle (or "war") against the war. This can lead to a different kind of blindness to negative consequences. One example might be California's drastic relaxation of drug policy that, while an understandable reaction to the "war," has been accused of ignoring consequences in terms of homelessness and crime.[3] Another might be the "defund the police" campaign that, despite its important calls for confronting racism and rethinking increasingly militarized policing, has shown frequent obliviousness to local calls for *better* policing, including from minorities in crime-affected neighborhoods.[4] A third example, as we have seen, would be how a similarly valid concern with addressing damaging false rumors and conspiracies during COVID-19 led to sometimes heavy-handed campaigns against "misinformation" affecting the ability to express dissenting views.

Increasingly, then, we may detect a "with us or against us" impulse forcing the debate into a binary—which is especially problematic when both ends of the binary lead down a route that is costly to the wider public good. In pandemic politics, we saw how the "economy versus health" framing was unhelpful to good-faith advocates on any side of the argument. It prevented us from seeing that the economy might be better served by a concerted attempt to get on top of the virus while it also stifled debate on how supporting health and well-being involves much more than simply confronting a virus.

De-escalation is a priority. As some securitization scholars have reminded us, this crucially involves ensuring that our heavily securitized
wars and fights are taken back into the ordinary arena of political debate and deliberation, from where they have to a large extent been
excised.[5] We mentioned that an important part of our methodology is
listening to the pattern, and *listening* is indeed key here. Only by "allowing in" the opponent's view can we hope to get beyond the standoff and escalation that tend to characterize both our actual wars and
fights and the public debate around them. That includes, of course,
listening to those who fiercely advocate for the interventions we have
criticized in this book! Where progress has been made toward another approach, it has come from an active search for friends rather
than enemies—including *especially* among those who could easily be
dismissed as part of the "enemy" category. We will return to this later.

If coalition building is crucial in our civilian-led interventions, it is
even more so when it comes to actual war. In the context of the war
on terror, we have already mentioned the remarkable work done by
the small NGO Saferworld in rigorously investigating the prospects
for war and peace worldwide. Saferworld rightly stresses that militarily
engaging the enemy is no substitute for tackling the corrupt and undemocratic systems that help to produce the enemy. In Saferworld's
global report on armed conflict involving proscribed groups or insurgents, the authors Larry Attree and Jordan Street suggest that such
groups are sometimes "more reconcilable than has been assumed."[6]
Of course, we should note that proscribed groups such as al-Shabaab
and the Taliban do a pretty good job of vilifying *themselves*. But the
report is surely correct to critique the obsession with waging war on
these groups and to highlight the extreme difficulty, perhaps even the
impossibility, of winning such contests. There are many wars in which
violence has tended to reproduce the problem while also helping
the enemy to gain support, notably when external support for counterinsurgency reinforces the corruption and repression of the state.
Attree and Street stress the need to "resist political and media pressure
to make attacking proscribed groups a priority, and avoid thinking

about conflicts with proscribed groups as something you can 'win.'"[7] Getting to some kind of political settlement will always be key, and the authors state, "Prioritising violent counter-terror approaches too often sidelines or hampers political dialogue and conflict resolution— not only with proscribed groups but also between other parties."[8]

It's not just NGOs making these points. When Ruben met officials from the African Union's Peace Support Operations Division, they were sharply critical of the fixation with defeating al-Shabaab rebels in Somalia. Sivuyile Bam, head of the division, said, "Al-Shabaab is not going to be resolved through a military-only option. The military can only hold and create space for negotiations." Bam continued by setting out the rules that the international community was largely failing to follow:

> First, you don't negotiate with your friend, you negotiate with your enemy. As unpalatable as your enemy is, he is part of the solution. Second, you must try by all means not to have a "winner takes all" attitude.... And thirdly, if possible try [to negotiate] without preconditions. The Somalis have to find each other, they have to start to talk to each other, and the more they talk, the less there's a specter of violence.

The "war fix" starts coming undone once we consciously open up the information and knowledge environment to dissent while consciously seeking out spaces of dialogue within this more open environment. Yet openness is not sufficient: rigor is also required. This takes us to our next "wreckommendation."

Make Externalities Count: Toward a Proper Cost-Benefit Analysis

Ideally, civil servants engage in a more or less continuous assessment of the costs and benefits of any intervention. Yet it remains striking how seldom our taxpayer-funded wars and fights are put through anything resembling a rigorous cost-benefit analysis. A first step forward would be to ensure that the typical policy cycle of formulation,

Figure 16 An idealized depiction of the policy cycle.

implementation, and evaluation is actually put into practice (see Figure 16).

However, it is not enough just to look at whether "value for money" has been achieved on some specific metric. We also need a wider kind of evaluation. Existing analyses rarely tell us enough about how benefits are *distributed* within a population.[9]

This is an intensely political question that habitually disappears from view. Crucially, a proper cost-benefit analysis must also entail a full accounting of costs. This means going beyond monetary costs to look at social costs. And it means looking at the distribution of these social costs. On whom do the costs of a particular policy fall? Who suffers, and who doesn't? Glossing over or, worse, ignoring different kinds of costs and benefits—and, crucially, their distribution—has routinely helped to sustain damaging policies rather than challenging them.

Thanks to the knowledge-fixing and distortion underlying our various wars and fights, politicians have often been able to exclude the negative effects of fighting terror, migration, crime, or drugs from the "balance sheet" (insofar as there is one). Negative effects are treated as "externalities," or as indirect costs. Success has often been defined as the number of enemies eliminated (as in the Vietnam War), some-times by invoking multiple and shifting goals (as in Afghanistan), and sometimes by using failure to underline the need for more security and more aggression (as when the defeat and then sacking of Saddam Hussein's army fed the rise of al Qaeda in Iraq and then ISIS). Often, moreover, politicians have been able to hide under the banner of "measurement"—anything that cannot easily be turned into a metric on a short timeframe is in danger of being left out of the equation, as we saw with COVID-19, as well as in our more violent wars. Assessments that have a narrow focus or a limited timeframe tend to obscure the full costs and consequences of interventions.

The distribution of costs and benefits—along with the misrepresen-tation of this distribution—goes a very long way toward explaining the persistence of ineffective and counterproductive policies. We have emphasized that conceptualizing a given intervention as a "war" or a "fight" makes it much more difficult to get a proper public account of this distribution. If you are in charge of a "war," you generally want it to be understood that "we are all in this together." You do not wel-come the news—particularly if it is public and prominent and particu-larly if you are one of the beneficiaries—that some are profiting and escaping the costs while others have costs loaded disproportionately upon them. This is where dissent is crucial: it helps unfix the discussion of costs and benefits by bringing different definitions and priorities into play. Encouragingly, we have seen how ordinary people have tried to put hidden costs and benefits on the map in all our interventions.

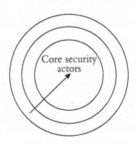

Figure 17 The centripetal mobilization around security.

Regarding costs, examples are plentiful: coca farmers protesting crop eradication, border communities complaining about the government's role in "migration crises" on their doorstep, migrant families taking governments to task over the death and suffering of their loved ones.

Part of moving toward a proper understanding of the appeal and longevity of a particular policy intervention is getting a better grip on the *gaming* of it. Who is manipulating or hijacking the intervention, and for what purposes? Do they have an interest in tackling the problem that is ostensibly being addressed? Do they have other priorities that take precedence? And, again, do they perhaps stand to benefit from a *failure* to address these underlying problems?

In the political systems analysis of *Wreckonomics*, we have identified a fairly consistent pattern. Many of the benefits have accrued within powerful institutions in instigating states, and some have percolated outward to a variety of state and nonstate actors. This includes poorer countries that claim to be cooperating in these various wars, as well as such ancillary groups as development, humanitarian, and international organizations, as we saw briefly in chapters 5 and 7. Through the vested interests that are nurtured in this process, a large range of actors has been drawn into the instigators' securitized framing of the problem. This can be depicted as a *centripetal* movement pulling peripheral and ancillary actors toward the core of the security system, thereby strengthening it (see Figure 17). Meanwhile, costs and risks have routinely been dispersed *centrifugally*—that is, away from the core security actors (Figure 18).[10] Risk has been transferred from

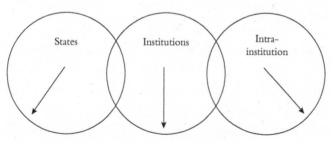

Figure 18 The centrifugal dispersal of costs and risks.

instigators to states that offer some kind of "partnership." Costs have trickled downward, away from headquarters to front-line officers dealing with the chaos, with these front-line responders increasingly themselves being from poorer "partner" (or "buffer") states. Costs have also dispersed toward humanitarian-oriented actors such as state welfare providers, NGOs, and UN agencies, which are left trying to ameliorate the consequences of these various wars. Finally, and most important, the immense *human* costs have been perversely distributed to ordinary people caught up in these "fights."

Mapping the distribution of costs and benefits is crucial for understanding why a given intervention persists despite not meeting its stated goals. But such an understanding has routinely fallen victim to the constraints on debate that we have identified—and sometimes to outright intimidation directed toward dissenters. Here a central question is who has the right to speak what counts as the truth. In practice, bureaucracies often have relatively narrow goals and become fixated on very particular targets. This is a process that tends to have important hidden costs. Highlighting these costs may be controversial (and indeed, for the whistleblowers or dissident workers concerned, costly). Highlighting hidden benefits may be similarly fraught with danger. An extreme case of a disaster where highlighting hidden costs ands benefits was risky is Mao's Great Leap Forward in China; a somewhat less extreme one is the same country's zero-COVID policy some sixty years later. In democracies, simply ignoring unwelcome evidence and voices is usually more effective than outright suppression. Yet the "emergency" mode of all our wars and fights greatly facilitates the full spectrum of knowledge-fixing. A holistic cost-benefit analysis can help to insure against this danger.

In any policy presented as being of supreme importance due to the urgency of the threat in question, public mapping of the full cost-benefit distribution should be mandatory. If this were to happen, the business of extracting success from failure would become much more difficult. This means resisting attempts by relatively powerful groups to shape the policy agenda—for example, by determining what can and cannot be discussed internally or publicly, or (more drastically) by framing dissent as disloyalty.[11] This takes us to our next point: strength in numbers.

Coalitions against Complicity: Or How to Turn the System against Itself

The fixation on a single and simplified threat has tended to generate a very large number of "games" that may run counter to the original stated purpose of the system. While holistic cost-benefit analyses will bring these games and their externalities into the open, such analyses may miss many of the *systemic* gains from the intervention. We noted above that our wars and fights have gained remarkable diversity and resilience through pulling a wide range of actors into a security framing. To break this pattern, it is not enough for dissidents to voice their views or for civil servants to concoct better evaluations. Broad coalitions for change must be built. This can be done, in part, by being good "wreckonomists" and using the system against itself.

There is a positive feedback loop between fuller public assessments of the skewed distribution of costs and benefits, on the one hand, and the building of broad coalitions for change, on the other. With irregular migration, we have seen how costs (and risks) have been pushed outward toward less powerful actors: from European capitals to border communities; from policing headquarters to Mediterranean and African "front lines"; from interior to health and social ministries; from border guards to humanitarians and, of course, to migrants themselves. Complicity has grown here, as in our other interventions—and part of the mechanism has been a kind of *compensation* for taking on costs and risks. From an evaluation standpoint, the key task is to identify these costs and risks. From a mobilization standpoint, the key task is to link up different struggles among those suffering the consequences of the intervention. Joining up these two tasks, there is a great opportunity to use a holistic analysis of costs to link up the actors who are shouldering them—building political momentum for coalitions from the "outside in." There are disgruntled voices within law enforcement, discontented civil servants in key ministries, and exhausted front-line workers inside the system who will be willing to listen (and often *are* listening) to target groups and "third parties" who suffer the gravest consequences of the intervention. In any intervention that is sufficiently destructive, the "cost-bearers" will eventually generate larger and more resilient coalitions than the "benefits-bearers." A key question is how long this is going to take. Once cost-bearers start joining forces with actors external or ancillary to the system on both national and international levels, the process can be accelerated (see Figure 19).

In building such "coalitions against complicity," there is also a huge amount of learning to be done *across our wars and fights.* Indeed, this is where it is so important to identify shared logics in different policy areas, as well as shared mobilizations against these destructive logics. We see this particularly in the war on drugs, where dialogue among unlikely partners has helped build large and diverse coalitions for change. A disparate assortment of actors—encompassing rights advocates, communities in coca-growing regions, drug users, academics,

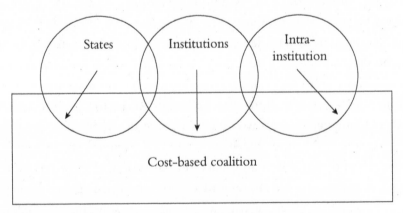

Figure 19 The export of costs (the arrows) has the potential to catalyze effective coalitions in which cost-bearers play a key role.

libertarian think tanks, and politicians from both right and left—has been pushing for a shift away from the war mentality. Together, these groups have pointed to the immense human costs of waging war on a substance. As these costs are increasingly acknowledged, it becomes easier to find another way forward that prioritizes public health and human well-being—and many governments are taking notice, from Uruguay to Switzerland. It has been a long process to dismantle the singular logic of war. Yet slowly, in some countries at least, the tide is turning. This includes Colombia, where the new leftist government is pushing for an end to the drug wars. That political shift would argu-ably not have been possible without the broad coalition-building and cost-benefit analyses of preceding decades.[12]

We may also learn from policy fields that have not tended to display the same level of "fixation" as our wars. We are thinking here above all of climate change and, more widely, campaigns that highlight the environment as a crucial public good. It was in relation to pollu-tion that unaccounted-for costs first rose to public prominence as "negative externalities." Even though measures to curb pollution and address global warming still fall drastically short of what's needed, the shift in public debate and policy toward accounting for such ex-ternalities has nevertheless been remarkable. Again, a great variety of actors—including not just scientists but activists, politicians, NGOs, and even corporations—eventually managed to shift the dial on *which costs count*. Barely a few decades ago, a fossil-fuel company could safely leave its pollution off the balance sheet and a government could safely ignore the consequences of promoting carbon-heavy industries. Today, the externalities generated by large polluters are increasingly accounted for publicly and politically—gradually, if imperfectly, ac-knowledging the wider costs not just to the public good but to the planetary good. And this is starting radically to shift policy, even if progress could be much faster.[13] A proper accounting of costs can alter incentives in helpful ways. A former governor of the Bank of England, Mark Carney, has pointed to the possibility that companies and indus-tries failing to push toward zero-carbon emissions could be penalized by investors and/or governments, so that the incentives for fossil fuel extraction may change very quickly.[14]

Climate/pollution policy and narcotics policy illustrate how an accurate diagnosis of the costs and benefits within a destructive system can open up pathways for coalition-building against it. In both cases, coalitions have been very loose and broad, ranging from corporate actors and regulators to academics, civil society groups, and affected people. It is a case here not so much of "finding one's enemy" (key to the unhelpful fixations of our wars and fights) as of "finding one's friends." And these are often *unexpected* friends.

This takes us back to our first point, on dialogue. In the migration field, there is a long-standing literature on the "strange bedfellows" that have cozied up in opposition to punitive border policies, reaching well beyond the usual suspects on the political left to employers and conservative tax advocates on the right.[15] Some of the harshest critics of our wars have hailed from the (economic) right, which often sees in them a stupendous misspend. A full public accounting of the costs and benefits of the wars is something voters of very diverse political colors can agree is of the essence. Such an accounting may well help to establish some long-lost trust in the probity of state institutions, besides the more fundamental objective of addressing the wars' stupendous costs in terms of the public good.

Yet we cannot afford for these coalitions to become technocratic. Legitimate calls for "peace" should not be allowed to "kill politics," to paraphrase Sharath Srinivasan's important book on war and peace in Sudan and South Sudan. There are of course also odd coalitions to be found among opponents to further migration, among opponents to the relaxation of drug laws, and so forth.[16] Coming back to dissent and dialogue, these coalitions clearly also need to be listened to and engaged.

We also cannot afford for peace-building efforts to be too "pure." There will be—and have been—some pretty queasy and uneasy bedfellows in any peace coalition. In the context of civil wars, a wealth of studies suggests that uneasy alliances are normal in any process of demobilization.[17] Peace is often uglier than we think, and those benefiting from a war may need to be cajoled into cooperation—or perhaps persuaded that they can benefit more from peace than from war. We may even suggest, in fact, that if all the "ugliness" (and all the self-interested or tainted allies) could actually be eliminated from the process, then peace would probably not happen at all. In self-consciously distancing ourselves from the claim that we are "on the side of the angels," we are also conscious—as Arendt made clear a long time ago—that when angels *believe they are angels*, this tends to be a huge part of the problem.[18] Self-righteousness has often invited fixation and obliviousness to a wider accounting of costs. Broad coalitions for change are important partly because they invite dissent and dialogue, and so help guard against the risk of reproducing a "wreckonomic" pattern in the proposed alternative. Indeed, any coming pandemic intervention or climate change net-zero policy would benefit from the kind of systems accounting and open debate that we have advocated.

In sum, complicity around the security fixations of the instigators is central to sustaining our belligerent systems of intervention—as well as to generating more costs and risks for weaker parties. But at the same time there is significant potential for building alternative international coalitions among the actors who are left to face the various costs and risks. The potential is immense: it ranges from skeptical front-line professionals to independent aid organizations, and from "Global South" governments and state agencies to local communities and, crucially, the families of those unjustly targeted by the wars.[19] Perverse gamings of the system and perverse distributions of costs and risks need further exposing, and this is an integral part of building coalitions against dysfunctional interventions that continuously reproduce human suffering.

Unfixing the Problem

It is a familiar refrain that wars and security interventions are failing to address the underlying drivers or "root causes" that they are ostensibly combating. Pushing back, instigators often claim that they *are* addressing root causes even as they run their wars and fights. This is part of the wonderful world that gave us WHAM (using aid to "win hearts and minds") as well as Europe's "Emergency Trust Fund" for addressing "root causes" of irregular migration in Africa while funding security forces that combat it.[20]

Yet with our systems lens, we can put the challenge in a more fundamental way: as one of unfixing a problem that has been "fixated" upon in such a narrow way. We've seen how war and security systems paradoxically depend upon rendering the "threat" as a simple—and often a *single*—threat. It is true that lip service is often paid to systems thinking, and policies to address "root causes" or build "resilience" are testament to this. Yet, as in Cold War times, such systems thinking tends to be shallow and rarely *accounts for the role of the intervention itself in changing the environment in which the "problem" manifests.* Even self-consciously "joined-up thinking" tends to obfuscate the oversimplified "war fix" that is driving the intervention.[21] In short, we may say that the system does not like to look at systems; it especially abhors casting a serious look at itself. It is, in this sense at least, antisystemic. Countering the simplistic fixation that lies at the heart of our wars, we need to appreciate the complexity of underlying problems while criticizing the simplicity of existing "solutions."

The "unfixing" we are advocating comes more clearly into focus if we look at approaches to conflict and counterterrorism that depart from the "war on terror." In their report on counterterror research for Saferworld, Attree and Street stressed the key role of underlying grievances and observed, "Reinforcing—and failing to transform—partners' abuse, corruption and exclusion is the single most important cause of failure in counter-terror and stabilisation strategies." Acknowledging that proscribed groups frequently have violent records, Attree and Jordan nevertheless stress the importance of bringing these groups into a peace process wherever possible, rather than excluding them, vilifying them, and waging an endless war on them.[22]

Again, this kind of approach redirects our focus from "the threat" to the intervention. It also directs our attention away from military confrontation to tentative dialogue (which crucially involves local communities as much as, or ideally more than, the people with guns). It uses an investigation of the intervention to get a better understanding of how the threat is renewing itself.

★★★

We are not trying to write a set of policy prescriptions here. However, if we lose the habit of embracing and laundering belligerent solutions that are manifestly not working, this in itself will create space and dialogue from which better solutions can emerge.[23] We are tempted to quote the old saying that when the pupil is ready, the guru will appear. Many of the most sensible and workable solutions are actually known already; they are not "rocket science," nor are they especially new. However, they have routinely been squeezed out by the erroneous—and habitually self-serving—belief that complex social problems can be addressed with an aggressive and single-minded supply-side approach. Addressing drug dependency means engaging in various forms of harm-reduction of a kind that has already been extensively trialed and rolled out for intoxicating substances (alcohol and drugs) in many parts of the world. Addressing insecure migrations involves adjusting labor market regulations in a way that protects both citizen and noncitizen workers, improving legal pathways, and working toward a better system of responsibility-sharing for refugees. Addressing insurgency and political violence involves supporting the criminal justice system, and it often means acting against corruption and supporting reform of the security sector (as we saw in Sierra Leone). All these fields of intervention must involve boosting economic security, education, and public health while tackling deep-seated inequality. If there is one lesson that our final crisis in this book—that of COVID-19—has taught us, it is that mending the fragility in our *social* systems is core to mitigating further crises.

Put simply, the "problem" must be reframed. Instead of seeing migration as a border issue, it can be treated as a labor market issue (or, when it comes to displacement, a protection issue). Drug policy does not have to be filed under public order but instead can come under public health. Terrorism can be treated as a policing issue, not as a reason for war. Shifting these frames will always be politically contentious—and it should be. However, a proper accounting for costs and benefits, combined with opening spaces for dialogue and disagreement, will push things in a healthy direction.

We need to get away from our collective fixation on singular "threats" and we need critically to examine the systems that respond to these various threats. Even as success is loudly proclaimed and evidence is marshaled to support this claim, it is very often precisely the response that is fueling the problem. If truth is indeed the first casualty of war, our hope is that war will be the first casualty of truth. More specifically, we hope that our "wreckonomics" may help in gaining a much better appreciation of the true costs and benefits of the various wars and fights that we have discussed in this book. Once we have such an appreciation and find ways of building coalitions around it, then the habit of the "war fix" will be more clearly revealed as destructive and self-defeating.

IO

Waging Peace

How (Not) to Fight the System

It should be obvious that we need a holistic approach that takes account of the many causes of complex social problems and challenges of the kind we have considered in this book. Yet the manifestly sensible nature of "unfixing" the problem has not prevented the ascendance of interventions focusing single-mindedly on combating a simplified existential "threat" across a wide range of policy spheres. Why is this?

In sifting through the "crime scene" with which we began, your systems detectives have tried to account for these continuing fixations and for the closely associated habit of securitized solutions or outright war. In particular, we have found that the persistence of our various wars and fights is closely linked to the gaming of these projects and the way in which costs and benefits have been rather systematically distributed within them. Dismantling a dysfunctional system demands a better understanding of the many ways in which failure has been turned into a peculiar kind of success. We might even think of an analogy to personal psychology. Advising someone to "stop their madness" may be of little help (as Freud understood) without an understanding of the diverse functions that are served by this "madness" in the first place.

But at this point your systems detectives also have an uneasy sense—and the reader may share these misgivings—that we need to push things further. We have clues to the crime, but its wider ramifications are still a little hazy. At this moment of escalating doubt, it so happens that our detectives are picking up the sound of a slurred voice at the doorway.

"Just one more thing," the voice drawls.

We realize that it is dear old Lieutenant Columbo paying us a final visit.

"Surely the big problem," he says, "is that by analyzing these systems on their own terms, you, my fellow detectives, are actively complicit with them?"

"How so?" we ask, alarmed at finding ourselves at the sharp end of an Agatha-Christie-style whodunnit, and so late in the story to boot.

Columbo flashes his weary smile. "You need to think," he adds gnomically, "about the beginning of wreckonomics—and the end."

At one level, of course, we would love for an end to *Wreckonomics*. Perhaps our patient readers, having heroically made it this far, will share this sensibility. But for the moment, we are perplexed and we ask Columbo for one more clue.

"Think about the case of the missing W," he says.

And with that, the man in the crumpled raincoat disappears from view.

Columbo leaves us with the sense that we must *widen* our investigation. As in many a crime series, the last episode opens the door to the larger picture. We have hinted at this wider context throughout the book. Yet throughout, we've had an uneasy feeling that we should be saying more about the wider economic system in which our various wars and fights play out. We're suddenly hit by the realization that it is indeed to the "end" of wreckonomics that we must look as we conclude: at economics.

The Politics of Distraction

How do we get to grips with the role of our war and security systems within wider systems? More specifically, how can we understand the complex relationships between inequality, grievance, and over-simplified solutions? We cannot hope to address particular tactics of political violence unless underlying grievances and power relations are addressed, including the vicious circle in which war spawns further grievances. We cannot hope to solve the genuine problems with drug addiction unless the wider social malaise that underpins both supply and demand is tackled. Similarly, we cannot hope to arrive at a just and sensible migration policy unless the underlying drivers—in particular, the economic inequalities and the wider structural factors that spur migration—are fully understood and addressed. These are all huge tasks! But we would be better equipped for them if we were not collectively distracted by the snake oil of magical and violent solutions.

Rampant inequality is feeding both the problem and the demand for a simple fix. On the one hand, *global* inequality is most obviously propelling international migration. While between-country inequality has softened on some counts, notably if we compare the West and East Asia, deep international inequalities persist while divides are frequently worsening *within* many countries.[1] In the United States in 1978, the richest 0.1 percent of the population owned 7 percent of the wealth; by 2012, this figure had risen to 22 percent, with the richest 1 percent owning an astonishing 42 percent.[2] One major paradox here is that, within a democracy, the majority has not simply voted itself—for example through taxation and redistribution—a greater share of the wealth. While there are many reasons for this (the American dream, the complexity of financial and taxation policies, the structure of the political system, and so on), the role of our various wars and fights should not be neglected. Particularly given the key role of the United States in instigating many of our global wars and fights, we here run up against *the politics of distraction*.

The fixation on simple solutions to simple problems—and the distortion of the information environment around these solutions—serves to distract voters and officials from the complex problems that underpin the "threat" in question. This fixation also provides a distraction from the wider malaise among citizens, a malaise that encourages the search for such simplistic solutions in the first place. In our "instigating" states, simplistic fixations have all too often worked as a sleight of hand, distracting the public from underlying crises of inequality and precarity, of climate change and environmental destruction, and of growing geopolitical tension. Fixating on hyped-up wars and fights often provides good cover for not addressing underlying crises.

Coining the term "polycrisis" amid the Ukraine invasion and galloping inflation in 2022, the economic historian Adam Tooze wrote, "What makes the crises of the past 15 years so disorientating is that it no longer seems plausible to point to a single cause and, by implication, a single fix."[3] We agree that it is unrealistic to point to a single fix, yet alarmingly, today's overlapping crises do not seem to have reduced the *plausibility* of such a move. Indeed, the more intractable our crises become, the more readily a quick fix seems to appeal. We all need a bit of fairground distraction, and our wars provide that in spades, with the added attraction of showing governments "getting tough." In a world where control always seems to slip out of the reach of politicians, as Wendy Brown has noted in her *Walled States,* the temptation to *stage* such control may be all the greater.[4]

The hyping and even manufacture of various threats has come to play a major role in an evolving politics of distraction.[5] We see this quite clearly if we head back, one last time, to the moment of the Cold War's end and the fate of the second "superpower." When President Boris Yeltsin's popularity plunged to single digits as ordinary Russians felt the brutal effects of privatization, corruption, and soaring inequality, his national security chief Oleg Labov confided to a legislator, "We need a small, victorious war to raise the President's ratings." This was part of the context—and indeed the function—of the first Chechen War of 1994, a human catastrophe that helped to launch Russia's own enduring "war on terror."[6] While the political instrumentalization of our wars and fights is rarely this explicit, the search for a rallying cry has time and again helped spur new versions of old wars and fights—including in more prosperous Western economies.

In chapter 2, we contrasted what we quite schematically called "conspiracy" and "complexity" views. While war does frequently *disrupt* economic activity, one thing that the "conspiracy" camp does well is to bring out some of the ways in which capitalism has often combined quite successfully with war and security interventions. We have seen variations of this destructive synergy in all our chapters. The securitization of emerging threats has fed the "military-industrial complex," most notably at points where political will seemed to wobble. "Fighting" migration has provided a bonanza for security companies and organizations while eroding migrant workers' rights and rendering migrants more deportable and exploitable. Wars on crime and drugs have suited large prison conglomerates just fine while helping to delegitimize political dissent. As we have seen from the Cold War to counterterror, even a "failing" war has sometimes furthered wider goals such as promoting business interests and projecting geostrategic power.

★★★

If these are some of the wider reasons why wars and fights are "offered," we also need a better understanding of the *demand* for simple and securitized solutions. Why does the "war fix" seem so appealing to so many of us? And is it really all that the political marketplace has to offer?

Answering this kind of question would require a separate investigation (and in the background, our detectives are readying themselves for another outing). So let us keep it short. If the popular demand for "security" is a fundamental feature of our political existence, as Thomas Hobbes suggested in his *Leviathan,* today we face an exceedingly complex world with multiple and sometimes quite amorphous risks and dangers to individual well-being.[7] Governments are frequently proving unable or unwilling to address the most significant risks, as in the financial crisis or with today's extraordinary levels of inequality.[8] When people do not feel safe across a range of spheres—money, health, crime, political violence—this is likely to heighten the demand for "security." As studies on nationalism, political emotion, and war suggest, this demand can often quite effectively be channeled into some kind of "war" or "fight."[9]

The particularly perverse aspect of this tendency is that a genuine *demand* for security frequently fails to be satisfied by the available *supply*. Instead, our wars and fights often exacerbate the underlying problems, not least inequality. In the case of migration, heavy border security—which has escalated on the back of popular concerns with migrants "taking jobs" and "reducing wages"—has tended to push migrants into a more precarious, deportable position, thereby arguably *worsening* the economic "race to the bottom" and labor market precarity (though citizens may also benefit from cheaper products and services). Meanwhile, there are also valid arguments around the impact of high levels of immigration on certain sectors, communities, and welfare nets. In sum, we face here a combination of seemingly "irrational" and "rational" motivations for the support that people routinely lend to one or another "war." This makes the wars and fights much harder to dismantle.

As Hannah Arendt recognized in *The Origins of Totalitarianism*, times of great uncertainty bring an especially strong temptation to sign up to oversimplified, bogus, and violent "solutions."[10] A key part of the politics of distraction would seem to be warding off introspection. In addition to the outright scapegoats (those with no connection to the problem at hand), we have seen a widespread demonization and vilification of groups with some *real* responsibility for harm done (from rebel groups embracing terror tactics to human smugglers) but who also serve a function in absorbing the lion's share of blame within a wider abusive system. We do not need to invoke the psychoanalytic concept of "projection" to realize that the constant identification of enemies and threats helps the system to ward off knowledge of itself; in many ways, this is simply a choice between taking responsibility and placing the blame elsewhere.

In *Wreckonomics,* we have seen that when this strategy either fails to tackle or actively worsens the named problem, this process is routinely turned to advantage. Perhaps the wars that are sold to us are not so different from other things that are sold to us; after all, when consumer goods do not bring us the lasting benefits that are promised, it can plausibly be argued that this—for the system of consumer capitalism—is not so much a problem as a solution. It's an invitation to *more of the same.*

At first sight (and probably the second one too), this is a rather depressing picture! Our initial conclusion from briefly "looking *up* the system" to wider economic relations may be that our war and security systems seem even more intractable than before. Precarity and inequality feed popular anxiety, which in turn feeds calls for strong measures and war fixes, which deepen crises and the underlying social malaise, which then feeds the anxiety further. In this infernal merry-go-round, genuine demands for social and economic security are conspicuously going unmet.

Amid this intractability, where to turn? Two tempting exit options loom. You may not be surprised to hear that we find both of them to be flawed—though we do at least find them stimulating when it comes to thinking on the margins of our wreckonomics framework. The first of them takes us back to Columbo's second cryptic clue: What's with the missing W?

The Case of the Missing W

At our various "crime scenes," there has often been a libertarian voice speaking up against the senseless war or fight in question. Milton Friedman—despite being a big "Chicago School" villain in Naomi Klein's account of disaster capitalism—actually criticized both the war on drugs and the Iraq invasion.[11] Like many on the economic right, he pointed to personal liberty and the misspending of taxpayer dollars as reasons for opposing heavy-handed interventions. Many advocates for deregulation and low taxation have pushed against the drug wars for years, with critics including libertarian think tanks such as the Cato Institute. Mass incarceration has relatedly been opposed on the grounds that it's too expensive. Liberal or libertarian voices as well as many employers have long pushed for openings to migrant labor and the good forces of the market. Particularly within the libertarian critique of "big government," there has been an emphasis on what we called, in chapter 2, "natural complexity" explanations of our social world. The idea has been that some version of Adam Smith's invisible hand will push toward beneficial outcomes when governments are wise enough to steer clear: you mess with complex market systems at your peril.

In short, the solution being offered by many economic liberals and libertarians is to counter securitization and overregulation with economic openness and deregulation. Especially in a context where all other avenues for change seem closed, this has frequently proven an attractive path—as seen, for instance, in proposals for refugee self-sufficiency and employment in special economic zones close to Syria, or in the swift liberalization of drug policy in California.[12] This presents a challenge for us. On the one hand, we share much of the caution around heavy and one-sided regulation, and especially around the huge human costs of the wars and fights. We find a dose of optimism refreshing in our anxiety-ridden times. Yet we must also reckon with how laissez-faire can lead to manifestly reckless outcomes, as we saw in our COVID-19 foray. And we are mindful that an increasingly unfettered capitalist system has fueled the phenomena being "targeted" in our wars and fights while simultaneously stoking the perceived need for distraction.[13]

When thinking across different contemporary crises as we worked on *Wreckonomics*, we sometimes found ourselves thinking about the global financial system—and especially the speculative bubble that caused the 2007–8 "credit crunch." Financial boom-and-boost seems to exhibit our wreckonomics mechanisms in spades, with one important exception. For a start, there have been multiple (and multibillion-dollar) **rigged** games within the complex and opaque system of global finance. The ability of wealthy groups to skew the "rules" in their own interest has been documented by authors such as Thomas Piketty, Jacob Hacker, and Paul Pierson.[14] Clearly, there has also been a great deal of **exporting** of costs and fixing of the fallout. Notoriously, the big banks were generally considered "too big to fail," and huge bonuses continued to be paid during the crisis. Meanwhile, the majority of costs were rather ruthlessly offloaded onto those who eventually lost their homes and those who were hit by austerity policies. Many of the important and damaging **cascades** within this fragile system were economic—for example when investors rushed for the exit within the "credit crunch" itself and when economic slumps subsequently spread quickly around the world. There were deeply damaging political cascades too. Mark Danner noted one of the most important when he observed, "Trumpism is partly the child of the 2008 Wall Street collapse and the vast sense of political corruption and self-dealing it brought in its wake."[15] As for **knowledge fixing**, the public faced not just a distorted mirror but a one-way mirror. As George Akerlof and Robert J. Shiller argued in their *Phishing for Phools,* the profitability of financial markets has depended on successfully rendering them opaque to the public. Focusing on the United States, the authors showed how wealthy individuals and big corporations have been able to skew the system to their advantage by exploiting information asymmetries, notably their own superior understanding of complex financial matters in contrast to a general public that struggles with such notions as "quantitative easing" and "collateralized debt obligations."[16] This takes us back to our familiar "principal-agent problem." Given that governments across the political spectrum have tended to protect these opaque systems, we may be tempted to conceptualize the "government-financial nexus" as a kind of "agent" routinely misleading the "principal" of the voters.[17]

So here—and in some abundance—were the R.E.C.K. elements in our W.R.E.C.K.onomics framework. At the same time, what was also striking us rather forcefully was *an absence.* At the risk of proliferating our detectives, we remembered that Sherlock Holmes had once attached great significance to "the dog that didn't bark in the night."

In the case of rampant global financial speculation, it was pretty clear that no one was framing the situation as a war; however hard we tried, we couldn't find a "war fix." So here at last was the missing W!

As with laissez-faire under COVID-19, leaving things to their own devices proved inadvisable in global finance and shadow banking—and not for the first time. Perverse gains reached astronomic proportions. Costs were pushed into the future and onto poorer people, to be paid back during years of austerity. Moral hazard was all round.

While various kinds of deregulation pushed through by governments were crucial in enabling the overborrowing and overlending that fueled the 2007–8 financial crisis,[18] there were additional kinds of knowledge fixing that helped to ensure that official responsibility went under the radar. One was the complexity of financial regulations that we referred to earlier. Another was the view that events were the result of a "free market" that was, in some rather fundamental sense, both *natural* and *apolitical*. On top of this, the knowledge fix included the idea that wealth was accruing to the "risk takers." It turned out that when the chips were down, most of the real risk takers had been poorer people; meanwhile (as with the habitual reverence for soldiers fighting a real war) respect for the "risk takers" in banking tended to legitimize the hidden imposition of risks and costs on others. Yet another important element of knowledge fixing was the (relatively subtle) suppression of dissent during the period of rampant financial speculation. Much of the boom was based on the assumptions of endlessly rising property prices and cheap money, and in practice expressions of doubt and dissent were discouraged when the money kept rolling in. As the political economist Robert Wade noted at the time, in lines that remind us of the "fix" of our wars:

> Almost everyone was in the grip of something like an addiction—the excitement-dopamine mechanism—and those who tried to draw attention to the growing dangers were squashed or derided. . . . Then,

after mid-September 2008 and the collapse of Lehman and Congress's rejection of the first Treasury plan, extreme anxiety took hold and events jumped off the known trend line altogether. It became clear that—thanks to financial globalization—toxic assets were hidden around the world and counterparty ability to meet liabilities could often not be determined; and that the export-dependent economies, far from "decoupling," were slowing sharply.[19]

There were "buy-ins" and games all through the system, as Wade and others showed when the reckoning came. Highly indebted households tried to "keep up" in a spiraling property market. There was surging inequality with stratospheric incomes and cheap money for individuals and investors at the top driving further speculation. Notable, too, was central bank lenience as well as "grossly overpaid bankers taking on ridiculous risks with borrowed money." "Confirmation bias" among economists, journalists, and politicians encouraged a wide range of players and observers to see "the best of all possible worlds" in financial globalization run wild.[20]

Yet for all that the W was largely missing as the crisis brewed and then broke, it turned out that the language of war was not to be entirely excluded from proceedings. Indeed, it crept steadily into the picture *when the costs of the crisis started to mount*. As policies of austerity were implemented in the wake of the financial crisis, in countries such as the United Kingdom the public were told that "sacrifice" would be necessary to ward off a greater disaster, with officials also stressing that "we are all in this together." The "warlike" language in some ways echoed the official discourse of the COVID-19 pandemic at a time when costs were mounting in that crisis. We can put this in broader terms: when highly uneven costs are seen to arise "naturally," there is less of a problem in legitimizing them. But where such costs are starting to be seen as the result of government policy, there is a bigger "legitimacy" problem—and it's a problem that the "war" framing can address. The war fix, in these cases, adds some aura of legitimacy to an existing system in which benefits and costs are being very unfairly distributed.

When our systems detectives are scrambling for clues to the wider picture, there always seems to be "just one more thing." In this briefest of forays into global finance, we have found further evidence of a wider "reckless" system in which our war fix makes occasional appearances. What this suggests—and it's something our COVID-19 chapter also indicated—is that simply countering wars or walls with radical laissez-faire is not a satisfactory solution. Further, we have identified a risk of a wider R.E.C.K. pattern when bureaucracies start to compete in the marketplace. Additional dangers are generated when such markets fuel inequality. While often seen as opposites, laissez-faire and the war fix are in many ways synergistic rather than antagonistic.

Revolution as the "Solution"?

We started this book by noting that much of our critique is aimed at the political right. We have nevertheless emphasized that "left" and "liberal" politicians (increasingly unstable terms as they are) have often gladly participated in, and even launched into, various wars and fights. The left may also bring its own brand of zeal and righteousness into new battlegrounds—perhaps wars-for-democracy or fights-for-the-climate. This is not surprising amid the intractability of our wars and fights, amid the deep crises of inequality and climate change, and amid our polarized politics. Given in particular the rather central role of capitalism in all these processes, one can be forgiven for asking: Do we need to overturn the whole system? Anyone for revolution?

Our framework should caution us greatly on this front. In fact, our destructive "wreckanisms" have kicked in with special force under systems that are self-consciously revolutionary. Such systems seem to invite many of the characteristics that have made our various wars and fights so difficult to reform. Among these characteristics are a sense of certainty, a sense of self-righteousness, and a willingness to relabel dissent as disloyalty.[21] It seems reasonable to suggest, for instance, that while communists rebelled against profoundly unjust systems, actually existing Communism became "wreckonomic" in spades.

Throughout the book, we have seen how righteous wars and fights have unraveled in practice—and we have stressed that such problems are predictable. Some forty years ago, Edward Clay and Bernard Schaffer looked at ambitious programs for development aid and argued, first, that success was routinely being claimed for floundering policies and, second, that factors like "political will" and "obstacles to implementation" needed to be built into the design of policy rather than listed in retrospect as reasons why things did not work out as hoped.[22] With any kind of revolutionary or righteous endeavor, it hardly seems helpful to suggest that good intentions were simply the victim of unforeseen obstacles and political wreckers.

In chapter 9, we tried to give a succinct account of our own policy "wreckommendations." We expressed our hesitation at the time. In trying to fix any social problem or any flawed intervention, one set of destructive blinkers may quickly replace another. In the twentieth century, there was no shortage of "solutions"—from whichever side of the political spectrum—that turned out to be worse than the problems they were trying (or claiming) to fix. As the twenty-first century has begun to unfold, the world has so far done a pretty good job of prolonging this dangerous dynamic.

The added problem is that many of the *alternative* causes for fixation are genuine crises needing urgent attention. Take climate change. Some climate activists have called for a "war" footing—and given the severity of the crisis, it's easy to see why. A strong case can be made that something approaching a "war on nature" has been waged with the assistance of corporate propaganda. In these circumstances, the instinct is to fight back. War *mobilizes*—if a senior politician were to stand before a large crowd and proclaim that there will be "a mild push on climate change" or "a moderately important attempt to erode poverty," we might not be impressed or inspired. And when politicians falter, activists step up. Prominent environmental writer George Monbiot has compared climate change to the Second World War effort, suggesting, "The difference between 1941 and 2021 is that now the mobilisation needs to come first. . . . Preventing Earth's systems from flipping means flipping our political systems."[23]

As wreckonomists, we urge caution. This book has shown repeatedly that the dangers in such language are grave indeed. The language of war can be relied upon to impede clear thinking, introspection, and dissent (as we saw with COVID-19 in both the "lockdown" and "let it rip" modes). One especially troubling mechanism here is that the language of war also invites rebellious violence, while such violence will inevitably invite violent repression along with the suppression of dissenting voices. We are reminded, too, that a war on *something* tends rather quickly to become a war on *someone*.

Wherever a war is declared or a fixation comes to the fore, there suddenly appears a quick and disorderly line of those who wish to jump on the bandwagon. It is notable that climate change is *already* being framed in militaristic terms—and often not in the way that some activists would hope. Revealingly, it is a sphere where the US military and its counterparts elsewhere have started positioning themselves as key "protectors" against what is said to be the threat of "climate migrants," "climate conflict," and so on.[24] Alongside the military instrumentalization of climate change, we are also seeing governments and corporations pushing through damaging initiatives in the name of responding to climate change. One example of this is people in poorer countries being pushed off their land for ostensibly climate-related ends.[25] Meanwhile, a range of governments around the world have started framing environmental and climate change protesters as some kind of threat or enemy. If climate change is to be the site of a "war," we may anticipate that two can play that game—and it will actually be more than two.

While revolution may be some way off, what we are increasingly seeing are relatively mundane and localized "fixes" around the climate—often with quite dramatic costs that may again go under the radar screen. Here, the *bureaucratic* fixation on zero-carbon strategies gives further grounds for caution. To see some of the problems that may lie ahead, let us return to the scene of our beloved fun-fair one last time. In the dull winter days of early 2023, a rather different cacophony was livening up St. Giles in central Oxford: a protest against zero-carbon restrictions had taken to the medieval city streets. The ire was against new road tolls, "low-traffic neigh-borhoods," and related antipollution measures that were being rolled out on an "experimental" basis. The protest combined with voices from the anti-lockdown right, inviting swift condemnations of con-spiratorial thinking and "misinformation." Yet a big part of the local concern was with the highly unequal and, to some, devastating im-pact on trade in one of Oxford's most multicultural and class-diverse neighborhoods. There is a sense, in such protests, of a concerted mobilization against the fixations of a detached elite all too happy with exporting costs onto ordinary citizens—whether in terms of COVID-19, zero-carbon, or both. In France, "yellow vests," for whom gas taxes were a key grievance, had earlier mobilized around the idea that "elites talk about the end of the world; we talk about the end of the month."[26] One takeaway is that unless extreme care is taken to minimize and mitigate costs of the carbon "fixation," further political trouble (possibly of a cascading kind) lies in store. We should not forget that the "pitch" of Trump and Johnson and similarly populist leaders was based in part on a conspicuous rejec-tion of liberal fixations and of a related bureaucratic quest for "over-regulation." If we are to try to rein in the world with well-meaning regulations (and accompanying condemnations of the "idiots" who resist), it may not go well. Again, whether we're dealing with a revo-lutionary fix or something altogether more mundane, the "obstacles to implementation" may not magically disappear.

Waging Peace

The habit of the war fix has proven remarkably adaptable, as we have seen here and throughout the book. This resilience is unfortunate, as our moment of geopolitical conflict and planetary crisis is in dire need of peace and de-escalation. Instead, we find ourselves buffeted by events. After all the fights and wars and existential struggles that we have been invited to embrace, to fund, and to applaud over so many decades, when we are finally confronted with a real war such as in Ukraine (and indeed with the real possibility of an escalation to *global war*), we are at risk of losing our bearings. Perhaps war has been sold to us so often as a costless "solution" that we have lost sight of what war actually *is*.

A core message of this book is that we need to abandon our addiction to the war fix and, more widely, to challenge the political and bureaucratic urge to simplify and magnify complex problems. Even a degree of success here will significantly expand the space for political debate. Such a shift will in turn help creative and constructive coalitions to flourish. And it will remove some of the self-righteousness that invites violence and intolerance among allies and enemies alike.

Our plea is not for a technocratic solution, replacing "counterproductive interventions" with "what works," in the manner of the old political Third Way (which itself brooked little dissent). Instead, we advocate waging peace, with an emphasis on the verb. This is an active process and struggle—the opposite, in many ways, of the stultifying "peace that kills politics." If our wars and fights are "co-created," the alternatives must be co-created too. Waging peace means actively seeking peaceful political *conflict*—avoiding the kind of fixations and knowledge fixes present in all our wars as well as in the bureaucracies that sustain them. It means opening up debate and the information environment. It means building novel coalitions and countercoalitions, actively seeking friends instead of enemies. As in the dirty yet successful peace processes in civil wars we touched upon in the previous chapter, it means actively bringing into the political and deliberative process those people most acutely affected by the *costs* of an intervention.

A "war" framing tends to suppress key critical voices, which in turn helps prolong bad interventions. Conversely, reforming these systems depends on bringing some key voices back into the frame—in many ways a Foucauldian project—so that these self-justifying systems can better be challenged. This is centrally about the voices of those who have had to bear the consequences. But here we also find other frequently suppressed voices such as insiders and officials charged with implementing our various interventions (or "wars"). These individuals have often developed their own sophisticated critique based on firsthand experience of deficiencies within the systems they are charged with implementing.

In this process, some very powerful vested interests will have to be confronted, challenged, and debated. Those interests, we have seen, include not only the familiar "bad guys" but also vast bureaucracies that feed on a strange mix of failure and success. Within a range of bureaucratic organizations (sometimes including private companies), the mixed message is often that "we are doing tremendously well" and at the same time that "we face an increasingly desperate struggle for survival and must redouble our efforts." This kind of doublespeak has become a pretty routine part of academia, for example—and readers may be thinking of their own versions. In this warped and often self-interested world, the little piggies' house is always getting bigger and better, but the wolf is always at the door. And looking forward, in the context of escalating crises and anxiety, the tendency to fixate on particular high-profile threats is likely to grow from left, right, and center. There is always one more wolf.

★★★

At this point, our systems detectives are beginning to feel quite good about their peacemaking and their broadsides against bureaucracy (and who doesn't like broadsides against bureaucracy?). However, our crumpled colleague Columbo's accusation is still niggling. Are we actively *complicit* in the systems we have spent so much time criticizing? Is there a danger that our somewhat cynical wreckonomic analysis of failing-but-succeeding systems will feed into a (functional) sense of despair and resignation?

We hope not. We have advocated for understanding what sustains damaging interventions from the "inside," and we have insisted that such an exercise (however cynical it might look) is crucial to the task of challenging and eventually dismantling them. There is a note of hope, here, in that while the *wider* systems discussed in this chapter may prove very hard to move, working on these co-created smaller systems of intervention is a very practical way forward. Co-creation works both ways here. We have largely fixed our attention on the fixers and the wreckers. But there is no shortage of allies and potential allies in a peace-waging project. Once we start looking, they are everywhere. Within state administrations, one can already find interventions that are run on relatively humane, rational, and transparent principles, with plenty of dedicated and civic-minded professionals carrying them out. A sense of civic duty is a real thing, and it seems to flourish best in circumstances where war language and single-minded fixations are put aside. There are many friends to find in such quarters for a coalition pushing back against our wars and fights—and with plenty of good ideas for the public money saved. In this chapter, we have also identified genuine concerns around inequality and insecurity across very different parts of the political spectrum. New friends and coalitions can be formed there, too, with some important bruising debate along the way. In international interventions, there is a huge reserve of knowledge and skill among aid workers, peacekeepers, local organizations, and crisis-affected populations. Listening to those voices has been key to *Wreckonomics*. It must be key to developing a path beyond our wars, too.

It's time to recognize that failure, while it has often been painted as success, is actually *failure*. And it's time to reject the "anything goes" mentality that surrounds our wars and fights. While a security lens has tended to push these interventions outside normal political and even legal channels, we need to push them back squarely into the *political* arena where costs and benefits can be subject to proper public discussion. Once we abandon the idea that the solution to complex social problems lies in waging some kind of war or fight, this will open the way for a more productive introspection. At the same time, a more far-reaching self-questioning and a more healthy culture of dissent will be needed if that process of abandoning easy and aggressive "fixes" is to be pushed along. Meanwhile, the body politic—if it can be steered away from unhelpful interventions and bogus remedies—may turn out to have remarkable powers of recovery. Ultimately, it's those powers of recuperation—and the potential for a revival of politics proper—that will allow us to emerge from our collective wreckage.

Notes

CHAPTER I

1. For the Saigon comparison, see, e.g., George Packer, "The Betrayal," *The Atlantic*, March 2022, https://www.theatlantic.com/magazine/archive/2022/03/biden-afghanistan-exit-american-allies-abandoned/621307/.

2. Defense stocks have significantly outperformed the overall market since the start of the war on terror: see Schwartz (2021). Figure of $2.3 trillion is from Brown University's Costs of War Project, September 2021, and covers the linked Afghan-Pakistan interventions. The project lists "war deaths" at a total of 243,000 in the Afghan-Pakistan theater, including deaths of serving personnel as well as civilians (70,000), aid workers, and other groups but excluding *indirect* war deaths from disease and loss of access to food and water: https://watson.brown.edu/costsofwar/figures/2021/human-and-budgetary-costs-date-us-war-afghanistan-2001-2022.

3. See the Afghanistan Papers, first exposed in the *Washington Post* (Whitlock, Shapiro, and Emamdjomeh 2019 and Whitlock 2021). Spending examples from ProPublica (2015) ($486 million) and Cockburn (2021) (B-1 bombers). The latter exemplifies a trend toward heavier and more expensive machinery positioned ever more remotely from the area of intervention, leading to large casualties at a distance. See, e.g., Shaw (2005), Andersson (2019), and Chamayou (2015) on remote military intervention.

4. Whitlock (2019, n.p.).

5. "Permacrisis" was at the top of Collins English Dictionary's words of the year for 2022, defined simply as "extended period of insecurity and instability." "Polycrisis" was popularized by historian Adam Tooze in the same year. Let us note that by no means do we accept "crisis" as a given: as our chapters will show, crises (and emergencies) are routinely manipulated and manufactured. See, e.g., Roitman (2013) for one critical

anthropological account of the politics of "crisis" and Keen (2023b) on disaster politics.

6. For the Costs of War figures, see https://watson.brown.edu/costsof war/. On Syria, see Keen (2017); compare Attree and Street (2022) on lessons from the global war on terror.

7. Andersson (2016); for further discussion see chapter 5.

8. For a compelling study of these much-discussed divides, see Mishra (2017).

9. See https://drugpolicy.org/issues/drug-war-statistics.

10. See, e.g., Baldwin, Methmann, and Rothe (2014) and Bettini (2013).

11. Additionally, military rearmament risks further setbacks to global warming measures.

12. As related in "Burnt Thumb Helps Convict Pizza Shop Owner Who Had Shop Torched for Insurance Money," ABC, April 12, 2017, https://www.abc.net.au/news/2017-04-12/mans-thumb-burnt-off-torch-pizza-restaurant-insurance/8440176.

13. Donnelly (2019: 904) admirably sets out a systems perspective in international relations, and we take the focus on connections, interdependencies, and relations from his critique of Kenneth Waltz's systems model. Notably, Donnelly goes on to criticize Waltz for replacing a genuine systems view (focused on such complexities) with "an analytic model of characterless units interacting with one another and with a reified structure."

14. Agnew (2015).

15. Keen (2023a) discusses further the power and politics of shame.

16. Kuzmarov (2008).

17. Klein (2007).

CHAPTER 2

1. Andersson (2014b, 2019); Keen (1994, 2012).

2. Keen (2005).

3. Andersson (2014b). We return to the wider gaming of migration crises and its literature in chapter 5.

4. An interesting if contested contribution here has come from Ian Shapiro (2005), who argues that both qualitative and quantitative social science fields have undergone a "flight from reality."

5. The literature here is vast, and some of it will be referenced as the chapters progress. See, e.g., Mbembe (2019) on neocolonial violence and "necropolitics"; Stannard (1993) on the violence inflicted on Native

Americans; Galeano's (2009) much read *The Open Veins of Latin America;*
Cardoso and Faletto (1979), Amin (1974), and Rodney ([1972] 2018) on
dependency and "underdevelopment."

6. For example, Rodney ([1972] 2018).
7. For example, Harvey (2004) and Chomsky (2003).
8. Agamben (2014); Cunningham and Warwick (2013).
9. Klein (2007). "Making a killing out of catastrophe" is the subtitle of
   Loewenstein (2015). See also his subsequent work on the war on drugs
   (Loewenstein 2019).
10. Hoyos (2012).
11. Chakrabarty (2012) has been a leading voice in seeking to "provin-
    cialize" Europe and the West while grappling lately with the challenge
    of climate change on a systemic level. Sainath (1995) provides a powerful
    analysis of many of the forces and "games" we discuss in this book in
    relation to rural poverty. On famine, Rangasami (1985) has been an in-
    spiration. See also Táíwò (2022), who has made a strong case for "taking
    African agency seriously" in discussions around contemporary power
    relations.
12. For example, Robinson and Gallagher (1982); Chabal and Daloz (1999).
13. Gall (1977: 12). The first version of his book was published two years
    previously under the title *General Systemantics.*
14. Gall (1977: xii).
15. Ramalingam and Jones (2008).
16. Ramalingam and Jones (2008).
17. Ramalingam and Jones (2008), citing Pidd (1996).
18. Ramalingam and Jones (2008: 60).
19. Duffield (2001, 2007, 2018), among other key works of inspiration to us.
20. For an eloquent plea for the importance of history in the study of war,
    see Berdal (2011).
21. Ahmed (2011); Tooze (2022). We have also discussed this ourselves in
    our recent work, including in Andersson (2019) and Keen (2023b).
22. Cf. Donnelly (2019).
23. The wider critique of holism and assuming systems coherence is dis-
    cussed by systems theory advocates such as Jervis (1997). See also the
    note below in relation to a similar "trap" in Foucault-inspired studies
    of power.
24. Compare critique in Keen (2012) regarding Kalyvas (2003).
25. We'll return to this point of displaced aims later, but should note here
    how our ground-up approach is less inspired by abstract complex sys-
    tems thinking than by Foucauldian approaches to power, including

studies of governmentality and security apparatuses (Foucault 2007) as well as the systems thinking behind Bourdieu's field theory (Bourdieu 2013; compare Donnelly 2019). In security studies, field theory and Foucauldian security come together in the important work of Bigo (2014) and others. Walters (2012) raises a cautious note on how governmentality studies sometimes risk reinforcing the coherence and strength of that which they criticize. This is a point that resonates with us and that the emphasis on co-creation and complexity helps to address. Further security scholarship is referenced in chapter 3.

26. See, e.g., Rothstein and Teorell (2008) for a critique of "public choice theory" and its assumptions around the preponderance of self-interest. See also chapter 7, which discusses new public management.

27. Securitization theory is discussed in chapter 3. We prefer the term "fixation" to "securitization" as it suggests we are facing a more general process. As examples beyond the security sphere will suggest, nonsecuritized fixation is quite common in state bureaucracies, where it may well inflect a similar "wreckonomics" process to what we see in our wars and fights. "Fixation" does two further things for our systems analysis. First, it highlights how threat selection and threat inflation are "antisystemic" moves in the sense that they strip away complexity. Second, it chimes with strands of psychological analysis: our wars and fights often become an "idée fixe" in political circles, making them harder to change. These points will be returned to in the latter parts of the book.

CHAPTER 3

1. Westad (2005: 396).
2. Ayoob (1995).
3. For example, Romero (2014).
4. Berdal (2003); Enzensberger (1994).
5. Berdal (2003).
6. For example, Woodward (1990); Keen (1994).
7. Keen (1994).
8. Duffield's work from this period includes the book *War and Hunger* coauthored with Joanna Macrae, Anthony Zwi, and Hugo Slim (Macrae et al. 1994); later works include the important *Global Governance and the New Wars* (Duffield 2001), referenced in the previous chapter, which further showed how the development industry had come to mesh with security concerns. Kaldor had already addressed the political economy of

the Cold War before she wrote her *New and Old Wars* (Kaldor 1981 and 1998), while de Waal was developing an influential political-economy analysis of famine and war in the Horn of Africa (e.g., Africa Watch and de Waal 1991). Specifically on our cases, the political economy of Sierra Leone's civil war was subject to an illuminating analysis in Lansana Gberie's (2005) *A Dirty War in West Africa*, while Sudan's local economic and political rivalries had earlier been highlighted in Frances Deng's (1986) *A Man Called Deng Majok*. Local tensions also formed a vital part of Stathis Kalyvas's (2012) analysis in *The Logic of Violence in Civil War*.

9. For example, Conetta and Knight (1998: n.p.).

10. Perlo-Freeman (2016), delineating data from the Stockholm Peace Research Institute.

11. Conetta (2010: v), emphasis in the original. Part of this concerns personnel costs, which have increased since 9/11; see Harper (2021).

12. Conetta (2010, v).

13. Securitization theory has been the subject of extensive debates in recent years, but we can identify three strands of relevance to the coming chapters—the "Copenhagen School" take on securitization as a political speech act, mentioned here and developed by Buzan, Waever, and de Wilde (1998), and the "Paris School" focus on securitization via *practice,* most prominent in the long-running work of Didier Bigo (e.g., 2014) on security practitioners in Europe (see also Côté-Boucher, Infantino, and Salter 2014 for an agenda-setting piece in the same special issue). A third strand has sought to highlight the colonial and racial dimensions of security (e.g., Ibrahim 2005 for an early example in migration studies). These perspectives have not always sat together easily. Some of the critique has come from war scholarship; for instance, Barkawi (2011a) has suggested a constructivist notion of securitization may be playing into the hands of states. Elsewhere, there has been a rather high-spirited debate among decolonial/race-critical and Copenhagen School theorists, an issue we won't go into further but that relates in some ways to our concluding discussions in the book on the perils of wars of words and the need for wide coalitions.

14. For an interesting aesthetic-historical analysis of this repurposing, called "imperial designs," see Hattam (2016).

15. Andersson (2014b). Important studies from this time include Nevins (2010) and Andreas (2009).

16. Giorgio Agamben (1998) was around this time also developing his analysis of the state of exception, which was to become hugely influential (if contested) in critical analyses of security. Our take on securitization

and fixation is broader in that it involves recognizing contexts where emergency or crisis is more subtly present than in formal "states of emergency."

17. Luttwak (1999).

18. Butler (1935, n.p.).

19. The literature on continuities and ruptures in colonial, Cold War, and more recent forms of warfare and organized violence is, of course, vast. See, e.g., Mbembe (2019) on "necropolitics" in relation to sovereignty and (neo)colonial power; Bauman (2001) and Shaw (2005) on patterns of remote warfare; and Duffield (2007) on the (re)emergence of nonterritorial threats after the demise of the Cold War.

20. US Department of Veterans Affairs, "America's Wars," May 2021, https://www.va.gov/opa/publications/factsheets/fs_americas_wars.pdf. For war deaths on the Vietnamese side, see, e.g., Hirschman, Preston, and Loi (1995).

21. Corson (1968: 75, 80).

22. Corson (1968: 97).

23. Corson (1968).

24. See also Byman (2006).

25. Corson (1968: 209).

26. Arendt (1973: 20).

27. Corson (1968: 81).

28. Kinnard (1991). Quotations reprinted in Cukier and Mayer-Schönberger (2013, n.p.), in a piece on "the dictatorship of data" that relates to the discussion of metrics and bureaucracy in chapter 7.

29. Turse (2013: 44).

30. Faludi (1999: 331–32).

31. Kalyvas (2004: 132).

32. Corson (1968: 102–3).

33. Faludi (1999: 337).

34. Westad (2005: 397).

35. Halperin's book, republished by Brookings in the 2000s (Halperin 2006), focuses on budget competition, institutional identity, and staff morale as he investigates how state institutions take positions on national security.

36. Shawcross (1980: 210).

37. See, e.g., Masco (2013) for a detailed anthropological account of the continuity in the generation of "national security affect" in the United States across the Cold War and the war on terror. For a recent journalistic investigation of the wider anti-Communist sentiment in the 1950s and beyond, see Bevins (2020).

38. Gravel and Lauria (2008: 131).

39. Carroll (2007: 225).

40. Elder (2014, n.p.).

41. See, e.g., Jervis (1997: 60), who incorporates the security dilemma with his system effects; see also Booth and Wheeler (2008). Walter and Snyder (1999) have applied the security dilemma to civil wars. The influence of game theory on international relations, and its relationship with systems thinking and with our political systems analysis, is a topic we have to set aside here.

42. Though analyzing escalation itself rather than mutual systemic interests, an interesting thinker here is Gregory Bateson, who deployed the notion of "schismogenesis" to refer to such processes from community up to interstate level. See Bateson (1958, 2000).

43. Carroll (2007).

44. Cockburn (2021).

45. Carroll (2007: 225–26).

46. Carroll (2007); Cockburn (2021).

47. Cockburn (2021: viii).

48. Cockburn (2021).

49. Cockburn (2021: 75) on the Last Supper and its aftermath.

50. Cockburn (2021: ix–x). Compare Shawcross (1980) on the growing role of the US Air Force between Korea and Vietnam.

51. Kaldor (1981).

52. Markusen (1997: 87, 94).

53. Markusen (1997: 87).

54. Porter (2021).

55. Cockburn (2021: 79).

56. George Kennan, "A Fateful Error," *New York Times*, February 5, 1997, https://www.nytimes.com/1997/02/05/opinion/a-fateful-error.html.

57. Cockburn cited in Kaldor (2021: n.p.).

58. Charles Dunlap, who rose to major general during his thirty-four years in the US Air Force, reported in 2011 that annual US defense expenditure was exceeding $700 billion (roughly half of the world's total), but he argued this was still not enough. He cited *Defense News* saying America's current bomber fleet was a "puny force against any serious adversary"; he said that China was challenging US air power in the Far East; and he noted that Russia and India were building a "fifth generation" of warplanes designed to better the US Air Force (Dunlap 2011: 142–43).

59. In March 2014, Republican Representative Mike Rogers, chair of the House Intelligence Committee, hosted a fundraising breakfast with a

crowd of mostly lobbyists for defense contractors. At the time, defense spending was under pressure with the Afghan war winding down and public opinion moving toward domestic spending priorities. But Putin had just invaded Crimea and on *Fox News,* Rogers took the chance to denounce what he said was President Barack Obama's weak response: "Putin is playing chess and I think we are playing marbles, and I don't think it's even close." One lobbyist described the mood of the meeting: "I'd call it borderline euphoric" (Cockburn 2021: 73).

60. For example, Matovski (2022).

61. This echoes Gall (1977), when he says that the system has a will to live. We return to this in chapter 7.

62. Jervis (2012: 403).

63. Berdal (2011: 117) points out, for example, that despite the prominence of criminal agendas in the wars in former Yugoslavia, there is "no reason to believe that Franjo Tudjman and his closest nationalist allies were not deeply committed to the *idea* of Great Croatia." Meanwhile, he notes how deaths among soldiers in Bosnia considerably exceeded deaths among civilians.

64. See Gaddis (2005) on figures such as John Foster Dulles, George F. Kennan, and Henry Kissinger as well as on symmetric and asymmetric forms of containment.

65. Bevins (2020).

CHAPTER 4

1. The work of investigative journalist Todd Miller is very illuminating for quite an "inside account" of the expansion of the security landscape in recent decades. See, e.g., Miller (2014).

2. The term "reality-based community" was applied derisively to war-on-terror critics by George W. Bush's senior aide Karl Rove (see, e.g., Keen 2012 and Andersson 2019).

3. Quoted in Barnett (2004: 108).

4. See Kristol and Kagan (1996) on the "monsters to destroy," reversing the dictum of nineteenth-century US president John Quincy Adams.

5. See Kaplan (1994) on the "coming anarchy." Barnett, just cited, was another such voice calling for US military engagement in what he termed the "non-integrating Gap" at the fringes of the "Core" of the world economy. See Keen (2012) and Andersson (2019) for a longer discussion of these figures at the turn of the Cold War.

6. This logic goes back to the early days of the "propaganda of the deed" in nineteenth-century Europe (Bolt 2012).

7. Gerges (2009).

8. See Attree and Street (2022) for a review.

9. Kerry's quote is from the first pre-election debate, 2004. See Robert Scheer, "US Is Its Own Worst Enemy in Iraq," *Los Angeles Times*, May 17, 2005, accessed at www.globalpolicy.org. See also Attree and Street (2022).

10. Attack data from Global Terrorism Index (2015, 2016). Data on insurgents from Goepner (2016: 113).

11. For example, Faguet (2021).

12. Gopal (2014); cf. Kalyvas (2012).

13. Gopal (2021, n.p.).

14. Gopal (2021, n.p.).

15. Rubin (2007); Human Rights Watch (2004).

16. For example, Gopal (2014); Forsberg (2010); Giustozzi (2004); Gordon (2011).

17. Gopal (2014, 2021). See also Forsberg (2010).

18. Gall (2014).

19. Rubin (2007: 69), who writes, "Counternarcotics efforts provide leverage for corrupt officials to extract enormous bribes from traffickers."

20. Gordon (2011); Chaudhuri and Farrell (2011); Forsberg (2010).

21. Cf. Reno (1995), who used the term "shadow state" in the case of Sierra Leone. On the warlords in Afghanistan's conflict, see, e.g., Forsberg (2010); Rubin (2007); Gordon (2011). Compare Weigand's (2022) careful comparative study of Taliban, state, and warlord claims to legitimacy in postoccupation Afghanistan.

22. Brinkley (2013: 15).

23. Brinkley (2013: 15).

24. Tierney (2010: 34–35).

25. Riechman and Lardner (2011).

26. Brinkley (2013: 16).

27. Wilder (2009).

28. On bunkering in Afghanistan, see Weigand and Andersson (2019); Duffield (2018) for the wider picture.

29. See Action on Armed Violence, https://aoav.org.uk/2019/military-age-males-in-us-drone-strikes/.

30. On blowback from counterterror, see Kilcullen (2009). For the hammer-and-nail quotation and the wider "freedom" of JSOC to wage its campaigns, see Scahill (2014: 107, 175).

31. We have sympathy for the position that war must be understood through the people participating in conflict, which means engaging deeply with the histories and sociopolitical realities of particular

conflicts (e.g., Thurston 2021). Yet our purpose is not to elucidate the dynamics of each of these conflicts *in their own right;* it is to understand the extent to which the systemic pattern we have highlighted has come to inflect these intricate conflict settings over time. Indeed, we see the two projects (of understanding systemic drivers and local contexts) as complementary, not mutually exclusive.

32. International Crisis Group (2009); Human Rights Watch (2009); Evans (2009).

33. Quoted in Sriyananda (2015, n.p.).

34. Keen (2014).

35. Of course, in Sri Lanka itself, the *national* "terrorist" enemy did not originate with the global war on terror: as is well known, the Tamil Tigers had once been global "innovators" in suicide bombing.

36. Prominent lawyer Alan Dershowitz (2002) argued that torture could be justifiable in the face of terrorism, giving the example of a "ticking bomb" and the possibility of getting crucial information via torture. Michael Ignatieff (2004, n.p.) suggested, "To defeat evil, we may have to traffic in evils: indefinite detention of subjects, coercive interrogations, targeted assassinations, even pre-emptive war."

37. For example, remarks by Sri Lanka's Permanent Representative to the UN in Geneva, Dr. Daya Jayatilleka (2009).

38. The quote comes from the "Mahinda Vision" manifesto during Mahinda Rajapaksa's successful 2005 campaign to become president, a victory that effectively relaunched the war in Sri Lanka (see International Crisis Group 2007). Mahinda's praise of China as respecting sovereignty was exemplified in his 2021 speech on the hundredth anniversary of the Communist Party (*Colombo Telegraph* 2021). See also Goodhand (2010) on the strategy of maximizing room for maneuver by playing donors off against one another.

39. Keen (2014).

40. Weiss (2011).

41. Wheeler (2012).

42. Venugopal (2018).

43. Welikala (2008).

44. Human Rights Watch (2013).

45. Weiss (2011: 170).

46. Most Muslims in Sri Lanka speak Tamil, but identification as Tamils is considerably less common than among Tamil-speaking Muslims in India.

47. International Crisis Group (2019).

48. International Crisis Group (2019).
49. International Crisis Group (2022).
50. Klem (2020: 210).
51. International Crisis Group (2019, 2022); Klem (2020).
52. BBC, January 8, 2023, https://www.bbc.co.uk/news/world-asia-64142694/.
53. Kanfash and Aljasem (2022); Martinez and Eng (2016).
54. Keen (2017); Droz-Vincent (2014); Leenders (2013).
55. See, e.g., Black (2021).
56. Arendt ([1951] 1979).
57. See, e.g., Abboud (2015); International Crisis Group (2012).
58. Weiss and Hassan (2015); Sands Vela and Maayeh (2014); Lister (2014). In its covert relationships with some violent jihadist groups, the Assad regime appears to have benefited from an earlier process by which it had facilitated the flow of jihadis from Syria into Iraq as part of an attempt to exert leverage over the US government at a time when Syria risked being added to the US "target list" along with Afghanistan and Iraq.
59. For example, Weiss and Hassan (2015).
60. Weiss and Hassan (2015).
61. See notably Turkmani et al. (2015).
62. Turkmani et al. (2015).
63. For example, Khalaf (2021).
64. "'More Than 90%' of Russian Airstrikes in Syria Have Not Targeted Isis, US Says," *The Guardian*, October 7, 2015; Dunn (2016).
65. Souleimanov, Aslan, and Petrtylova (2015). One of the important functions of violence—as we have seen in many contexts, including above in Afghanistan—is that you can exert influence, whether nationally or in international diplomacy, by offering to rein in the trouble you are stirring up. This is also part of gaming the system, as we will see in disturbing detail when turning to the "fight against irregular migration" in chapter 5.
66. U.S. State Department, "Terms of Reference for the Joint Implementation Group," 2016, accessed at https://www.washingtonpost.com/r/2010-2019/WashingtonPost/2016/07/13/Editorial-Opinion/Graphics/terms_of_reference_for_the_Joint_Implementation_Group.pdf (published as a link in Rogin 2016b).
67. For example, Syrian Observatory for Human Rights (2016).
68. Morrison (2016).
69. Rogin (2016a).
70. "Aleppo: Russia Ready to 'Fight Together' with US in Shattered Syrian City," *The Guardian*, August 16, 2016.

71. There is a detailed discussion in Keen (2017).

72. Ellis (2004: 460).

73. The argument around Algeria's "export" and insertion into the war on terror is pushed most strongly, e.g., in Keenan (2009). Scholars of Mali have contested his argument, with Soares (2012: 2) for instance asserting that it "cannot explain the success and appeal of Islamists in northern Mali." While Keenan's conclusions thus need to be taken with a pinch of salt, the wider imbrication of Algeria in the insecurity of northern Mali has been widely noted (e.g. Strazzari 2015). Thurston (2018: 16), for instance, observes how "political settlements [with jihadists] in Algeria, and later in Mauritania, exacerbated some of the conditions that made Mali the regional epicentre of jihadism, as did the participation of other governments and actors in the kidnapping economy."

74. Lacher (2012: 13).

75. Whitehouse (2012).

76. See Andersson (2019); Whitehouse (2012).

77. Solomon (2013).

78. Bagayoko (2019).

79. Sangaré (2016).

80. UNHCR (2022).

81. Intellectuals in Mali and the wider region had long been accusing France of colonial attitudes in its interventions: see, e.g., Traoré and Diop (2014) on French involvement in the early stages of Mali's conflict.

82. Klein (2007).

83. Saadawi (2018).

84. Attree and Street (2022: i–ii).

85. Attree and Street (2022: 56).

86. See also Attree (2016).

CHAPTER 5

1. Dave Goldenberg, "Chicanery on the Midway," 2001 article captured at https://archive.ph/20080610084215/http://www.pac-c.org/Carnies.htm.

2. See, e.g., Walia (2013) and Besteman (2020), exemplary of a wider trend of identifying global systems of exploitation and violence and identifying particular (Western and/or US-led) imperial patterns behind these systems.

3. The remote relationship is powerfully rendered in Duffield's (2018) *Post-humanitarianism*. See also Andersson (2019).

4. During Ruben's time with former deportees in 2010, he heard many stories of this atrocity. One man, stuck in the very reception camp in Ceuta that he had tried to reach five years earlier, showed Ruben a big scar on his thigh from the Moroccan forces' bullets that night. Like him, many of the survivors were still en route five years later. "The adventure, it's like war," said another veteran in a safe house in Mali's capital, Bamako, referring to their long journeys north. "And we're like soldiers." See Andersson (2014b).

5. A wealth of literature on US border enforcement has emphasized how the escalating securitization of migration since the 1990s has reshaped routes and rendered the passage ever more dangerous; see, e.g., Nevins (2010) on "Operation Gatekeeper"; Andreas (2009) on the different layers of the evolving border game; Donato, Wagner, and Patterson (2008) on gendered patterns to the "cat-and-mouse game" over time; and Cornelius (2001) and De León (2015) on its increasingly deadly consequences.

6. Andersson (2014b).

7. The stark parallels were being seen already by the turn of the century; see, e.g., Andreas and Snyder (2000).

8. For an early study of European externalization policies, see Lahav and Guiradon (2000). Akkerman (2018) notes that, by 2018, the EU borders and coast guard agency Frontex had working arrangements with eighteen non-EU countries as well as with two regional organizations, the CIS Border Troop Commanders Council for Central Asian states and the MARRIO Regional Centre for the Balkans. On top of this, Frontex and in particular EU member states have long-running working arrangements with a range of Sahelian states. Frontex's working arrangements are listed in the public register of documents on the Frontex website.

9. See Andersson (2014b) for details on this episode.

10. Of course, the European externalization of migration controls was racially charged on a much more general level. Lack of space precludes further details on the particular dynamics of the Mauritanian role in fighting migration, or the racial and colonial histories that underlie it; two particularly useful studies on this are Frowd (2018) and Ould Moctar (2020). Specifically, Ould Moctar extensively discusses the racialization of illegality in the context of colonial legacies and border externalization.

11. See Andersson (2005) on the context and consequences of Plan Sur, implemented at the time.

12. On militias and their political maneuvering, see Reitano and Micaleff (2017). We discuss Libya more thoroughly, and with further referencing, in Andersson and Keen (2019).

13. See independent journalist Nancy Porsia's investigations, "The Kingpin of Libya's Human Trafficking Mafia," *TRT World*, February 20, 2017, https://www.trtworld.com/magazine/libya-human-trafficking-mafia-in-zawiya-301505/.

14. Greenhill (2016); also on the EU–Turkey deal, Amnesty (2017). Notably, some policymakers and academics have only very belatedly woken up to these games. Léonard and Kaunert (2021: 729), in a study of Turkey's exploitation of Europe's vulnerability on migration, suggest erroneously that securitization by external actors "has not been considered to date."

15. Greenhill (2010).

16. Daniel Howden's Lighthouse Reports has conducted a remarkable investigation of this horrific incident, as well as of many other instances of violence and cover-ups at Europe's borders. See https://www.lighthousereports.nl/investigation/reconstructing-the-melilla-massacre/.

17. In her view, checks and balances, rights considerations, and conflicting electoral politics create a dilemma for governments steering between crackdowns and humanitarianism in the face of "engineered" migrations (Greenhill 2010). These are important considerations but, as we suggest here, only one part of a much wider picture in which the securitization of migration in the instigating state (treating it as an urgent and sometimes even existential threat) generates incentives to use the resultant threat among neighboring and "partner" states.

18. Greenhill (2010).

19. On India's border and migration controls targeting supposed Bangladeshi "intruders," see Ghosh (2019) and Samaddar (2020). On the global trend, the literature is vast: e.g., Jones (2016) and Andersson (2014a).

20. Vallet (2017).

21. Akkerman (2021).

22. Budget figures retrieved from the Frontex website in 2022: https://frontex.europa.eu. EU lawmakers refused to sign off on the 2022 budget over pushbacks and financial question marks, which is indicative of the perverse incentives and games operative in the border security industry: see https://euobserver.com/migration/154639. In July of that year, a leaked report from the EU's anti-fraud office, Olaf, found that Frontex "covered up and helped to finance illegal pushbacks of asylum-seekers in Greece" (Christides and Lüdke 2022, n.p.).

23. See https://www.americanimmigrationcouncil.org/research/the-cost-of-immigration-enforcement-and-border-security. See Miller (2019) for a journalistic investigation of the US "export" of its border security worldwide (paralleled, as we see in this chapter, by a similarly expansive European project).

24. For example, see Larsson (2020) on civil security as a façade for the arms industry.

25. Massey et al. (2016).

26. E.g., Cornelius and Tsuda (2004). Specifically, Chebel d'Appollonia (2012: 223) writes that "the gap between official rhetoric (which professes the will to manage flows) and the actual outcomes may not be understood as a policy failure, but alternatively as the result of the competition between various pro- and anti-immigrant factions." From a different perspective, Brown (2017) has considered the political psychology of walling and sovereignty in an influential study.

27. Andreas (2009).

28. See, e.g., Chavez (2008); Ngai (2004); FitzGerald and Cook-Martín (2014).

29. Massey (2015: 288, 295). See also his quantitative study together with colleagues on "why border enforcement backfired" (Massey, Pren, and Durand 2016).

30. For example, De Genova (2002).

31. On how Spanish conservatives came to find in irregular migration a political boon, see Gabrielli (2011).

32. "Protecting" turned to "promoting" after the controversies around the former—yet the aims on migration within this "promotional" landscape remain just as security-oriented as before, or as the EU stated in 2019, "Strong borders, modernisation of the EU's asylum system and cooperation with partner countries are important to achieve a fresh start on migration." https://ec.europa.eu/info/strategy/priorities-2019-2024/promoting-our-european-way-life_en.

33. The *Daily Mail* headline on "we're from Europe" was later "corrected": https://www.huffingtonpost.co.uk/entry/daily-mail-correction-were-from-europe-eu-referendum_uk_5763cfe6e4b01fb6586374d8.

34. See, e.g., Hansen and Pettersson (2022: 118), who argue that irregular migration by means of visa overstaying "has largely, and routinely, been left out of the securitised discussion on migration," drawing on evidence of Frontex risk analyses.

35. On this "graveyard," where thousands have perished by Border Patrol omission or commission, see de León (2015).

36. On these interactions between migrant and policing tactics, see, e.g., de Genova (2017).

37. Massey et al. (2016).

38. On the deadly "game" between Italy, Malta, and other coastal states over avoiding responsibility for search-and-rescue, see, e.g., Gammeltoft-Hansen and Aalberts (2010); Heller and Pezzani (2012); also Albahari (2016).

39. One report summarizes the changes thus: "Tighter security in recent years has made other forms of clandestine or irregular entry—such as travelling through the Channel Tunnel concealed in a lorry—more difficult, increasing the appeal of using small boats. The end of the Dublin Regulation's application post-Brexit has also reduced the number of safe and legal routes for asylum seekers with family in the UK. And crucially, the initial success of using small boats has appeared to create a snowball effect, encouraging more and more to follow suit, and making the route increasingly hard to contain" (Morris and Qureshi 2022: 4). See also Keen (2020) on the human consequences of this game in Calais, specifically the functions of suffering.

40. IOM Missing Migrants project, https://missingmigrants.iom.int/reg ion/mediterranean. See also the painstaking work of UNITED List of Deaths over a longer time period, cataloging some forty-eight thousand deaths related to "Fortress Europe" policies since 1993: https://uniteda gainstrefugeedeaths.eu.

41. "Trafficking" is a separate legal category and "mafia" is an incorrect descriptor for most smuggling networks (with exceptions such as the Mexican cartels), most being organized in a dispersed fashion. For a global analysis of the growth of human smuggling, delineating dynamics such as those covered in this paragraph, see Sanchez and Achilli (2019).

42. Wogt (2013: 764, 774). See also Andreas (1998) on "narcocorruption," linking into migration-related corruption.

43. On the evolving smuggling market in Libya and its direct relation with the counterproductive "war on smugglers," see Albahari (2018). On violence and extraction mirroring the Mexico route, see Achtnich (2022).

44. Research interview with CBP officials, as related in Andersson (2018).

45. Reitano and Micaleff (2017: 3).

46. Reitano and Micaleff (2017); Andersson and Keen (2019).

47. Kenan Malik, writing in the *Observer* amid the Belarus crisis of 2021, did not mince his words: "To maintain Fortress Europe, the EU has funded a huge kidnap and detention industry right across Africa from

the Atlantic to the Red Sea, from the Mediterranean to beyond the Sahara. The 'Khartoum process' is a deal the EU stitched together with countries in the north and east of Africa to detain migrants before they can reach the Mediterranean. . . . Europe's policies have turned migrants into a resource to be exploited" (Malik 2021, n.p.).

48. Jaspars and Buchanan-Smith (2018: 30).

49. Amnesty (2016).

50. See Jaspars and Buchanan-Smith (2018: 30), who write, "The RSF attacked, looted and destroyed large numbers of villages in North and South Darfur throughout 2014. In 2015 and 2016, the government (with the RSF) launched major offensives on the Jebel Marra region, the last rebel stronghold. . . . Some 380,000 people were newly displaced in 2013, 430,000 in 2014 and 247,000 in 2015."

51. Morgan (2017, n.p.).

52. Amnesty (2016: 2).

53. Though the EU policy was to engage the police and not work with either the security forces or irregular forces, the reality was much more complicated; as one report put it, "The fact is, however, that *janjawid* militias have also been integrated into the so-called Central Reserve Police, whose record is no better than the RSF's. Further, whether distinctions between regular and irregular forces, and between police and army, are sufficient to avoid abuses can be questioned. It is perhaps for this reason that the EU itself acknowledges that in a context such as Sudan, it is very difficult to mitigate all risks, including 'the risk of unintentionally involving members of the Rapid Support Forces (RSF)/ Janjaweed in project activities'" (Tubiana, Warin, and Saeneen 2018: 54).

54. See de Waal's (2015) framework for understanding the "business of power" in the Horn of Africa, as well as de Waal and Ibreck (2016: 9).

55. Tubiana, Warin, and Saeneen (2018: 55–56).

56. Tubiana, Warin, and Saeneen (2018: 53).

57. De Waal (2022).

58. On Mali, see chapter 4. On Niger, see the in-depth reportage of Howden and Zandonini (2018) on what they rightly call "Europe's migration laboratory." In Niger, on one occasion in 2016, the foreign minister said the country needed "a billion euros to fight against clandestine migration." The gamble paid off: in December the following year, the EU announced it would support Niger with assistance of precisely 1 billion euros by 2020. Perhaps more important, the president, Mahamadou Issoufou, gained very substantial leverage and political support with his European "allies" at a delicate time of dwindling democratic legitimacy.

On Niger's gambit, see Reuters, May 3, 2016, https://www.reuters.com/article/us-europe-migrants-idUSKCN0XU1P9. Both Niger and Mali are discussed more extensively in Andersson (2019).

59. Andersson and Keen (2019).

60. On humanitarian borders, see Walters (2011); Pallister-Wilkins (2022); Cuttitta (2018); Andersson (2014b).

61. On the debacle, see the *Guardian,* https://www.theguardian.com/world/2021/nov/09/eu-condemns-belaruss-gangster-style-tactics-in-polish-border-crisis. As noted, studies on border violence worldwide are extensive, reaching from academic work (e.g., Albahari 2016; Jones 2016; de León 2015) to advocacy reports (e.g., Amnesty 2008), journalistic accounts (e.g., Trilling 2021; Rivkin 2021), and activist initiatives such as Border Violence Monitoring Network.

62. See the EU briefing on instrumentalization at https://www.europarl.europa.eu/RegData/etudes/BRIE/2022/739204/EPRS_BRI(2022)739204_EN.pdf.

63. On the Lampedusa "border play" over many years, including the Berlusconi administration's role in it, see Cuttitta (2014).

64. After the terrible fatal shipwreck of February 2023, Médecins Sans Frontières stated that its rescue vessel, *Geo Barents,* had been "unfairly detained and fined by the Italian government. Even though this measure directly targets MSF, the real price will be paid by those fleeing across the central Mediterranean who will be left without assistance." https://msf.org.uk/article/italy-msf-provides-support-survivors-deadly-shipwreck.

CHAPTER 6

1. Davies (2022) gives some clues to the "dark nudges" of gambling.

2. Important here is anthropologist Rebecca Cassidy's (2020) work on the *production* of gambling (and addiction) by governments and corporations as well as historian Jonathan Cohen's (2022) work on US state lotteries.

3. Cohen (2022); Vermeys and Elliott (2022) on Nevada.

4. Hari (2019).

5. Amnesty International, press release, May 18, 2020, https://www.amnesty.org.uk/philippines-president-duterte-war-on-drugs-thousands-killed.

6. CNN, September 30, 2016, https://edition.cnn.com/2016/09/30/asia/duterte-hitler-comparison/index.html.

7. HRW (2017).
8. Confidential transcript released by *The Intercept,* available at https://www.documentcloud.org/documents/3729123-POTUS-RD-Doc.html#document/p1.
9. Hari (2019: 14).
10. A poem by Franklin P. Adams (much cited since) at the time summed up why alcohol prohibition nevertheless persisted for some time: "Prohibition is an awful flop. / We like it. / It can't stop what it's meant to stop. / We like it. / It's left a trail of graft and slime, / It won't prohibit worth a dime, / It's filled our land with vice and crime. / Nevertheless, we're for it." https://druglibrary.net/schaffer/History/e1930/adamsprohibition.htm.
11. That was also true of the Supreme Court of the day.
12. Hari (2019) discusses how certain problematic cases were brought to national prominence as part of this campaign.
13. Hari (2019).
14. Hari (2019: 53–54).
15. While a war by name, the war on poverty was not quite a war by nature. On its longer-term impacts (which remain contested), see, e.g., Bailey and Danziger (2013).
16. Friedman (1998) returned to this argument some years later in a piece titled "There's No Justice in the War on Drugs." While we agree with much of this critique, especially as concerns the injustices of the war, we also take issue with the free-market ideology underpinning Friedman's position, as should be clear from our discussion in chapters 8–10.
17. The Carter administration took steps toward decriminalizing marijuana, building on an earlier committee recommendation that Nixon had ignored.
18. A brief history of the drug wars is to be found at the Drug Policy Alliance website, https://drugpolicy.org/issues/brief-history-drug-war.
19. Alexander (2012).
20. Alexander (2012: 335); also Nadelmann (1990).
21. Miron (2004) offers the argument that prohibition has historically increased levels of violent crime. In Mexico, the start of the drug war of 2006 notably coincided with such a rise. According to one relevant study, "[I]n 2005, the total rate of homicides was close to 11 per 100,000 individuals; by 2010, it was 18.5 per 100,000 individuals" (Enamorado et al. 2016: 129).
22. Parenti (2008).
23. Kuzmarov (2008).

24. Parenti (2008).

25. Baum (2017, n.p.).

26. Parenti (2008).

27. See Jude Joffe-Block and Terry Greene Sterling, "Joe Arpaio: Inside the Fallout of Trump's Pardon," *The Guardian*, April 8, 2021, https://www.theguardian.com/us-news/2021/apr/08/joe-arpaio-sheriff-arizona-donald-trump.

28. See Hari (2019) on horrific cases of sadistic violence. See Boyd (2001) on "the new Jim Crow." In 2021, the UN Working Group on Arbitrary Detention found that the "war on drugs" had resulted in "widespread rights violations associated with the enforcement of drug laws, including unlawful imprisonment, the trial of children and adolescents as 'adults,' torture and ill-treatment, lack of fair trial guarantees, extra-judicial killings, and the abusive use of the death penalty." https://www.ohchr.org/en/statements/2022/06/end-war-drugs-and-promote-policies-rooted-human-rights-un-experts/; UN Working Group on Arbitrary Detention (2021).

29. Blumenson and Nilsen (1998: 68).

30. *Harvard Law Review* (2015: 1734).

31. Blumenson and Nilsen (1998: 36).

32. Boyd (2001, n.p.).

33. Blumenson and Nilsen (1998).

34. Alexander (2012: 60).

35. On racial disparities and US imprisonment in a global perspective, see Drug Policy Alliance (2016); Rothwell (2015). See also the Sentencing Project's 2023 summary of "Mass Incarceration Trends" in the United States: https://www.sentencingproject.org/reports/mass-incarceration-trends/. On growth in imprisonment from the Reagan years to the 2010s, see Cullen (2018).

36. Caulkins et al. (2005: 7).

37. LSE IDEAS (2014: 3, 9) on price elasticity; Carpenter (2014) on dangerous pattern of consumption.

38. Blumenson and Nilsen (1998: 37–39).

39. Blumenson and Nilsen (1998: 39).

40. Blumenson and Nilsen (1998: 39).

41. Alexander (2012).

42. "The Corrections Corporation of America, by the Numbers," *Mother Jones,* July–August 2016, https://www.motherjones.com/politics/2016/06/cca-corrections-corperation-america-private-prisons-company-profile/. A similar phenomenon is the "bed mandate" in US migrant detention, guaranteeing occupancy rates and so incentivizing further detentions.

43. *Harvard Law Review* (2015).
44. *Harvard Law Review* (2015).
45. *Harvard Law Review* (2015: 1724).
46. Compare Andersson (2018) on predatory "bioeconomies" in migration control and more widely.
47. The term was coined by Cowan (1996). See Beletsky and Davis (2017) on fentanyl as well as on the "Iron Law" more widely.
48. For a summary, see LSE IDEAS (2014).
49. Castillo, Mejía, and Restrepo (2014: 70).
50. Arbour and ElBaradei (2019, n.p.).
51. Hari (2019).
52. Andreas (1998), who also describes the shifting of routes.
53. LSE IDEAS (2014: 3).
54. Idler and Garzón Vergara (2021: 406–8).
55. Council on Foreign Relations, 2021, https://www.cfr.org/backgroun der/mexicos-long-war-drugs-crime-and-cartels/.
56. Alejandro Celorio Alcántara, legal adviser of the Mexican Ministry of Foreign Affairs, paraphrased in Mineo (2022).
57. HRW, letter to the editor, *Washington Post,* reprinted at https://www. hrw.org/news/2009/08/18/human-rights-mexicos-drug-war#.
58. LSE IDEAS (2014: 29); Castillo, Mejía, and Restrepo (2014).
59. Agnew (2015). There is considerable uncertainty around these murders, as Agnew acknowledges.
60. Lee (2020: n.p.) for the overview and quote; see Dube and Naidu (2015) on the link between US military aid and paramilitary attacks.
61. Andreas (1998: 161).
62. Andreas (1998), building on the work of Lupsha (1991).
63. Fiorentini and Peltzman (1995); McCoy and Block (1992); Bertram et al. (1996).
64. Ribando Seelke and Finklea (2017: 11).
65. Keen (2012).
66. Hari (2019); Agnew (2015).
67. Fajardo (2003); Restrepo and Spagat (2005). Compare Gordon (2011) on similar patterns in Afghanistan, touched upon in chapter 4.
68. Keen (2003); Andersson (2005).
69. Schirmer (1999); Keen (2003).
70. Saunders-Hastings (2015).
71. For instance, Caulkins in LSE IDEAS (2014) raises some arguments in favor of enforcement.
72. This point is powerfully made by Hari (2019).

73. Public health approaches, as we have seen earlier in the chapter, are far from new (e.g., Buning et al. 1991; Mosher and Yanagisako 1991). For a recent evaluation of Portugal's influential model, warts and all, see Rêgo et al. (2021). We would need a much longer chapter to discuss the promises and pitfalls of liberalization; some of this filters into our reflections on ways forward in chapters 9 and 10.

CHAPTER 7

1. Andersson and Keen (2019).
2. Arendt (1994).
3. UNICEF (2017). On containment via camps and the EU's "hotspot" approach, see, e.g., Tazzioli and Garelli (2020).
4. Part of the controversy revolved around the "Remain in Mexico" or MPP policy, challenged in court by the Biden administration: see *Al Jazeera*, August 9, 2022, https://www.aljazeera.com/news/2022/8/9/us-scraps-remain-in-mexico-policy-after-supreme-court-ruling/. For the Biden administration's proposal on cracking down on asylum applications at the southern border, see US Department of Homeland Security, February 2023, https://public-inspection.federalregister.gov/2023-03718.pdf.
5. Andreas (2009: 9). See also, e.g., Massey (2015), cited in chapter 5.
6. Gall (1977).
7. Andersson (2016); see also studies by Oxford's Determinants of International Migration Project on these effects.
8. This was actively conveyed in the Brussels meeting and is of a piece with the longer-running "securitization of development" discussed, e.g., by Duffield (2001).
9. Muggah and Aguirre (2021: 381–83).
10. Thrall and Goepner (2017: 8); see also Gerges (2021).
11. UNDP (2017); see also Dodge and Wasser (2014).
12. Lemieux (2017).
13. See Elden (2013) on vertical forms of power; Chamayou (2015) on drones and force protection; also Andersson (2019). See Duffield (2018) for the wider picture.
14. Shaw (2005).
15. Drug Policy Alliance, "About Us," accessed April 23, 2023, https://drugpolicy.org/about-us/.
16. UN news service on migrant deaths, citing IOM data: https://news.un.org/en/story/2022/11/1130997. Notoriously, deaths in desert areas

(including the Sahara and Sonora) are severely under-reported: e.g., de León (2015).

17. This argument has of course been made repeatedly in our wars: see, e.g., Johnson and Tierney (2006) and Goepner (2016) on the war on terror; Andersson (2016) and Albahari (2018) on migration.

18. The literature here is extensive: for one influential perspective on global containment policies, see Agier (2011).

19. We touched upon studies of the racial dimensions of policing migration in the Maghreb in chapter 5. See, e.g., Gross-Wyrtzen and El Yacoubi (2022).

20. See, e.g., Weigand (2022) on the struggle over legitimacy in Afghanistan. We discuss Niger in Andersson and Keen (2019).

21. Arendt ([1951] 1979); this is discussed further in Keen (2023b).

22. For example, Bradbury (2010); Attree (2016); Walker (2016).

23. Whitlock (2019).

24. Whitlock, Shapiro, and Emamdjomeh (2019).

25. Chandrasekaran (2006).

26. *Omertà* is the Mafia's code of silence.

27. For example, Howell (2014); while herself critical of securitization in relation to the aid world, Howell also offered an interesting twist on this literature in considering some positive aspects of securitization in relation to NGOs in particular.

28. Quoted in Woodward (2002: 137).

29. Quoted in Whitlock (2019, n.p.).

30. Woodward (2002).

31. This was an idiom used, for instance, by ordinary people in Mali when discussing corruption and conflict in the country; see Whitehouse (2012).

32. Quoted in Whitlock (2019, n.p.). Flynn, according to investigative journalist Jeremy Scahill (2014: 104–5), was "on the knife's edge of the intelligence technology that would be at the center of the mounting, global kill/capture campaign" of Joint Special Operations Command. See chapter 4. Flynn was later convicted under Special Prosecutor Robert Mueller's investigation into Russian election interference and eventually pardoned by Trump.

33. Akam (2022, n.p.).

34. Keen (2012: 90); see also chapter 4.

35. Hayek (2001).

36. Becker (1997).

37. In his short and very readable piece, Barkawi (2011b, n.p.) also calls neo-liberalism "a mass production facility for self-licking cones." While we agree with his sentiment, putting the focus more squarely on aspects of NPM makes the critique more precise, which is important given how loosely "neoliberalism" is sometimes blamed for all the world's ills. Interestingly, and as an aside, Barkawi goes on to compare military and academic reactions to the SLICC system, and the result is not in scholars' favor. "A university system that took decades to build was dismantled by its own hands in less than a generation," he says of the UK university sector. "As for principled resistance, one was more likely to find it among the US officer corps in Vietnam than among British academics."

38. Lorenz (2012: 600).

39. Halperin (2006).

40. De Waal (1997). Over time, a number of more subtle crossovers into aid territory developed, for instance with programs to "counter violent extremism" or "build resilience," dragging a range of think tanks and NGOs into the system of security and military intervention.

41. The "humanitarianization" of border security has been widely studied; see, e.g., Walters (2011); Andersson (2014b); Cuttitta (2018); and Pallister-Wilkins (2022).

42. To take an example, Ruben heard firsthand how, in the Spanish case, the authorities had at an early stage of sea arrivals sought to replace the independent-minded Médecins Sans Frontières with the more emollient Spanish Red Cross.

43. For a critical take on the IOM's role around the Mediterranean, see Heller and Pécoud (2018). Despite some recent advances, IOM's growing clout on migration remains insufficiently analyzed yet points to the ways in which we must expand our view of crisis and security narratives away from the usual state-level suspects.

44. Marshall-Denton (2023). Compare the "refugee rentier state" argument of Freier, Micinski, and Tsourapas (2021), which shows how many refugee-hosting countries in the "Global South" are increasingly "commodifying" displaced populations, relating us back to the bargaining of chapter 5. Taking a wider view, however, highly unequal global refugee responsibilities combined with destination-state containment efforts (with UN buy-in) suggests the existence of a refugee rentier *system*.

45. To our knowledge no firm evidence exists to back up the value of these "sensitization" campaigns, which is unsurprising given how high-risk

migration tends to be framed by those engaging in it as active risk-taking and sacrifice (e.g., Melly 2011).

46. Similarly to Sudan, lines between state officials and militia groups are blurred indeed in Libya. See, e.g., Pacciardi and Berndtsson (2021).

47. See, for instance, "Refugee rescuers charged in Italy with complicity in people smuggling," *The Guardian,* March 4, 2021, https://www.theg uardian.com/global-development/2021/mar/04/refugee-rescuers-charged-in-italy-with-complicity-in-people-smuggling/.

48. This includes the framing of migration as a "borders problem." As Walters (2015) has perceptively noted in his discussion of academic "border-centrism," the political centering of borders when it comes to (unwanted) migration is a fairly recent historical phenomenon in many parts of the world. See Andersson (2017) on impact metrics and the "refugee crisis."

49. The debate around an influential anthropological article criticizing the "ambulance-chasing" tendencies of research on migration is interesting here, with one respondent suggesting that, besides returning to a more low-key ethnographic mode, researchers would do well to "study up" and "focus on the politicians who construct refugees as a problem, research those who vote for them, analyze the conditions that create displacement, study those who labor within systems that constrain mobility," and so forth (Besteman 2019: 283; Cabot 2019). *Wreckonomics* is one such attempt.

50. On this, see, e.g., Calhoun (2010).

51. Andersson (2019); Keen (2023a).

52. See, e.g., McChesney (2014); Davies (2009).

53. Bolt (2012).

54. Smith (2005).

55. Part of this is intentional, and part is not. Academics are keen to explore what Foucault called "power-knowledge," but we would join forces with those who have highlighted how we need to understand the "will to ignorance" as well: see McGoey (2019).

56. Gordon (2022).

CHAPTER 8

1. While both of us were alarmed by the UK government's lax attitude to COVID-19 in the spring of 2020 (as well as the Swedish one, in Ruben's case), there was subsequently a period when our views were significantly different. Part of this may have reflected personal circumstances that, as

for everybody else, fed into different experiences of the pandemic and its responses, particularly once lockdown hit. No doubt our own intellectual background also played some role. David had long worked on humanitarian operations and complex emergencies (including in a book of that name), while Ruben had focused on security and surveillance, including on hard risk-management "lockdown" in international operations in his 2019 book *No Go World*. Our perspectives eventually reconverged to a large degree, as the chapter illustrates. Key to that convergence was precisely the kind of open, no-holds-barred debate that we are advocating for—and hopefully "modeling"—in this chapter.

2. De Waal (2021), who also intriguingly explores how epidemiologists can usefully begin to see like a virus.

3. This is one reason why disease metaphors are so popular in actual war fighting.

4. Levitt and Dubner (2006). See also our chapter 2.

5. Horton (2020a: 935).

6. Stewart and Busby (2020).

7. Shipman and Wheeler (2020); see also Jukes (2020).

8. Walker (2020).

9. Hancock (2021, n.p.).

10. See, e.g., Roberts (2020).

11. Ryan (2021).

12. Booth (2020).

13. Pegg et al. (2020).

14. See, e.g., this blog post, from which the quote is taken: Isabel Frey, "'Herd Immunity' Is Epidemiological Neoliberalism," *The Quarantimes*, March 19, 2020, https://thequarantimes.wordpress.com/2020/03/19/herd-immunity-is-epidemiological-neoliberalism/. Another take looked at the three countries mentioned here as representative of neoliberal policies: https://www.aljazeera.com/opinions/2020/4/14/coronavirus-herd-immunity-and-the-eugenics-of-the-market/.

15. Keen (2021).

16. When Johnson finally did close the pubs, his expressions of regret invoked the "freedom-loving instincts" of the British people; see O'Toole (2020).

17. See Mintrom et al. (2021) on interesting differences in the political narrative in Germany and the United Kingdom.

18. Colombo (2021: 576).

19. Serwer (2020).

20. Serwer (2020).

21. Horton (2020b: 1178).

22. Schwartz (2020).

23. Horton (2020b: 1178).

24. Cadwalladr (2020, n.p.).

25. *The Lancet* (2020).

26. Singh (2020, n.p.).

27. Gustavsson (2021) takes issue with the public health patriotism of Sweden, linking it to particular elements of Swedish nationalism and exceptionalism.

28. Rocha, Pelayo, and Rackimuthu (2021).

29. For example, Jagannathan and Rai (2022); Naomi Grimley, Jack Cornish, and Nassos Stylianou, "Covid: World's True Pandemic Death Toll Nearly 15 Million, Says WHO," BBC, May 5, 2022, https://www.bbc.co.uk/news/health-61327778/.

30. BBC, May 7, 2020, https://www.bbc.co.uk/news/world-us-canada-52568405.

31. Reidy (2021).

32. SAGE Secretariat (2020).

33. To illustrate the critiques, one *Lancet Microbe* commentary suggested in 2021 that "[i]nitial projections built worst-case scenarios that would never happen as a means of spurring leadership into action" (Biggs and Littlejohn 2021).

34. While we are not epidemiologists, the main point we wish to make is that at the time, there was little public scope for debating these forecasts, whereas with time the space to engage in scientific debate did open up to a degree—a key point we return to in our third section. For instance, one study coauthored by John Ioannidis (a prominent scientific lockdown opponent) argued in 2022 that "forecasting COVID-19 has failed" overall: "Failure in epidemic forecasting is an old problem. In fact, it is surprising that epidemic forecasting has retained much credibility among decision-makers, given its dubious track record. . . . Predictions may work in 'ideal,' isolated communities with homogeneous populations, not the complex current global world." Instead, "the asymmetry of risks need[s] to be approached in a holistic fashion," a point very much related to our suggestions in the next chapter. See Ioannidis, Cripps, and Tanner (2022: 425, 428).

35. UK House of Commons, Science and Technology Committee (2021).

36. Sur (2021).

37. It is worth noting that, in the United States, the "herd immunity" strategy was not highlighted in the same way as in the United Kingdom.

More prominent in America was the simple insistence—spearheaded by Trump himself—that the virus was not a grave threat and that businesses should be either kept open or reopened very quickly. Inconsistently with his railing against the threat of the "Chinese virus," Trump regularly played down risks from COVID-19. In September 2020, he declared that, as time passed, the virus would go away even without a vaccine, adding, "And you'll develop—you'll develop herd—like a herd mentality." So the concept—albeit in characteristically mangled form—had clearly percolated to the president. See discussion in Keen (2021).

38. Hellewell et al. (2020).

39. Tapper (2020).

40. In academia, as in the wider debate (or shouting match), there has been a stark divide between those seeing "health security" as a threat to democracy and those finding a progressive biopolitics in the rollout of pandemic controls. Compare Agamben (2021) and Bratton (2021). Duffield (Unpublished) has reflected on the wider implications in a piece under preparation. See also Lyon (2022) for a thoughtful "first response" review on the "pandemic" of surveillance during the pandemic.

41. Sur (2021).

42. Notoriously, when quizzed on the negative effects that Brexit could have on British businesses, the leader of the United Kingdom's traditionally pro-business party said, "Fuck business."

43. Swinford (2021).

44. Blake (2020).

45. On Macron, see BBC, March 16, 2020, https://www.bbc.co.uk/news/av/51917380. On Guterres, see UN, press release, https://unric.org/en/covid-19-we-are-at-war-with-a-virus-un-secretary-general-antonio-guterres/.

46. Horton (2020b).

47. See, e.g., BBC reporting on the UK health minister's leaked WhatsApp communications, March 5, 2023, https://www.bbc.co.uk/news/uk-64848106/.

48. The UK Department of Health and Social Care incurred £8.7 billion of losses on £12.1 billion worth of PPE purchased in 2020–21. Besides the dubious contracts listed here, a very large part of the loss was due to overspending on PPE in the early part of the pandemic: see report by Peston (2022).

49. Monbiot (2020).

50. McKee (2021).

51. Case brought by the Good Law Project, https://goodlawproject.org/update/high-court-vip-lane-ppe-unlawful/.

52. The fraud write-off triggered the resignation of a junior minister early in 2022. Reuters, January 24, 2022, https://www.reuters.com/world/uk/uk-minister-resigns-over-woeful-attempts-stop-covid-19-loan-fraud-2022-01-24/.

53. Howden et al. (2021: n.p.) write in their cross-country investigative report that Palantir was pitching widely across Europe amid the pandemic, often offering "free trials." In Greece, "[t]he zero-cost agreement was not registered on the public procurement system, neither did the Greek government carry out a data impact assessment—the mandated check to see whether an agreement might violate privacy laws."

54. See, e.g., Ovide (2021).

55. Tréguer (2021: 27).

56. Klein (2020).

57. For example, Costello (2021).

58. Rizvi (2021).

59. See https://brownstone.org/articles/the-zoom-class-gets-covid/.

60. Ofsted chief inspector on BBC Radio 4, conveyed in Rachel Hall, "Pandemic Has Delayed Social Skills of Young Children, Says Ofsted Chief," *The Guardian,* April 4, 2022, https://www.theguardian.com/society/2022/apr/04/pandemic-has-delayed-social-skills-of-young-children-says-ofsted-chief. Ofsted's briefings on education recovery, providing the grounds for the chief inspector's assessment, are available at https://www.gov.uk/government/collections/ofsted-education-recovery-series.

61. Colombo (2021: 579).

62. This issue was raised already in the summer of 2020 by the oncologist Karol Sikora, including in an interview with *The Times* of London, August 22, 2020, https://www.thetimes.co.uk/article/saturday-interview-karol-sikora-zr3qxsn6f/.

63. Citation from summary of report in the *British Medical Journal.* The difficulty of separating out excess deaths due to different (yet often overlapping) causes has made a fuller account of the costs and benefits of different approaches difficult. The report, by Collateral Global, suggests that "the pandemic only highlighted and exacerbated a long-running problem: underfunding, poor structural layout, undertraining, underskilling, under-equipping, and finally, lack of humanity in dealing with the most vulnerable members of society. Neglect, thirst, and hunger were—and possibly still are—the biggest killers" (Heneghan et al. 2021: 2).

64. See, e.g., United Nations (2020).

65. Sun et al. (2022: 4).

66. HRW (2021, n.p.) on Sri Lanka; HRW (2020, n.p.) on Kenya; HRW (2022) on Greece and stop-and-search; Farahat and Markard (2020) on Mediterranean closures of ports to people rescued in the Mediterranean.

67. Vikram Dodd, "Black people were three times more likely to receive Covid fines in England and Wales," *The Guardian,* May 31, 2023, https://www.theguardian.com/uk-news/2023/may/31/black-people-england-and-wales-more-likely-issued-pandemic-fines-police-study/.

68. On links between Maoist population control and the People's War against COVID-19, see Jiang (2022). On social (as opposed to the more widely publicized technological) forms of control in employment and internal migration settings, see Xing and Xiang (2022).

69. For example, report by Chung (2022).

70. News reports later said the officials in charge had been fired due to the incident: https://www.theguardian.com/world/2022/jan/06/china-fires-hospital-officials-after-pregnant-woman-loses-baby-due-to-covid-lockdown-rules/.

71. News report by *Bloomberg* (2022).

72. Leung and Zoo (2022).

73. See McMorrow, Liu, and Yu (2023) on the absence of COVID-19 on death certificates.

74. Sur (2021).

75. On mortality in South Asia, see UNICEF (2021); BBC, March 17, 2021, https://www.bbc.co.uk/news/world-asia-56425115. On education, see UNESCO, UNICEF, and the World Bank (2021), and *Guardian* report summarizing the findings, January 25, 2022, https://www.theguardian.com/global-development/2022/jan/25/un-data-reveals-nearly-insurmountable-scale-of-lost-schooling-due-to-covid.

76. De Waal (2021).

77. See Kihato and Landau (2020) on COVID-19 regulation and spatial injustice in African cities. On African death tolls and differential levels of preparedness, see Ezeh et al. (2021).

78. Meagher (2022); Mkandawire (2010). Mkandawire highlighted colonial economic history as a major factor in settings regions apart, a point also taken up by De Waal (2021) in the context of various epidemics.

79. Robinson et al. (2021).

80. Even the idea that policy should be "somewhere in the middle" may be a kind of surrender to the binary rather than creatively thinking through

solutions in the light of complex policy problems and impacts—a point that gains importance in our final two chapters.

81. Green and Fazi (2023), discussed by Seymour (2023).

82. BBC, January 5, 2022, https://www.bbc.co.uk/news/world-europe-59873833.

83. For a curious take on the trucker situation, see Lyons (2022).

84. Weiss (2022).

85. This reminded us of "Better dead than red" and "Better red than dead" slogans during the Cold War. The mutual reinforcement and differentiation through cumulative interaction in both cases echoes Gregory Bateson's (1958) notion of *schismogenesis,* which we referenced briefly in chapter 3.

86. One prominent example was of Jay Bhattacharya, professor at Stanford Medical School and one of the authors of the Great Barrington Declaration, advocating "focused protection" instead of lockdowns, who faced various rounds of trouble on Twitter for his position; news reports include Ensor (2022). In terms of abuse, *Science* reported that 38 percent of researchers who had published multiple papers on COVID-19 said they had experienced at least one type of harassment related to their COVID-19 work, and a *Nature* news survey found 81 percent of respondents said that they had experienced personal verbal attacks or some kind of "trolling" after talking to the media about COVID-19. See Van Noorden (2022).

87. Foa et al. (2022).

88. WHO stated in May 2022 that "the full death toll associated directly or indirectly with the COVID-19 pandemic (described as 'excess mortality') between 1 January 2020 and 31 December 2021 was approximately 14.9 million (range 13.3 million to 16.6 million)." WHO press release, May 5, 2022, https://www.who.int/news/item/05-05-2022-14.9-million-excess-deaths-were-associated-with-the-covid-19-pandemic-in-2020-and-2021.

89. Ruben encountered this kind of language in EU-funded awareness-raising campaigns on irregular migration in Senegal, where participants were said to be vaccinated or inoculated against the risks.

90. De Waal (2021).

91. Foucault (1991).

92. Mitchell (2022).

93. For example, Keen (2008).

94. On hospital beds, see Mueller (2020). On intensive care units, see, e.g., Jacobs (2021).

95. Quote from Buzelli and Boyce (2021: 501). On the war-like triage (and more on the privatization problem), see, e.g., De Falco (2021).
96. Yong (2020).
97. Luce (2020).
98. Reicher (2021, n.p.).
99. Colombo (2021: 575).
100. Colombo (2021: 578).
101. Interestingly, de Waal (2021) finds in the global response to AIDS some cause for hope, in that through activism and advocacy, there was eventually a shift toward a humanized rather than a "martial" response.
102. Jervis uses this phrase frequently, citing Garett Hardin (e.g., Jervis 2012).

CHAPTER 9

1. Keen (2012).
2. Compare Keen (2023a) on the politics of shame.
3. Kinder and Hammond (2023).
4. Notably, in Minneapolis in 2021, polls showed that despite grave concerns about the quality of policing, a larger proportion of Black residents were in favor of increasing the police force and not replacing it with a department for public safety (*Star Tribune* 2021).
5. "Copenhagen School" authors emphasized the need for "desecuritization" since their early days of theorizing securitization. See Aradau (2004) for a critical reflection.
6. Attree and Street (2022: i).
7. Attree and Street (2022: 57).
8. Attree and Street (2022: 57).
9. Hammitt (2020).
10. For further discussion of these tendencies in the migration case, see Andersson (2016).
11. Clay and Schaffer (1982).
12. LSE IDEAS (2014); Idler and Garzón Vergara (2021).
13. In the United Kingdom, the Stern (2007) review on the economics of climate change was particularly influential. On the serious limits of corporate climate accounting, see, e.g., Livsey (2021).
14. Carrington (2019).
15. As noted in brief later in the chapter, there are of course also strange bedfellows *opposing* further migration, linking trade unions to the conservative right, for example. These coalitions also need to be listened to, allowing potentially for even larger coalitions that move away from a securitized approach while protecting all workers.

16. Srinivasan (2021).
17. For example, Torjesen and Macfarlane (2007); Venugopal (2018).
18. This is a point we draw from Hannah Arendt.
19. Compare Beck (1999) on cosmopolitan risk communities.
20. On pseudo-causal narratives in the EU's Emergency Trust Fund for Africa, see Zaun and Nantermoz (2021). On WHAM, see chapters 4 and 7.
21. We're indebted, here as elsewhere, to Duffield's (2001) work on how, for instance, security and development thinking presents a seemingly "holistic" frame for frequently self-serving ends.
22. Cf. Stedman (1997).
23. Cf. Srinivasan (2021).

CHAPTER 10

1. Milanovic (2018) argues that a more open global migration regime would help to reduce inequality further. Others, notably George Borjas, have argued that migration negatively impacts native workers, while still others highlight costs at origin. This debate is a complex and at times a heated one, and we don't have the space to go into it further here. For one prominent controversy, summarized from the perspective of one of the advocates of a more open regime, see Clemens (2017).
2. Saez and Zucman (2016); Piketty (2018).
3. Tooze (2022, n.p.).
4. See Brown's (2017) interesting argument on wall-building and waning sovereignty. Other academics, notably Saskia Sassen (1996), have suggested that sovereignty is transforming in important respects. Our wars and fights can certainly be seen as part of this transformation.
5. See also Andersson (2019); Keen (2023b).
6. Carlotta Gall and Thomas De Waal (1997) memorably called Moscow's military intervention in Chechnya a "small victorious war." See also Klein (2007).
7. See Beck (1999) on world risk society.
8. For example, Ahmed (2011).
9. For a small sample of this literature, which extends into studies of populism and political emotion, see, e.g., Kinnvall (2019) on ontological (in) security and muscular nationalism in India; Mishra (2017) on the steering of anger and anxiety in South Asia as well as worldwide; Chebel d'Appollonia (2012) on border security, anxiety, and fear. Our own work on the political mobilization of fear (Andersson 2019) and shame

(Keen 2023a) has also engaged these dimensions of security and war, with further investigations to come.

10. Arendt ([1951] 1979).

11. Klein (2007).

12. We discussed drug liberalization in earlier chapters. The refugee proposals were prominently part of the book *Refuge* (Betts and Collier 2017).

13. Compare Fraser's (2022) searing indictment of capitalism on numerous counts.

14. Piketty (2018); Hacker and Pierson (2011).

15. Danner (2016).

16. Akerlof and Shiller (2015).

17. Hacker and Pierson (2011).

18. For example, Wade (2009).

19. Wade (2009: 1167).

20. Wade (2009: 1169–70).

21. Underlining the dangers of a "war" framing was the language of existential struggle, of "enemies," and of sacrifice that infused the drive for "development" in Communist China, Cambodia, and the Soviet Union, situations where variations of a "war on poverty" facilitated and legitimized terrible famines and persecutions. In a huge drive for "development," China's Great Leap Forward saw Communist bureaucrats competing to meet and exceed their targets for requisitioning grain; in the process, they helped to create a massive famine that was hushed up through extreme violence and intimidation against "counterrevolutionary" enemies—including anyone who tried to present a more realistic picture of what was going on. See Becker (1997).

22. Clay and Schaffer (1982).

23. Monbiot (2021, n.p.).

24. For example, Baldwin, Methmann, and Rothe (2014); Bettini (2013).

25. Alex de Waal has stressed this point in relation to food security: "Already you see investors, particularly from the Middle East and Asia but also from North America and Europe, buying up huge tracts of land in Africa because they see it as a limited resource that we better grab as much as we can. And that's causing all sort of problems by displacing farmers." Investors, de Waal observes, "are thinking of this as a hedge against food shortages — but actually you're creating the problem now." As cited by NPR, "What Today's Headlines About Famine Get Wrong," January 19, 2018, https://www.cpr.org/2018/01/19/what-todays-headlines-about-famine-get-wrong/.

26. Azmanova (2021, n.p.).

References

Abboud, Samer. 2015. *Syria*. Cambridge, UK: Polity.

Achtnich, Marthe. 2022. "Bioeconomy and Migrants' Lives in Libya." *Cultural Anthropology* 37(1): 9–15.

Africa Watch and Alex de Waal. 1991. *Evil Days: Thirty Years of War and Famine in Ethiopia*. New York: Human Rights Watch.

Agamben, Giorgio. 1998. *Homo Sacer: Sovereign Power and Bare Life*. Stanford, CA: Stanford University Press.

Agamben, Giorgio. 2014. "For a Theory of Destituent Power." *Critical Legal Thinking*, February 5. https://criticallegalthinking.com/2014/02/05/the ory-destituent-power/.

Agamben, Giorgio. 2021. *Where Are We Now? The Epidemic as Politics*. 2nd ed. London: Eris.

Agier, Michel. 2011. *Managing the Undesirables: Refugee Camps and Humanitarian Government*. Cambridge: Polity.

Agnew, Heather Robin. 2015. "Reframing 'Femicide': Making Room for the Balloon Effect of Drug War Violence in Studying Female Homicides in Mexico and Central America." *Territory, Politics, Governance* 3(4): 428–45.

Ahmed, Nafeez Mosaddeq. 2011. "The International Relations of Crisis and the Crisis of International Relations: From the Securitisation of Scarcity to the Militarisation of Society." *Global Change Peace & Security* 23(3): 335–55.

Akerlof, George A., and Robert J. Shiller. 2015. *Phishing for Phools: The Economics of Manipulation and Deception*. Princeton, NJ: Princeton University Press.

Akkerman, Mark. 2018. *Expanding the Fortress: The Policies, the Profiteers, and the People Shaped by EU's Border Externalisation Programme*. Report. Amsterdam: Stop Wapenhandel/Transnational Institute, May.

Akkerman, Mark. 2021. "Financing Border Wars: The Border Industry, Its Financiers and Human Rights." Briefing. Amsterdam: Stop Wapenhandel/ Transnational Institute, April.

Akram, Simon. 2022. "A Surfeit of Rank." *London Review of Books* 44(5), March 10. https://www.lrb.co.uk/the-paper/v44/no5/simon-akam/a-surfeit-of-rank.

Albahari, Maurizio. 2016. *Crimes of Peace: Mediterranean Migrations at the World's Deadliest Border.* Philadelphia: University of Pennsylvania Press.

Albahari, Maurizio. 2018. "From Right to Permission: Asylum, Mediterranean Migrations, and Europe's War on Smuggling." *Journal on Migration and Human Security* 6(2): 121–30.

Alexander, Michelle. 2012. *The New Jim Crow: Mass Incarceration in the Age of Colorblindness.* New York: New Press.

Amin, Samir. 1974. "Accumulation and Development: A Theoretical Model." *Review of African Political Economy* 1(1): 9–26.

Amnesty International. 2008. *Mauritania Report: Arrests and Collective Expulsions of Migrants Denied Entry into Europe.* Report. London: Amnesty International, July.

Amnesty International. 2016. "Human Rights Impacts and Risks Associated with the Khartoum Process." Submission to the UK All-Party Parliamentary Group For Sudan and South Sudan, October.

Amnesty International. 2017. *A Blueprint for Despair: Human Rights Impact of the EU-Turkey Deal.* Report. London: Amnesty International, February.

Andersson, Ruben. 2005. "The New Frontiers of America." *Race Class* 46(3): 28–38.

Andersson, Ruben. 2012. "A Game of Risk: Boat Migration and the Business of Bordering Europe." *Anthropology Today* 28(6): 7–11.

Andersson, Ruben. 2014a. "A Global Front: Thoughts on Enforcement at the Rich World's Borders." Online appendix to *Illegality, Inc: Clandestine Migration and the Business of Bordering Europe.* Oakland: University of California Press.

Andersson, Ruben. 2014b. *Illegality, Inc.: Clandestine Migration and the Business of Bordering Europe.* Oakland: University of California Press.

Andersson, Ruben. 2016. "Europe's Failed 'Fight' against Irregular Migration: Ethnographic Notes on a Counterproductive Industry." *Journal of Ethnic and Migration Studies* 42(7): 1055–75.

Andersson, Ruben. 2017. "The Price of Impact: Reflections on Academic Outreach amid the 'Refugee Crisis.'" *Social Anthropology/Anthropologie Sociale* 26(2): 222–37.

Andersson, Ruben. 2018. "Profits and Predation in the Human Bioeconomy." *Public Culture* 30(3): 413–39.

Andersson, Ruben. 2019. *No Go World: How Fear Is Redrawing Our Maps and Infecting Our Politics.* Oakland: University of California Press.

Andersson, Ruben, and David Keen. 2019. *Partners in Crime? The Impact of Europe's Outsourced Migration Controls on Peace, Stability and Rights.* Report. London: Saferworld, July.

Andreas, Peter. 1998. "The Political Economy of Narco-Corruption in Mexico." *Current History* 97(618): 160–65.

Andreas, Peter. 2009. *Border Games: Policing the U.S.-Mexico Divide*. Ithaca, NY: Cornell University Press.

Andreas, Peter, and Timothy Snyder. 2000. *The Wall around the West: State Borders and Immigration Controls in North America*. Lanham, MD: Rowman & Littlefield.

Aradau, Claudia. 2004. "Security and the Democratic Scene: Desecuritization and Emancipation." *Journal of International Relations and Development* 7: 388–413.

Aradau, Claudia, and Martina Tazzioli. 2020. "Biopolitics Multiple: Migration, Extraction, Subtraction." *Millennium: Journal of International Studies* 48(2): 198–220.

Arbour, Louise, and Mohamed ElBaradei. 2019. "The Campaign for a 'Drug-Free World' Is Costing Lives." *The Guardian*, March 20.

Arendt, Hannah. (1951) 1979. *The Origins of Totalitarianism*. San Diego, CA: Harvest.

Arendt, Hannah. 1973. *Crises of the Republic*. Harmondsworth: Penguin.

Arendt, Hannah. 1994. *Essays in Understanding, 1930–1954*. New York: Harcourt, Brace.

Attree, Larry. 2016. *Blown Back: Lessons from Counter-Terror, Stabilisation and Statebuilding in Yemen*. Report. London: Saferworld, February.

Attree, Larry, and Jordan Street. 2022. *No Shortcuts to Security: Learning from Responses to Armed Conflicts Involving Proscribed Groups*. Report. London: Saferworld, May.

Ayoob, Mohammed. 1995. *Third World Security Predicament: State Making, Regional Conflict and the International System*. Boulder, CO: Lynne Rienner.

Azmanova, Albena. 2021. "Precarity, Populism, and Prospects for a Green Democratic Transformation." openDemocracy, January 18. https://www.opendemocracy.net/en/rethinking-populism/precarity-populism-and-prospects-green-democratic-transformation/.

Bagayoko, Niagalé. 2019. "La réforme du système de sécurité malien à l'épreuve des mutations du nexus 'défense/sécurité intérieure' dans l'espace sahélien." *Canadian Journal of African Studies* 53(3): 463–68.

Bailey, Martha J., and Sheldon Danziger, eds. 2013. *Legacies of the War on Poverty*. New York: Russell Sage Foundation.

Baldwin, Andrew, Chris Methmann, and Delf Rothe. 2014. "Securitizing 'Climate Refugees': The Futurology of Climate-Induced Migration." *Critical Studies on Security* 2(2): 121–30.

Barkawi, Tarak. 2011a. "From War to Security: Security Studies, the Wider Agenda and the Fate of the Study of War." *Millennium: Journal of International Studies* 39(3): 701–16.

Barkawi, Tarak. 2011b. "The West's Self-Licking Ice Cream Cones." *Al Jazeera*, September 15.

Barnett, Thomas P. M. 2004. *The Pentagon's New Map: War and Peace in the Twenty-first Century*. New York: G. P. Putnam's Sons.

Bateson, Gregory. 1958. *Naven*. Stanford, CA: Stanford University Press.

Bateson, Gregory. 2000. *Steps to an Ecology of Mind*. Chicago: University of Chicago Press.

Baum, D. 2017. "Legalize It All: How to Win the War on Drugs." *Harper's*, April.

Bauman, Zygmunt. 2001. "Wars of the Globalization Era." *European Journal of Social Theory* 4(1): 11–28.

Beck, Ulrich. 1999. *World Risk Society*. Cambridge, UK: Polity.

Becker, Jason. 1997. *Hungry Ghosts: Mao's Secret Famine*. London: Simon & Schuster.

Beletsky, Leo, and Corey S. Davis. 2017. "Today's Fentanyl Crisis: Prohibition's Iron Law, Revisited." *International Journal of Drug Policy* 46: 156–59.

Berdal, Mats. 2003. "How 'New' are 'New Wars'? Global Economic Change and the Study of Civil War." *Global Governance* 9 (4): 477–502.

Berdal, Mats, and David Malone, eds. 2000. *Greed and Grievance: Economic Agendas in Civil Wars*. Boulder: Lynne Rienner/International Peace Academy.

Berdal, Mats. 2011. "The 'New Wars' Thesis Revisited." In *The Changing Character of War*, edited by Hew Strachan and Sibylle Scheipers. New York: Oxford University Press.

Bertram, Eva, Morris Blachman, Kenneth Sharpe, and Peter Andreas, eds. 1996. *Drug War Politics: The Price of Denial*. Berkeley: University of California Press.

Besteman, Catherine. 2019. "A Comment on Heath Cabot's 'The Business of Anthropology and the European Refugee Regime.'" *American Ethnologist* 46(3): 282–83.

Besteman, Catherine. 2020. *Militarized Global Apartheid*. Durham, NC: Duke University Press.

Bettini, Giovanni. 2013. "Climate Barbarians at the Gate? A Critique of Apocalyptic Narratives on 'Climate Refugees.'" *Geoforum* 45: 63–72.

Betts, Alexander, and Paul Collier. 2017. *Refuge: Transforming a Broken Refugee System*. London: Allen Lane.

Bevins, Vincent. 2020. *The Jakarta Method: Washington's Anticommunist Crusade and the Mass Murder Program That Shaped Our World*. New York: PublicAffairs.

Biggs, Adam T., and Lanny F. Littlejohn. 2021. "Revisiting the Initial COVID-19 Pandemic Projections." *The Lancet Microbe* 2(3): E91–E92.

Bigo, Didier. 2002. "Security and Immigration." *Alternatives* 27: 63–92.

Bigo, Didier. 2014. "The (In)securitization Practices of the Three Universes of EU Border Control." *Security Dialogue* 45(3): 209–25.

Black, Ian. 2021. "Russian Foreign Minister Urges End to Calls for Assad to Stand Down." *The Guardian*, November 18.

Blake, Aaron. 2020. "Trump's Continually Strange Comments on Possibly 'Overrated' Coronavirus Testing." *Washington Post*, May 15.

Bloomberg. 2022. "This Is What Life's Like in the World's Strictest Covid Zero City." September 23.

Blumenson, Eric, and Eva Nilsen. 1998. "Policing for Profit: The Drug War's Hidden Economic Agenda." *University of Chicago Law Review* 65(1): 35–114.

Bolt, Neville. 2012. *The Violent Image: Insurgent Propaganda and the New Revolutionaries*. London: Hurst.

Booth, Robert. 2020. "Why Did So Many People Die of Covid-19 in the UK's Care Homes?" *The Guardian*, May 28.

Booth, Ken, and Nicholas Wheeler. 2008. *The Security Dilemma: Fear, Cooperation, and Trust in World Politics*. Basingstoke: Palgrave Macmillan.

Bourdieu, Pierre. 2013. *Outline of a Theory of Practice*. Cambridge: Cambridge University Press.

Boyd, Graham. 2001. "The Drug War Is the New Jim Crow." *NACLA Report on the Americas*, July–August. https://www.aclu.org/other/drug-war-new-jim-crow/.

Bradbury, Mark. 2010. "State-Building, Counterterrorism, and Licensing Humanitarianism in Somalia." Report. Boston: Feinstein International Center, Tufts University, September.

Bratton, Benjamin. 2021. *The Revenge of the Real: Politics for a Post-Pandemic World*. London: Verso.

Brinkley Joel. 2013. "The Monstrous Failure of US Aid to Afghanistan." *World Affairs* 175(5): 13–23.

Brown, Wendy. 2017. *Walled States, Waning Sovereignty*. 2nd ed. New York: Zone Books.

Buning, E. C., E. Drucker, A. Matthews, R. Newcombe, and P. A. O'Hare, eds. 1991. *The Reduction of Drug-Related Harm*. Abingdon: Routledge.

Burnett, John. 2004. "In the Line of Fire." *New York Times*, August 4.

Butler, Smedley D. 1935. *War Is a Racket*. https://www.ratical.org/ratville/CAH/warisaracket.html.

Buzan, Barry, Ole Wæver, and Jaap de Wilde. 1998. *Security: A New Framework for Analysis*. Boulder, CO: Lynne Rienner.

Buzelli, Maria Luisa, and Tammy Boyce. 2021. "The Privatization of the Italian National Health System and Its Impact on Health Emergency Preparedness and Response: The COVID-19 Case." *International Journal of Social Determinants of Health and Health Services* 51(4): 501–8.

Byman, Daniel. 2006. "Friends Like These: Counterinsurgency and the War on Terrorism." *International Security* 31(2): 79–115.

Cabot, Heath. 2019. "The Business of Anthropology and the European Refugee Regime." *American Ethnologist* 46(3): 261–75.

Cadwalladr, Carole. 2020. "'They Can't Get Away with This': Doctor Who Took Protest to No 10." *The Guardian*, April 20.

Calhoun, Craig. 2010. "The Idea of Emergency: Humanitarian Action and Global (Dis)order." In *Contemporary States of Emergency: The Politics of Military and Humanitarian Interventions*, edited by Didier Fassin and Mariella Pandolfi, 123–45. New York: Zone.

Cardoso, Fernando Henrique, and Faletto, Enzo. 1979. *Dependency and Development in Latin America*. Berkeley: University of California Press.

Carpenter, Ted G. 2014. *Bad Neighbor Policy: Washington's Futile War on Drugs in Latin America*. Basingstoke: Palgrave Macmillan.

Carrington, Damian. 2019. "Firms Ignoring Climate Crisis Will Go Bankrupt, Says Mark Carney." *The Guardian*, October 13.

Carroll, James. 2007. *House of War: The Pentagon and the Disastrous Rise of American Power*. London: HarperCollins.

Cassidy, Rebecca. 2020. *Vicious Games: Capitalism and Gambling*. London: Pluto.

Castillo, Juan Camilo, Daniel Mejía, and Pascual Restrepo. 2014. "Scarcity without Leviathan: The Violent Effects of Cocaine Supply Shortages in the Mexican Drug War." Working Paper 356. Washington, DC: Center for Global Development.

Caulkins, Jonathan P., Peter Reuter, Martin Y. Iguchi, and James Chiesa. 2005. "How Goes the 'War on Drugs'? An Assessment of U.S. Drug Problems and Policy." Occasional Paper. Santa Monica, CA: RAND Drug Policy Research Center.

Chabal, Patrick, and Jean-Pascal Daloz. 1999. *Africa Works: Disorder as Political Instrument*. London: James Currey.

Chakrabarty, Dipesh. 2012. "Postcolonial Studies and the Challenge of Climate Change." *New Literary History* 43(1): 1–18.

Chamayou, Gregoire. 2015. *Drone Theory*. London: Penguin.

Chandrasekaran, Rajiv. 2006. *Imperial Life in the Emerald City: Inside Baghdad's Green Zone*. London: Bloomsbury.

Chaudhuri, Rudra, and Theo Farrell. 2011. "Campaign Disconnect: Operational Progress and Strategic Obstacles in Afghanistan, 2009–2011." *International Affairs* 87(2): 271–96.

Chavez, Leo. 2008. *The Latino Threat: Constructing Immigrants, Citizens, and the Nation.* Palo Alto, CA: Stanford University Press.

Chebel d'Appollonia, Ariane. 2012. *Frontiers of Fear: Immigration and Insecurity in the United States and Europe.* Ithaca, NY: Cornell University Press.

Chomsky, Noam. 2003. *Hegemony or Survival: America's Quest for Global Dominance.* London: Penguin.

Chung, Nathan. 2022. "'We Won't Survive': China's Migrant Workers Fear More Lockdowns as Covid Threat Remains." *The Guardian,* June 16.

Christides, Giorgos, and Steffen Lüdke. 2022. Classified Report Reveals Full Extent of Frontex Scandal. *Der Spiegel,* July 29.

Clemens, Michael. 2017. "There's No Evidence That Immigrants Hurt Any American Workers." *Vox.com,* August 3.

Cockburn, Andrew. 2021. *The Spoils of War: Power, Profit and the American War Machine.* London: Verso.

Cohen, Jonathan D. 2022. *For a Dollar and a Dream: State Lotteries in Modern America.* New York: Oxford University Press.

Colombo, Enzo. 2021. "Human-Rights Inspired Governmentality: Covid-19 from a Human Dignity Perspective." *Critical Sociology* 47(4–5): 571–81.

Colombo Telegraph. 2021. "The 100th Anniversary of the Communist Party of China: PM Mahinda Rajapaksa's Speech—Full Text," July 7.

Conetta, Carl. 2010. "An Undisciplined Defense: Understanding the $2 Trillion Surge in US Defense Spending." Briefing Report 20. Cambridge, MA: Project on Defense Alternatives, January.

Conetta, Carl, and Charles Knight. 1998. "Dueling with Uncertainty: The New Logic of American Military Planning." Report. Cambridge, MA: Project on Defense Alternatives, Commonwealth Institute.

Cornelius, Wayne A. 2001. "Death at the Border: The Efficacy and 'Unintended' Consequences of U.S. Immigration Control Policy 1993–2000." Working Paper. San Diego, CA: Center for Comparative Immigration Studies, December 2001.

Cornelius, Wayne A., and Takeyuki Tsuda. 2004. "Controlling Immigration: The Limits of Government Intervention." In *Controlling Immigration: A Global Perspective,* edited by Wayne A. Cornelius, Philip L. Martin, and James F. Hollifield, 3–48. Stanford, CA: Stanford University Press.

Corson, William R. 1968. *The Betrayal.* New York: W. W. Norton.

Costello, Anthony. 2021. "'Living with the Virus' Makes No Sense." *The Guardian*, July 7.

Côté-Boucher, Karine, Federica Infantino, and Mark B. Salter. 2014. "Border Security as Practice: An Agenda for Research." *Security Dialogue* 45(3): 195–208.

Cowan, Richard C. 1986. "How the Narcs Created Crack." *National Review* 38: 26–31.

Cukier, Kenneth, and Viktor Mayer-Schönberger. 2013. "The Dictatorship of Data." *MIT Technology Review*, May 31. https://www.technologyreview.com/2013/05/31/178263/the-dictatorship-of-data/.

Cullen, James. 2018. *The History of Mass Incarceration*. Report. New York: Brennan Center for Justice, July 20.

Cunningham, David, and Alexandra Warwick. 2013. "Unnoticed Apocalypse." *City* 17(4): 433–48.

Cuttitta, Paolo. 2014. "'Borderizing' the Island: Setting and Narratives of the Lampedusa 'Border play.'" *CME: An International e-Journal for Critical Geographies* 13(2): 196–219.

Cuttitta, Paolo. 2018. "Delocalization, Humanitarianism, and Human Rights: The Mediterranean Border between Exclusion and Inclusion." *Antipode* 50(3): 783–803.

Danner, M. 2016. "The Magic of Donald Trump." *New York Review of Books*, May 26.

Davies, Nick. 2009. *Flat Earth News*. London: Vintage.

Davies, Rob. 2022. "What Gambling Firms Don't Want You to Know—and How They Keep You Hooked." *The Guardian*, February 12.

De Falco, Rosella. 2021. "Italy's Experience during COVID-19: The Limits of Privatisation in Healthcare." Policy Brief: Global Initiative for Economic, Social and Cultural Rights, June 1.

De Genova, Nicholas. 2002. "Migrant Illegality and Deportability in Everyday Life." *Annual Review of Anthropology* 31: 419–47.

De Genova, Nicholas, ed. 2017. *The Borders of "Europe": Autonomy of Migration, Tactics of Bordering*. Durham, NC: Duke University Press.

De León, Jason. 2015. *The Land of Open Graves: Living and Dying on the Migrant Trail*. Oakland: University of California Press.

Deng, Frances. 1986. *The Man Called Deng Majok: A Biography of Power, Polygyny and Change*. New Haven, CT: Yale University Press.

Dershowitz, Alan. 2002. *Why Terrorism Works*. New Haven, CT: Yale University Press.

De Waal, Alex. 1997. *Famine Crimes: Politics and the Disaster Relief Industry in Africa*. Oxford: African Rights & the International African Institute in association with James Currey.

De Waal, Alex. 2014. "When Kleptocracy Becomes Insolvent: Brute Causes of the Civil War in South Sudan." *African Affairs* 113(452): 347–69.

De Waal, Alex. 2015. *The Real Politics of the Horn of Africa: Money, War and the Business of Power*. Cambridge, UK: Polity.

De Waal, Alex. 2021. *New Pandemics, Old Politics: Two Hundred Years of War on Disease and Its Alternatives*. Medford, UK: Polity.

De Waal, Alex. 2022. "Reaping the Whirlwind: The Fall of Al-Bashir." In *Sudan's Unfinished Democracy*, edited by Willow Berridge, Justin Lynch, Raga Makawi, and Alex de Waal, 37–78. London: Hurst.

De Waal, Alex, and Rachel Ibreck. 2016. "A Human Security Strategy for the European Union in the Horn of Africa." Research Paper. London: LSE Security in Transition/Friedrich Ebert Stiftung, February.

Dodge, Toby, and Becca Wasser. 2014. "The Crisis of the Iraqi State." In *Middle Eastern Security, the US Pivot and the Rise of ISIS,* edited by Toby Dodge and Emile Hokayem, 447–48. London: International Institute for Strategic Studies.

Donato, K. M., B. Wagner, and E. Patterson. 2008. "The Cat and Mouse Game at the Mexico-U.S. Border: Gendered Patterns and Recent Shifts." *International Migration Review* 42(2): 330–59.

Donnelly, Jack. 2019. "Systems, Levels, and Structural Theory: Waltz's Theory Is *Not* a Systemic Theory (and Why That Matters for International Relations Today)." *European Journal of International Relations* 25(3): 904–30.

Droz-Vincent, Philippe. 2014. "'State of Barbary' (Take Two): From the Arab Spring to the Return of Violence in Syria." *Middle East Journal* 68(1): 33–58.

Drug Policy Alliance. 2016. "The Drug War, Mass Incarceration and Race." Note, February.

Dube, Oeindrila, and Suresh Naidu. 2015. "Bases, Bullets and Ballots: The Effect of U.S. Military Aid on Political Conflict in Colombia." *Journal of Politics* 77(1): 249–67.

Duffield, Mark. 2001. *Global Governance and the New Wars: The Merging of Development and Security*. London: Zed Books.

Duffield, Mark. 2007. *Development, Security and Unending War: Governing the World of Peoples*. Cambridge, UK: Polity Press.

Duffield, Mark. 2018. *Post-Humanitarianism: Governing Precarity in the Digital World*. Cambridge, UK: Polity.

Duffield, Mark. Unpublished (2022). "Thinking Like an Object: Connectivity, Behavioural Robotics and Pandemic Politics." Unpublished manuscript.

Dunlap, Charles. 2011. "The Military-Industrial Complex." *Daedalus* 140(3): 135–47.

Dunn, Andrew. 2016. "Obama Envoy: 70 Percent of Russian Strikes Don't Hit ISIS." *The Hill*, October 2.

Elden, S. 2013. "Secure the Volume: Vertical Geopolitics and the Depth of Power." *Political Geography* 34: 35–51.

Elder, Sean. 2014. "Cold War Roadshow." *Newsweek*, November 15.

Ellis, Stephen. 2004. "Briefing: The Pan-Sahel Initiative." *African Affairs* 103(412): 459–64.

Enamorado, Ted, Luis F. López-Calva, Carlos Rodríguez-Castelán, and Hernán Winkler. 2016. "Income Inequality and Violent Crime: Evidence from Mexico's Drug War." *Journal of Development Economics* 120: 128–43.

Ensor, Josie. 2022. "Stanford Anti-Lockdown Professor Jay Bhattacharya Secretly Blacklisted on Twitter, New Leak Shows." *Daily Telegraph*, December 9.

Enzensberger, Hans Magnus. 1994. *Civil Wars: From L.A to Bosnia*. New York: The New Press.

Evans, Gareth. 2009. "Falling Down on the Job." *Foreign Policy*, May 1.

Ezeh, Alex, Michael Silverman, and Saverio Stranges, with Janica Adams. 2021. "The Impact of COVID-19 Has Been Lower in Africa: We Explore the Reasons." *The Conversation*, August 17.

Faguet, Jean-Paul. 2021. "Chronicle of a Collapse Foretold: Why Democracy Died in the Afghan Desert." LSE blog post, September 9.

Fajardo, Luis E. 2003. "From the Alliance for Progress to the Plan Colombia." Working Paper. London: LSE: Crisis States Research Centre.

Faludi, Susan. 1999. *Stiffed: The Betrayal of the Modern Man*. London: Chatto & Windus.

Farahat, Anuscheh, and Nora Markard. 2020. "Closed Ports, Dubious Partners: The European Policy of Outsourcing Responsibility." e-paper. Heinrich Böll Stiftung, May.

Fiorentini, Gianluca, and Sam Peltzman, eds. 1995. *The Economics of Organized Crime*. Cambridge: Cambridge University Press.

FitzGerald, Scott, and David Cook-Martín. 2014. *Culling the Masses: The Democratic Origins of Racist Immigration Policy in the Americas*. Cambridge, MA: Harvard University Press.

Foa, Roberto S., Xavier Romero-Vidal, Andrew J. Klassen, Joaquin Fuenzalida Concha, Marian Quednau, and Lisa Sophie Fenner. 2022. "The Great Reset: Public Opinion, Populism and the Pandemic." Report. Cambridge: Bennett Institute for Public Policy, Cambridge University.

Forsberg, Carl. 2010. "Politics and Power in Kandahar." Afghanistan Report 5. Washington, DC: Institute for the Study of War, April.

Foucault, Michel. 1991. *Discipline and Punish: The Birth of the Prison*. London: Penguin.

Foucault, Michel. 2007. *Security, Territory, Population: Lectures at the Collège de France, 1977–78*. New York: Palgrave Macmillan.

Fraser, Nancy. 2022. *Cannibal Capitalism: How Our System Is Devouring Democracy, Care, and the Planet—and What We Can Do About It*. London: Verso.

Freier, Luisa F., Nicholas R. Micinski, and Gerasimos Tsourapas. 2021. "Refugee Commodification: The Diffusion of Refugee Rent-Seeking in the Global South." *Third World Quarterly* 42(11): 2747–66.

Friedman, Milton. 1998. "There's No Justice in the War on Drugs." *New York Times*, January 11.

Frowd, Philippe M. 2018. *Security at the Borders: Transnational Practices and Technologies in West Africa*. Cambridge: Cambridge University Press.

Gabrielli, Lorenzo. 2011. "La construction de la politique d'immigration espagnole: Ambiguïtés et ambivalences à travers le cas des migrations ouest-afric- aines." PhD dissertation, Université de Bordeaux.

Gaddis, John Lewis. 2005. *Strategies of Containment: A Critical Appraisal of American National Security Policy during the Cold War*. Revised and expanded ed. New York: Oxford University Press.

Galeano, Eduardo. 2009. *Open Veins of Latin America: Five Centuries of the Pillage of a Continent*. London: Serpent's Tail.

Gall, Carlotta. 2014. *The Wrong Enemy: America in Afghanistan, 2000–2014*. Boston: Houghton Mifflin Harcourt.

Gall, Carlotta, and Thomas de Waal. 1997. *Chechnya: A Small Victorious War*. London: Picador.

Gall, John. 1977. *How Systems Work and Especially How They Fail*. London: Times Books.

Gammeltoft-Hansen, Thomas, and Tanja E. Aalberts. 2010. "Sovereignty at Sea: The Law and Politics of Saving Lives in the Mare Liberum." DIIS Working Paper 18. Copenhagen: University of Copenhagen.

Gberie, Lansana. 2005. *A Dirty War in West Africa: The RUF and the Destruction of Sierra Leone*. London: Hurst.

Gerges, Fawaz A. 2009. *The Far Enemy: Why Jihad Went Global*. Cambridge: Cambridge University Press.

Gerges, Fawaz A. (2016) 2021. *ISIS: A History*. Princeton, NJ: Princeton University Press.

Ghosh, Sahana. 2019. "'Everything Must Match': Detection, Deception, and Migrant Illegality in the India-Bangladesh Borderlands." *American Anthropologist* 121(4): 870–83.

Giustozzi, Antonio. 2004. "Respectable Warlords? The Politics of State-Building in Post-Taliban Afghanistan." Working Paper 33. London: Crisis States Programme, DESTIN, LSE.

Global Terrorism Index. 2015. *Measuring and Understanding the Impact of Terrorism.* Sydney: Institute for Economics and Peace.

Global Terrorism Index. 2016. *Measuring and Understanding the Impact of Terrorism.* Sydney: Institute for Economics and Peace.

Goepner, Erik W. 2016. "Learning from Today's Wars: Measuring the Effectiveness of America's War on Terror." *Parameters* 46(1): 107–20.

Goodhand, Jonathan. 2010. "Stabilising a Victor's Peace? Humanitarian Action and Reconstruction in Eastern Sri Lanka." *Disasters* 34(s3): S342–S367.

Gopal, Anand. 2014. *No Good Men among the Living: America, the Taliban and the War through Afghan Eyes.* New York: Metropolitican Books/Henry Holt and Company.

Gopal, Anand. 2021. "The Other Afghan Women." *New Yorker,* September 6. https://www.newyorker.com/magazine/2021/09/13/the-other-afghan-women.

Gordon, Gavin. 2022. "Suella Braverman Says She Will Fix UK's 'Broken' Asylum System." *The Independent,* November 1.

Gordon, Stuart. 2011. *Winning Hearts and Minds? Examining the Relationship between Aid and Security in Afghanistan's Helmand Province.* Report, April. Boston: Feinstein International Center, April.

Gravel, Mike, and Joe Lauria. 2008. *A Political Odyssey: The Rise of American Militarism and One Man's Fight to Stop It.* New York: Seven Stories Press.

Green, Toby, and Thomas Fazi. 2023. *The COVID Consensus: The Global Assault on Democracy and the Poor: A Critique from the Left.* London: Hurst.

Greenhill, Kelly M. 2010. *Weapons of Mass Migration: Forced Displacement, Coercion, and Foreign Policy.* Ithaca, NY: Cornell University Press.

Greenhill, Kelly M. 2016. "Open Arms behind Barred Doors: Fear, Hypocrisy and Policy Schizophrenia in the European Migration Crisis." *European Law Journal* 22(3): 317–32.

Gross-Wyrtzen, Leslie, and Zineb Rachdi El Yacoubi. 2022. "Externalizing Otherness: The Racialization of Belonging in the Morocco-EU Border." *Geoforum,* https://doi.org/10.1016/j.geoforum.2022.103673.

Gustavsson, Gina. 2021. *Du stolta du fria: Om svenskarna, Sverigebilden och folkhälsopatriotismen.* Stockholm: Kaunitz-Olsson.

Hacker, Jacob, and Paul Pierson. 2011. *Winner-Take-All Politics: How Washington Made the Rich Richer—and Turned Its Back on the Middle Class.* London: Simon & Schuster.

Halperin, Morton H., with Priscilla A. Clapp and Arnold Kanter. 2006. *Bureaucratic Politics and Foreign Policy.* Washington, DC: Brookings Institution Press.

Hammitt, James. 2020. "Accounting for the Distribution of Benefits and Costs in Benefit-Cost Analysis." *Journal of Benefit Cost Analysis* 12(1): 64–84.

Hancock, Sam. 2021. "Who Do We Not Save?" *The Independent*, May 26.

Hansen, Froda, and Johanna Pettersson. 2022. "Contradictory Migration Management? Differentiated Security Approaches to Visa Overstay and Irregular Border Crossings in the European Union." *European Security* 31(1): 117–34.

Hari, Johann. 2019. *Chasing the Scream*. London: Bloomsbury.

Harper, John. 2021. "Pentagon Personnel Costs at Historic High." *National Defense*, October 19.

Harvard Law Review. 2015. "Policing and Profit." 128(1723): 1723–46.

Harvey, David. 2004. "The 'New' Imperialism: Accumulation by Dispossession." *Socialist Register* 40: 63–87.

Hattam, Victoria. 2016. "Imperial Designs: Remembering Vietnam at the US-Mexico Border Wall." *Memory Studies* 9(1): 27–47.

Hayek, Friedrich. 2001. *The Road to Serfdom*. Abingdon: Routledge.

Heller, Charles, and Antoine Pécoud. 2018. "Counting Migrants' Deaths at the Border: From Civil Society Counter-statistics to (Inter)governmental Recuperation." Working Paper 143. Oxford: IMI.

Heller, Charles, and Lorenzo Pezzani. 2012. "Report on the 'Left-to-Die Boat.'" Forensic Architecture. https://forensic-architecture.org/investigat ion/the-left-to-die-boat/.

Hellewell, Joel, Sam Abbott, Amy Gimma, Nikos I. Bosse, Christopher I. Jarvis, Timothy W. Russell, James D. Munday, Adam J. Kucharski, and W. John Edmunds. 2020. "Feasibility of Controlling COVID-19 Outbreaks by Isolation of Cases and Contacts." *The Lancet*, February 28.

Heneghan, C., M. Dietrich, J. Brassey, and T. Jefferson. 2021. "CG Report 6: Effects of COVID-19 in Care Homes—A Mixed Methods Review." *Collateral Global* Version 1, December 3. https://collateralglobal.org/arti cle/effects-of-covid-19-in-care-homes/.

Hirschman, Charles, Samuel Preston, and Vu Manh Loi. 1995. "Vietnamese Casualties during the American War: A New Estimate." *Population and Development Review* 21(4): 783–812.

Horton, Richard. 2020a. "Offline: COVID-19—A Reckoning." *The Lancet* 395(10228): 935.

Horton, Richard. 2020b. "Offline: COVID-19—Bewilderment and Candour." *The Lancet* 395: 1178.

Howden, Daniel, Apostolis Fotiadis, Ludek Stavinoha, and Ben Holst. 2021. "Seeing Stones: Pandemic Reveals Palantir's Troubling Reach in Europe." *The Guardian*, April 2.

Howden, Daniel, and Giacomo Zandonini. 2018. "Niger: Europe's Migration Laboratory." *New Humanitarian*, May 22.

Howell, Jude. 2014. "The Securitisation of NGOs Post-9/11." *Conflict, Security & Development* 14(2): 151–79.

Hoyos, Héctor. 2012. "Aftershock: Naomi Klein and the Southern Cone." *Third Text* 26(2): 217–28.

Human Rights Watch. 2004. *"Enduring Freedom": Abuses by U.S. Forces in Afghanistan*. Report. New York: Human Rights Watch, March.

Human Rights Watch. 2009. *War on the Displaced: Sri Lankan Army and LTTE Abuses against Civilians in the Vanni*. Report. New York: Human Rights Watch, February 20.

Human Rights Watch. 2013. *Human Rights Failings Detailed, Justice for War Crimes Blocked, Civil Society Attacked*. Report. New York: Human Rights Watch, February 1.

Human Rights Watch. 2017. *"License to Kill": Philippine Police Killings in Duterte's "War on Drugs."* Report. New York: Human Rights Watch, March 2.

Human Rights Watch. 2020. *Kenya: Police Brutality during Curfew*. Report. New York: Human Rights Watch, April 22.

Human Rights Watch. 2021. *Sri Lanka: Police Abuses Surge amid Covid-19 Pandemic*. Report. New York: Human Rights Watch, August 6.

Human Rights Watch. 2022. *Greece: New Biometrics Policing Program Undermines Rights*. Report. New York: Human Rights Watch, January 18.

Ibrahim, Maggie. 2005. "The Securitization of Migration: A Racial Discourse." *International Migration* 43(5): 163–87.

Idler, Annette, and Juan Carlos Garzón Vergara, eds. 2021. *Transforming the War on Drugs: Warriors, Victims and Vulnerable Regions*. London: Hurst.

Ignatieff, Michael. 2004. "Could We Lose the War on Terror? Lesser Evils." *New York Times Magazine*, May 2.

Institute for Economics and Peace. 2017. Global Terrorism Index 2017. Report, November.

International Crisis Group. 2007. "Sri Lanka: Sinhala Nationalism and the Elusive Southern Consensus." Asia Report 141. Brussels: International Crisis Group, November 7.

International Crisis Group. 2009. *Conflict Risk Alert: Sri Lanka*. Report. Brussels: International Crisis Group, March 9.

International Crisis Group. 2012. "Syria's Mutating Conflict." Middle East Report 128. Brussels: International Crisis Group, August 1.

International Crisis Group. 2018. *Migration and Displacement from Darfur: Conflict, Livelihoods and Food Security*. Report. Brussels: International Crisis Group.

International Crisis Group. 2019. "After Sri Lanka's Easter Bombings: Reducing Risks of Future Violence." Asia Report 302. Brussels: International Crisis Group, September 27.

International Crisis Group. 2022. "'In a Legal Black Hole': Sri Lanka's Failure to Reform the Prevention of Terrorism Act." Report. Brussels: International Crisis Group, February 7.

Ioannidis, John P. A., Sally Cripps, and Martin A. Tanner. 2022. "Forecasting for COVID-19 Has Failed." *International Journal of Forecasting* 38: 423–38.

Jacobs, Sherelle. 2021. "We Are Reaping the Whirlwind of a Historic Failure to Solve Britain's Deadly ICU Crisis." *Daily Telegraph*, January 18.

Jagannathan, Srinath, and Rajnish Rai. 2022. "The Necropolitics of Neoliberal State Response to the Covid-19 Pandemic in India." *Organization* 29(3): 426–48.

Jaspars, Susanne, and M. Buchanan-Smith. 2018. "Migration and Displacement from Darfur: Conflict, Livelihoods and Food Security."

Jayatilleka, Dayan. 2009. "Stand Up for Others, They Stand Up for You." Interview. June 3. wannioperation.com.

Jervis, Robert. 1997. *System Effects: Complexity in Political and Social Life.* Princeton, NJ: Princeton University Press.

Jervis, Robert. 2012. "System Effects Revisited." *Critical Review* 24(3): 393–415.

Jiang, Jue. 2022. "A Question of Human Rights or Human Left? The 'People's War against COVID-19' under the 'Gridded Management' System in China." *Journal of Contemporary China* 31(136): 491–504.

Jones, Reece. 2016. *Violent Borders: Refugees and the Right to Move.* London: Verso.

Jukes, Peter. 2020. "The Coronavirus Crisis: Herd Immunity Infected UK Policy, but Who Was Patient Zero for This Toxic Transatlantic Idea?" *Byline Times*, April 3.

Kaldor, Mary. 1981. *The Baroque Arsenal.* New York: Hill & Wang.

Kaldor, Mary. 1998. *New and Old Wars: Organized Violence in a Global Era.* Stanford, CA: Stanford University Press.

Kaldor, Mary. 2021. "Book Review: The Spoils of War." OpenDemocracy, October 3. https://www.opendemocracy.net/en/book-review-the-spoils-of-war/.

Kalyvas, Stathis N. 2003. "The Ontology of 'Political Violence': Action and Identity in Civil Wars." *Perspectives on Politics* 1(3): 475–94.

Kalyvas, Stathis N. 2004. "The Paradox of Terrorism in Civil War." *Journal of Ethics* 8(1): 97–138.

Kalyvas, Stathis N. 2012. *The Logic of Violence in Civil Wars.* Cambridge: Cambridge University Press.

Kanfash, Mohammad, and Ali Aljasem. 2022. "Starvation as Strategy in the Syrian Armed Conflict: Siege, Deprivation, and Detention." In *Accountability* for *Mass Starvation: Testing the Limits of the Law,* edited by Bridget Conley, Alex de Waal, Catriona Murdoch and Wayne Jordash, 195–216. Oxford: Oxford University Press.

Kaplan, Robert D. 1994. "The Coming Anarchy." *Atlantic Monthly,* February.

Keen, David. 1994. *The Benefits of Famine: A Political Economy of Famine and Relief in Southwestern Sudan, 1983–1989.* Princeton, NJ: Princeton University Press.

Keen, David. 2003. "Demobilising Guatemala." Working Paper Series 1, 37. London: Crisis States Research Centre, LSE.

Keen, David. 2005. *Conflict and Collusion in Sierra Leone.* Oxford: James Currey and International Peace Academy.

Keen, David. 2008. *Complex Emergencies.* Cambridge, UK: Polity.

Keen, David. 2012. *Useful Enemies: When Waging Wars Becomes More Important Than Winning Them.* New Haven, CT: Yale University Press.

Keen, David. 2014. "The Camp and 'the Lesser Evil': Humanitarianism in Sri Lanka." *Conflict, Security and Development* 14(1): 1–31.

Keen, David. 2017. *Syria: Playing Into Their Hands: Regime and International Roles in Fuelling Violence and Fundamentalism in the Syria War.* London: Saferworld.

Keen, David. 2020. "The Functions and Legitimization of Suffering in Calais, France." *International Migration* 59(3): 9–28.

Keen, David. 2021. "Does Democracy Protect? The United Kingdom, the United States, and Covid-19." *Disasters* 45(S1): S26–S47.

Keen, David. 2023a. *Shame: The Power and Politics of an Emotion.* Princeton, NJ: Princeton University Press.

Keen, David. 2023b. *When Disasters Come Home: Making and Manipulating Emergencies in the West.* Cambridge, UK: Polity.

Keen, David, and Ruben Andersson. 2018. "Double Games: Success, Failure and the Relocation of Risk in Fighting Terror, Drugs and Migration." *Political Geography* 67: 100–110.

Keenan, Jeremy. 2009. *The Dark Sahara: America's War on Terror in Africa.* London: Pluto Press.

Khalaf, Rana. 2021. "Governance without Government in Syria: Civil Society and State Building during Conflict." *Syria Studies* 7(3): 37–72.

Kihato, Caroline W., and Loren Landau. 2020. "Coercion or the Social Contract? COVID 19 and Spatial (In)justice in African Cities." *City & Society* DOI: 10.1111/ciso.12265.

Kilcullen, David. 2009. *The Accidental Guerilla: Fighting Small Wars in the Midst of a Big One.* Oxford: Oxford University Press.

Kinder, Tabby, and George Hammond. 2023. "What if San Francisco Never Pulls Out of Its 'Doom Loop'?" *The Financial Times,* May 18.

Kinnard, Douglas. 1991. *The War Managers: American Generals Reflect on Vietnam*. New York: Da Capo Press.

Kinnvall, Catarina. 2019. "Populism, Ontological Insecurity and Hindutva: Modi and the Masculinization of Indian Politics." *Cambridge Review of International Affairs* 32(3): 283–302.

Klein, Naomi. 2007. *The Shock Doctrine: The Rise of Disaster Capitalism*. London: Allen Lane.

Klein, Naomi. 2020. "How Big Tech Plans to Profit from the Pandemic." *The Guardian*, May 13.

Klem, Bart. 2020. "Sri Lanka in 2019: The Return of the Rajapaksas." *Asian Survey* 60(1): 207–12.

Kristol, William, and Robert Kagan. 1996. "Toward a Neo-Reaganite Foreign Policy." *Foreign Affairs* 75(4): 18–32.

Kuzmarov, Jeremy. 2008. "From Counter-Insurgency to Narco-Insurgency: Vietnam and the International War on Drugs." *Journal of Policy History* 20(3): 344–78.

Lacher, Wolfram. 2012. *Organized Crime and Conflict in the Sahel-Sahara Region*. Report. Washington, DC: Carnegie Endowment for International Peace, September.

Lahav, Gallya, and Virginie Guiraudon. 2000. "Comparative Perspectives on Border Control: Away from the Border and outside the State." In *The Wall around the West: State Borders and Immigration Control in North America and Europe*, edited by Peter Andreas and Timothy Snyder, 55–77. Lanham, MD: Rowman & Littlefield.

La Vanguardia. 2022. "Sánchez sobre el asalto en Melilla: Si hay un responsable son las mafias." June 25.

Larsson, Sebastian. 2020. "The Civil Paradox: Swedish Arms Production and Export and the Role of Emerging Security Technologies." *International Journal of Migration and Border Studies* 6(1–2): 26–51.

Lee, Brendon. 2020. "Not-So-Grand Strategy: America's Failed War on Drugs in Colombia." *Harvard International Review*, January 9. https://hir.harvard.edu/americas-failed-war-on-drugs-in-colombia/.

Leenders, Reynoud. 2013. "How the Syrian Regime Outsmarted Its Enemies." *Current History* 112(758): 331–37.

Lemieux, Frederic. 2017. "What Is Terrorism? What Do Terrorists Want?" *The Conversation,* May 23.

Léonard, Sarah, and Christian Kaunert. 2021. "De-centring the Securitisation of Asylum and Migration in the European Union: Securitisation, Vulnerability and the Role of Turkey." *Geopolitics* 27: 729–51.

Leung, Kanis, and Zen Soo. 2022. "China Lockdown Protests Pause as Police Flood City Streets." Associated Press, November 29.

Levitt, Stephen D., and Stephen J. Dubner. 2006. *Freakonomics: A Rogue Economist Explores the Hidden Side of Everything*. London: Penguin.

Lister, Charles. 2014. "Assessing Syria's Jihad." Report. Adelphi Series 54, no. 447–48. London: International Institute for Strategic Studies.

Livsey, Alan. 2021. "Accounting Needs to Be Stepped Up for Climate Change Costs." *Financial Times*, March 15.

Loewenstein, Antony. 2015. *Disaster Capitalism: Making a Killing out of Catastrophe*. London: Verso.

Loewenstein, Antony. 2019. *Pills, Powder and Smoke: Inside the Bloody War on Drugs*. London: Scribe.

Lorenz, Chris. 2012. "If You're So Smart, Why Are You under Surveillance? Universities, Neoliberalism, and New Public Management." *Critical Inquiry* 38(3): 599–629.

LSE IDEAS. 2014. *Ending the Drug Wars*. Report. London: LSE, May.

Luce, Edward. 2020. "Premature US Reopening Plays Russian Roulette with Its Workers." *Financial Times*, May 6.

Lupsha, Peter. 1991. "Drug Lords and Narco-Corruption: The Players Change but the Game Continues." *Crime, Law and Social Change* 16: 41–58.

Luttwak, Edward N. 1999. "Give War a Chance." *Foreign Affairs* 78(4): 36–44.

Lyon, David. 2022. *Pandemic Surveillance*. Cambridge, UK: Polity.

Lyons, N. S. 2022. "Reality Honks Back." *The Upheaval* blog, February 16. https://theupheaval.substack.com/p/reality-honks-back/.

Macrae, Joanna, Anthony Zwi, Mark Duffield, and Hugo Slim. 1994. *War and Hunger: Rethinking International Responses to Complex Emergencies*. London: Zed Books/Save the Children.

Malik, Kenan. 2021. "Lukashenko Is a Handy Villain to Mask the Cruelty of Fortress Europe." *The Observer*, November 14.

Markusen, Ann. 1997. "How We Lost the Peace Dividend." *American Prospect*, 33 (July–August): 86–95.

Marshall-Denton, Chloe. 2023. "Mixed Migration, Fragmented Protection: Refugee and Migrant Protection in the 'Field' of Mixed Migration." DPhil thesis, University of Oxford.

Martinez, José, and Brent Eng. 2016. "The Unintended Consequences of Emergency Food Aid: Neutrality, Sovereignty and Politics in the Syrian Civil War, 2012–15." *International Affairs* 92(1): 153–73.

Masco, Joseph. 2013. *The Theater of Operations: National Security Affect from the Cold War to the War on Terror*. Durham, NC: Duke University Press.

Massey, Douglas S. 2015. "A Missing Element in Migration Theories." *Migration Letters* 12(3): 279–99.

Massey, Douglas S., Karen A. Pren, and Jorge Durand. 2016. "Why Border Enforcement Backfired." *American Journal of Sociology* 121(5): 1557–600.

Matovski, Aleksandar. 2022. "How Does the Weak Strongman Stay in Power? Exposing the Roots of Vladimir Putin's Rule in Russia." *Asia Policy* 17(3): 182–85.

Mbembe, Achille. 2019. *Necropolitics*. Durham, NC: Duke University Press.

McChesney, Robert. 2014. "Not Silent, but Deadly." *Monthly Review*, June, 66.

McCoy, Alfred W., and Alan A. Block, eds. 1992. *War on Drugs: Studies in the Failure of U.S. Narcotics Policy*. Boulder, CO: Westview.

McGoey, Linsey. 2019. *The Unknowers: How Strategic Ignorance Rules the World*. London: Zed Books.

McKee, Martin. 2021. "The UK's PPE Procurement Scandal Reminds Us Why We Need Ways to Hold Ministers to Account." *British Medical Journal* 372(639). https://www.bmj.com/content/bmj/372/bmj.n639.full.pdf.

McMorrow, Ryan, Nian Liu, and Sun Yu. 2023. "Relatives Angry as Covid Kept Off Chinese Death Certificates: 'What Are You Trying to Hide?'" *Financial Times*, January 20.

Meagher, Kate. 2022. "Crisis Narratives and the African Paradox: African Informal Economies, COVID-19 and the Decolonization of Social Policy." *Development and Change* 53(6): 1200–29.

Melly, Caroline M. 2011. "Titanic Tales of Missing Men: Reconfigurations of National Identity and Gendered Presence in Dakar, Senegal." *American Ethnologist* 38(2): 361–76.

Milanovic, Branko. 2018. *Global Inequality: A New Approach for the Age of Globalization*. Cambridge, MA: Harvard University Press.

Miller, Todd. 2014. *Border Patrol Nation: Dispatches from the Front Lines of Homeland Security*. San Francisco: City Lights Press.

Miller, Todd. 2019. *Empire of Borders: The Expansion of the US Border around the World*. London: Verso.

Mineo, Liz. 2022. "Stopping Toxic Flow of Guns from U.S. to Mexico." *Harvard Gazette*, February 18.

Mintrom, Michael, Maria Rost Rublee, Matteo Bonotti, and Steven T. Zech. 2021. "Policy Narratives, Localisation, and Public Justification: Responses to COVID-19." *Journal of European Public Policy* 28(8): 1219–37. DOI: 10.1080/13501763.2021.1942154.

Miron, Jeffrey A. 2004. *Drug War Crimes: The Consequences of Prohibition*. Independent Institute.

Mishra, Pankaj. 2017. *Age of Anger: A History of the Present*. London: Farrar, Straus & Giroux.

Mitchell, Tom. 2022. "Li Qiang, Xi's Right-hand Man." *Financial Times*, October 28.

Mkandawire, Thandika. 2010. "On Tax Efforts and Colonial Heritage in Africa." *The Journal of Development Studies* 46(10): 1647–69.

Monbiot, George. 2020. "When Secret Coronavirus Contracts Are Awarded without Competition, It's Deadly Serious." *The Guardian,* July 15.

Monbiot, George. 2021. "Think Big on Climate: The Transformation of Society in Months Has Been Done Before." *The Guardian,* October 20.

Morgan, Hiba. 2017. "Sudan's RSF Unit Accused of Abuses against Migrants." *Al Jazeera,* November 17.

Morris, Marley, and Amreen Qureshi. 2022. "Understanding the Rise in Channel Crossings." Briefing Paper. London: IPPR.

Morrison, David. 2016. "Who Broke the Syria Ceasefire?" openDemocracy, October 17. https://www.opendemocracy.net/en/what-russia-and-rest-of-us-are-doing-in-syria/.

Mosher, J., and K. Yanagisako. 1991. "Public Health, Not Social Warfare: A Public Health Approach to Illegal Drug Policy." *Journal of Public Health Policy* 12: 278–323.

Mueller, Benjamin. 2020. "Doctors Say U.K. Is Ill Prepared for Coronavirus." *New York Times,* March 5.

Muggah, Robert, and Katherine Aguirre. 2021. "Rethinking Drug Policy Metrics to Move beyond the War on Drugs." In *Transforming the War on Drugs: Warriors, Victims and Vulnerable Regions,* edited by Annette Idler and Juan Carlos Garzón Vergara, 377–401. Oxford: Oxford University Press.

Nadelmann, Ethan A. 1990. "Global Prohibition Regimes: The Evolution of Norms in International Society." *International Organization* 44(4): 479–526.

Nevins, Joseph. 2010. *Operation Gatekeeper and Beyond: The War on "Illegals" and the Remaking of the U.S.-Mexico Boundary.* 2nd ed. Abingdon: Routledge.

Ngai, Mae M. 2004. *Impossible Subjects: Illegal Aliens and the Making of Modern America.* Princeton, NJ: Princeton University Press.

Niva, Steve. 2013. "Disappearing Violence: JSOC and the Pentagon's New Cartography of Networked Warfare." *Security Dialogue* 44(3): 185–202.

O'Toole, Fintan. 2021. Coronavirus Has Exposed the Myth of British Exceptionalism. *The Irish Times,* April 11.

Ould Moctar, Hassan. 2020. "Border Externalisation and the Postcolonial Conditioning of Contemporary Capitalism in Mauritania." PhD dissertation, SOAS.

Ovide, Shira, 2021. "How Big Tech Won the Pandemic." *New York Times,* April 30.

Pacciardi, Agnese, and Joakim Berndtsson. 2021. "EU Border Externalisation and Security Outsourcing: Exploring the Migration Industry in Libya." *Journal of Ethnic and Migration Studies* 48(17): 4010–28.

Pallister-Wilkins, Polly. 2022. *Humanitarian Borders: Unequal Mobility and Saving Lives.* London: Verso.

Parenti, C. 2008. *Lockdown America: Police and Prisons in the Age of Crisis*. London: Verso.

Pegg, David, Robert Booth, and David Conn. 2020. "Revealed: The Secret Report That Gave Ministers Warning of Care Home Coronavirus Crisis." *The Guardian*, May 7.

Pengely, Martin. 2020. "Trump Pardons Former National Security Adviser Michael Flynn." *The Guardian,* November 25.

Perlo-Freeman, Sam. 2016. "65 Years of Military Spending: Trends in SIPRI's New Data." SIPRI, November 21. https://sipri.org/commentary/blog/2016/65-years-military-spending/.

Peston, Robert. 2022. "Covid: ITV News Reveals £8.7 Billion of Losses on PPE in Government Accounts." ITV, February 2.

Pidd, Michael. 1996. *Tools for Thinking: Modelling in Management Science*. Chichester: John Wiley and Sons.

Piketty, Thomas. 2018. *Capital in the Twenty-First Century*. Cambridge, MA: Harvard University Press.

Porter, Gareth. 2021. "How the 'Self Licking Ice Cream Cone' Prolonged the 20-Year War." *Responsible Statecraft*, October 4.

ProPublica. 2015. "We Blew $17 Billion in Afghanistan. How Would You Have Spent It?" Report. December 17. https://projects.propublica.org/graphics/afghan/.

Ramalingam, Ben, and Harry Jones, with Toussaint Reba and John Young. 2008. "Exploring the Science of Complexity: Ideas and Implications for Development and Humanitarian Efforts." Working Paper 285. London: ODI, October.

Rangasami, Amrita. 1985. "'Failure of Exchange Entitlements' Theory of Famine: A Response." *Economic and Political Weekly*, 12 and 19 October: 1747–51, 1797–800.

Rêgo, Ximene, Maria João Oliveira, Catarina Lameira, and Olga S. Cruz. 2021. "20 years of Portuguese Drug Policy: Developments, Challenges and the Quest for Human Rights." *Substance Abuse Treatment, Prevention, and Policy* 16 (59): 1–11.

Reicher, Stephen. 2021. "Cop26 Leaders Blame Individuals, while Supporting a Far More Destructive System." *The Guardian,* November 9.

Reidy, Eric. 2021. Briefing: Coronavirus and the Halting of Asylum at the US-Mexico Border. *New Humanitarian*, June 29.

Reitano, Tuesday, and Mark Micaleff. 2017. "Human Smuggling and Libya's Political End Game." Report. Institute for Security Studies. https://globalinitiative.net/wp-content/uploads/2018/01/2017-12-13-pamphlet-migration.pdf.

Reno, William. 1995. *Corruption and State Politics in Sierra Leone*. Cambridge: Cambridge University Press.

Restrepo, J., and M. Spagat. 2005. "Colombia's Tipping Point?" *Survival* 47(2): 131–52.

Ribando Seelke, C., and K. Finklea. 2017. *U.S.-Mexican Security Cooperation: The Merida Initiative and Beyond*. Report. Washington, DC: Congressional Research Service, June.

Riechman, Deb, and Richard Lardner. 2011. "U.S. $360M Lost to Corruption in Afghanistan." *Army Times*/Associated Press, August 16.

Rivkin, Amanda. 2021. "Violent Migrant 'Pushbacks' at Croatian Border Exposed by Media." *Deutsche-Welle*, October 7.

Rizvi, Zain. 2021. "Pfizer's Power." Report. Public Citizen Access to Medicines, October 19.

Roberts, Joe. 2020. "Telegraph Journalist Says Coronavirus 'Cull' of Elderly Could Benefit Economy." *Metro*, March 11.

Robinson, Alice, Peter Justin, Naomi Pendle, Linda Ahimbisibwe, Chot Biel, Latjor Dang, Benjamin Dut Dut Tong, Chuol Gew, Rose Mabu, Ngot Mou, and Umba Peter. 2021. "This Is Your Disease": Dynamics of Local Authority and NGO Responses to Covid-19 in South Sudan. Report, June. London: Firoz Lalji Institute, LSE.

Robinson, Alice, Peter Justin, Naomi Pendle, Linda Ahimbisibwe, Chot Biel, Latjor Dang, Benjamin Dut Dut Tong, Chuol Gew, Rose Mabu, Ngot Mou, and Umba Peter. 2021. "This Is Your Disease: Dynamics of Local Authority and NGO Responses to Covid-19 in South Sudan." Report. London: LSE, June.

Robinson, Ronald, and John A. Gallagher. 1982. *Africa and the Victorians: The Official Mind of Imperialism*. London: Macmillan.

Rocha, Ian Christopher N., Marie Grace A. Pelayo, and Sudhan Rackimuthu. 2021. "Kumbh Mela Religious Gathering as a Massive Superspreading Event: Potential Culprit for the Exponential Surge of COVID-19 Cases in India." *American Journal of Tropical Medicine and Hygiene* 105(4): 868–71.

Rodney, Walter. (1972) 2018. *How Europe Underdeveloped Africa*. London: Verso.

Rogin, Josh. 2016a. "Kerry Touts the Russian Line on Syrian Rebel Groups." *Washington Post*, July 12.

Rogin, Josh. 2016b. "Obama's Syria Plan Teams Up American and Russian Forces." *Washington Post*, July 13.

Roitman, Janet. 2013. *Anti-crisis*. Durham, NC: Duke University Press.

Romero, Federico. 2014. "Cold War Historiography at the Crossroads." *Cold War History* 14(4): 685–703.

Rothstein, Bo, and Jan Teorell. 2008. "What Is Quality of Government? A Theory of Impartial Government Institutions." *Governance:An International Journal of Policy,Administration, and Institutions* 21(2): 165–90.

Rothwell, Jonathan. 2015. *Drug Offenders in American Prisons: The Critical Distinction between Stock and Flow.* Report. Washington, DC: Brookings Institution, November.

Rubin, Barnett. 2007. "Saving Afghanistan." *Foreign Affairs* 86(1): 57–78.

Ryan, Frances. 2021. "During Covid, to Be 'Vulnerable' Is to Be Told Your Life Doesn't Matter." *The Guardian,* June 24.

Ryan, Maria. 2011. "'War in Countries We Are Not at War With': The 'War on Terror' on the Periphery from Bush to Obama." *International Politics* 48(2–3): 364–89.

Saadawi, Ahmed. 2018. *Frankenstein in Baghdad.* New York: Penguin.

Saez, Emmanuel, and Gabriel Zucman. 2016. "Wealth Inequality in the United States since 1913." *Quarterly Journal of Economics* 131(2): 519–78.

SAGE Secretariat. 2020. "Current Understanding of COVID-19 Compared with NSRA Pandemic Influenza Planning Assumptions." Report. London: SAGE, February 26.

Sainath, Palagummi. 1995. *Everybody Loves a Good Drought: Stories from India's Poorest Districts.* New Delhi: Penguin.

Samaddar, Ranabir. 2020. *The Postcolonial Age of Migration.* Abingdon: Routledge.

Sands, Phil, Justin Vela, and Suha Maayeh. 2014. "Assad Regime Set Free Extremists from Prison to Fire Up Trouble during Peaceful Uprising," *The National,* January 21.

Sangaré, Boukary. 2016. "Le Centre du Mali épicentre du djihadisme?" Analysis. Brussels: GRIP, May 20.

Sassen, Saskia. 1996. *Losing Control: Sovereignty in an Age of Globalization.* New York: Columbia University Press.

Saunders-Hastings, K. 2015. "Order and Insecurity under the Mara:Violence, Coping, and Community in Guatemala City." DPhil thesis, Oxford University.

Sanchez, Gabriella, and Luigi Achilli, eds. 2019. *Critical Insights on Irregular Facilitation: Global Perspectives.* Fiesole: Robert Schuman Centre, European University Institute.

Scahill, Jeremy. 2014. *Dirty Wars:The World Is a Battlefield.* London: Serpent's Tail.

Schwartz, Ian. 2020. "Trump Rips CNN Reporter at Briefing." Realclear Politics, April 19.

Schwartz, Jon. 2021. "$10,000 Invested in Defense Stocks When Afghanistan War Began Now Worth Almost $100,000." *The Intercept,* August 16.

Schirmer, Jennifer. 1999. "The Guatemalan Politico-Military Project: Legacies for a Violent Peace?" *Latin American Perspectives* 26(2): 92–107.

Serwer, Adam. 2020. "The Coronavirus Was an Emergency Until Trump Found Out Who Was Dying." *The Atlantic*, May 8.

Seymour, Richard. 2023. "Three Years On, There is a New Generation of Lockdown Sceptics—and They're Rewriting History." *The Guardian*, March 23.

Shapiro, Ian. 2005. *The Flight from Reality in the Human Sciences*. Princeton, NJ: Princeton University Press.

Shaw, Martin. 2005. *The New Western Way of War: Risk-Transfer War and Its Crisis in Iraq*. Cambridge, UK: Polity.

Shawcross, William. 1980. *Sideshow: Kissinger, Nixon and the Destruction of Cambodia*. London: Fontana.

Shipman, T., and C. Wheeler. 2020. "Ten Days That Shook Britain—and Changed the Nation For Ever." *Sunday Times*, March 22.

Singh, Guddi. 2020. "We Are Being Treated as Cannon-Fodder." openDemocracy, March 19. https://www.opendemocracy.net/en/opendemocrac yuk/treating-the-crisis-we-are-being-treated-as-cannon-fodder/.

Smith, Michael. 2005. "Blair Planned Iraq War from Start." *Sunday Times*, May 1.

Soares, Benjamin F. 2012. "On the Recent Mess in Mali." *Anthropology Today* 28(5): 1–2.

Solomon, Hussein. 2013. "Mali: West Africa's Afghanistan." *RUSI Journal* 158(1): 12–19.

Soudan, François. 2017. "Ibrahim Boubacar Keïta: 'Le Mali est une digue. Si elle rompt, l'Europe sera submergée.'" *Jeune Afrique*, December 15.

Souleimanov, Emil Aslan, and Katarina Petrtylova. 2015. "Russia's Policy toward the Islamic State." *Middle East Policy* 32(3): 66–78.

Srinivasan, Sharath. 2021. *When Peace Kills Politics: International Intervention and Unending Wars in the Sudans*. London: Hurst.

Sriyananda, Shanika. 2015. "'I Am a Very Religious Person; the Truth Will Prevail': Gotabaya." *Daily FT*, May 21.

Stannard, David E. 1993. *American Holocaust: The Conquest of the New World: Columbus and the Conquest of the New World*. New York: Oxford University Press.

Star Tribune. 2021. "Minnesota Poll Results: Minneapolis Policing and Public Safety Charter Amendment." September 18.

Stedman, Stephen. 1997. "Spoiler Problems in Peace Processes." *International Security* 22(2): 5–53.

Stewart, Heather, and Mattha Busby. 2020. "Coronavirus: Science Chief Defends UK Plan from Criticism." *The Guardian*, March 13.

Stern, Nicholas H. 2007. *The Economics of Climate Change: The Stern Review*. Cambridge, UK: Cambridge University Press.

Strazzari, Francesco. 2015. "Azawad and the Rights of Passage: the Role of Illicit Trade in the Logic of Armed Group Formation in Northern Mali." Report, January. Oslo: Norwegian Peacebuilding Resource Centre.

Sun, Nina, Emily Christie, Luisa Cabal, and Joseph J. Amon. 2022. "Human Rights in Pandemics: Criminal and Punitive Approaches to COVID-19." *BMJ Global Health* 7:e008232.

Sur, Malini. 2021. "Viral Nationalism." *Cultural Anthropology*, Hot Spots series, March 16.

Swinford, Steven. 2021. "Boris Johnson 'Said He Would Let Covid Rip' in Lockdown Row." *The Times*, April 27.

Syrian Observatory for Human Rights. 2016. "About 600 Civilian Casualties between 6000 Killed by Coalition Airstrikes in 23 Months." Report. Coventry: Syrian Observatory for Human Rights, August 24.

Táíwò, Olúfẹ́mi. 2022. *Against Decolonisation: Taking African Agency Seriously*. London: Hurst.

Tapper, James. 2020. "Recruit Volunteer Army to Trace Coronavirus Contacts Now, Urge Top Scientists." *The Guardian*, April 4.

Tazzioli, Martina, and Glenda Garelli. 2020. "Containment beyond Detention: The Hotspot System and Disrupted Migration Movements across Europe." *Society and Space* 38(6): 1009–27.

The Guardian. 2020. "'Chaos and Panic': Lancet Editor Says NHS Was Left Unprepared for Covid-19." March 28.

The Lancet. 2020. "Covid-19: Protecting Health-care Workers." Editorial, March 21.

Thrall, A. Trevor, and Erik Goepner. 2017. "Step Back: Lessons for U.S. Foreign Policy from the Failed War on Terror." Policy Analysis 814. Washington, DC: Cato Institute, June.

Thurston, Alex. 2018. "Political Settlements with Jihadists in Algeria and the Sahel." *West African Papers* 18. Paris: OECD Publishing.

Thurston, Alex. 2021. "Five Ways Not to Analyze War." *Foreign Exchanges*, May 21.

Tierney, John. 2010. "Warlord, Inc.: Extortion and Corruption along the U.S. Supply Chain in Afghanistan." Report of the Majority Staff, Subcommittee on National Security and Foreign Affairs, Committee on Oversight and Government Reform, US House of Representatives, June.

Tooze, Adam. 2022. "Welcome to the World of the Polycrisis." *Financial Times*, October 28.

Torjesen, Stina, and Neil MacFarlane. 2007. "R before D: The Case of Post Conflict Reintegration in Tajikistan." *Conflict, Security and Development* 7(2): 311–32.

Traoré, Aminata, and Boubacar Boris Diop. 2014. *La gloire des imposteurs*. Paris: Philippe Rey.

Tréguer, Félix. 2021. "The Virus of Surveillance: How the COVID-19 Pandemic Is Fuelling Technologies of Control." *Political Anthropological Research on International Social Sciences* 2: 16–46.

Trilling, Daniel. 2021. "Dark Things Are Happening on Europe's Borders. Are They a Sign of Worse to Come?" *The Guardian,* November 8.

Tubiana, Jerôme, Clotilde Warin, and Gaffar Mohammud Saeneen. 2018. *Multilateral Damage: The Impact of EU Migration Policies on Central Saharan Routes*. Report. The Hague: Clingendael, September.

Turkmani, Rim, Ali Ali, Mary Kaldor, and Vesna Bojicic-Dzelilovic. 2015. "Countering the Logic of the War Economy in Syria." Report. London: Civil Society and Human Security Research Unit, LSE, July 30.

Turse, Nick. 2013. *Kill Everything That Moves: The Real American War in Vietnam*. New York: Henry Holt.

UK House of Commons, Science and Technology Committee. 2021. "The UK Response to Covid-19: Use of Scientific Advice." January 8. https://publications.parliament.uk/pa/cm5801/cmselect/cmsctech/136/13605.htm.

UK's All Party Parliamentary Group for Sudan and South Sudan.

UNDP. 2017. *Journey to Extremism in Africa: Drivers, Incentives and the Tipping Point for Recruitment*. Report. New York: UNDP. https://journey-to-extremism.undp.org/enter.

UNESCO, UNICEF, and the World Bank. 2021. *The State of the Global Education Crisis: A Path to Recovery*. Report. New York: UN.

UNICEF. 2017. *A Deadly Journey for Children: The Central Mediterranean Migration Route*. Report. New York: UN, February.

UNICEF. 2021. *Direct and Indirect Effects of the COVID-19 Pandemic and Response in South Asia*. Report. New York: UN, March.

UNHCR. 2022. "Decade of Sahel Conflict Leaves 2.5 Million People Displaced." Summary of spokesperson statement. New York: UN, January 14.

United Nations. 2020. *COVID-19 and Human Rights*. Report. New York: UN, April.

UN Working Group on Arbitrary Detention. 2021. A/HRC/47/40: Arbitrary Detention relating to Drug Policies. Study. New York: UN.

Vallet, Elizabeth. 2017. "Border Walls Are Ineffective, Costly and Fatal—but We Keep Building Them." *The Conversation*, July 4.

Van Noorden, Richard. 2022. "Higher-Profile COVID Experts More Likely to Get Online Abuse." *Nature*, April 4. https://www.nature.com/articles/d41586-022-00936-4/.

Venugopal, Rajesh. 2018. *Nationalism, Development and Ethnic Conflict in Sri Lanka*. Cambridge: Cambridge University Press.

Vermeys, Sonia Church, and Erin Elliott. 2022. "The Gambling Law Review: USA—Nevada." https://thelawreviews.co.uk/index.php/title/the-gambling-law-review/usa-nevada/.

Wade, Robert. 2009. "Robert Wade on the Global Financial Crisis, Interviewed by Alex Izurieta." *Development and Change* 40(6): 1153–90.

Walia, Harsha. 2013. *Undoing Border Imperialism*. Chico, CA: AK Press.

Walker, Justine. 2016. "Study on Humanitarian Impact of Syria-Related Unilateral Restrictive Measures." Report. UN Economic and Social Commission for Western Asia, May. https://www.voltairenet.org/IMG/pdf/Humanitarian_Impact_of_Syria-Related_Unilateral_Restrictive_Measures.pdf.

Walker, Peter. 2020. "No 10 Denies Claim Dominic Cummings Argued to 'Let Old people Die.'" *The Guardian*, March 22.

Walter, Barbara F., and Jack Snyder. 1999. *Civil Wars, Insecurity, and Intervention*. New York: Columbia University Press.

Walters, William. 2011. "Foucault and Frontiers: Notes on the Birth of the Humanitarian Border." In *Governmentality: Current Issues and Future Challenges*, edited by U. Bröckling, S. Krasmann, and T. Lemke, 138–64. New York: Routledge.

Walters, William. 2012. *Governmentality: Critical Encounters*. Abingdon: Routledge.

Walters, William. 2015. "Reflections on Migration and Governmentality." *Movements: Journal for Critical Migration and Border Regime Studies* 1(1): 1–25.

Waltz, Kenneth N. 1979. *Theory of International Politics*. New York: Random House.

Weigand, Florian. 2022. *Waiting for Dignity: Legitimacy and Authority in Afghanistan*. New York: Columbia University Press.

Weigand, Florian, and Ruben Andersson. 2019. "Institutionalized Intervention: The 'Bunker Politics' of International Aid in Afghanistan." *Journal of Intervention and Statebuilding* 13(4): 503–23.

Weiss, Gideon. 2022. "COVID-19 and the Far Right's Diminishing Memory of the Holocaust." *Think Global Health,* February 28.

Weiss, Gordon. 2011. *The Cage: The Fight for Sri Lanka and the Last Days of the Tamil Tigers.* London: The Bodley Head.

Weiss, Michael, and Hassan Hassan. 2015. *ISIS: Inside the Army of Terror.* New York: Regan Arts.

Welikala, Asanga. 2008. *A State of Permanent Crisis.* Colombo: Centre for Policy Alternatives.

Westad, Odd Arne. 2005. *The Global Cold War: Third World Interventions and the Making of Our Times.* Cambridge: Cambridge University Press.

Wheeler, Thomas. 2012. *China and Conflict-Affected States: Between Principle and Pragmatism: Sri Lanka.* Report. London: Saferworld, January.

White House. 2020. Task Force Briefing, April 19.

Whitehouse, Bruce. 2012. "What Went Wrong in Mali?" *London Review of Books* 34(16): 17–18.

Whitlock, Craig. 2019. "At War with the Truth." *Washington Post,* December 9.

Whitlock, Craig. 2021. *The Afghanistan Papers: A Secret History of the War.* New York: Simon & Schuster.

Whitlock, Craig, Leslie Shapiro, and Armand Emamdjomeh. 2019. "The Afghanistan Papers: A Secret History of the War." *Washington Post,* December 9.

Wilder, Andrew. 2009. "A 'Weapons System' Based on Wishful Thinking." *Boston Globe,* September 16.

Wogt, Wendy A. 2013. "Crossing Mexico: Structural Violence and the Commodification of Undocumented Central American Migrants." *American Ethnologist* 40(4): 764–80.

Woodward, Bob. 2002. *Bush at War.* London: Simon and Schuster.

Woodward, Peter. 1990. *Sudan, 1898–1989.* Boulder, CO: Lynne Rienner.

Xing, Chaoguo, and Biao Xiang. 2022. "Migrant Care Labour Agencies as Actors of Social Control: Case Studies from China." Halle: MoLab Inventory of Mobilities and Socioeconomic Changes, March.

Yong, Ed. 2020b. "How the Pandemic Defeated America." *The Atlantic,* September.

Zaun, Natascha, and Olivia Nantermoz. 2021. "The Use of Pseudo-Causal Narratives in EU Policies: The Case of the European Union Emergency Trust Fund for Africa." *Journal of European Public Policy* 29(4): 510–29.

Index

For the benefit of digital users, indexed terms that span two pages (e.g., 52–53) may, on occasion, appear on only one of those pages.

Tables and figures are indicated by *t* and *f* following the page number